SUPERNATURAL CHRISTIANITY

Stories and Reflections

Alden Marshall

Verses not otherwise marked are KJV.

Photo credits Alden Marshall.

Cover design by Lauren Harris

ISBN 978-1-970037-90-6

Library of Congress Control Number: 2021924890

Knoxville, Tennessee
crippledbeaglepublishing.com

Published and printed in the United States of America.

CONTENTS

The white church pictured above is The Little Country Church in Rogersville, Tennessee, USA, where I was saved as a boy.

The church pictured above is The Church of the Spilled Blood, Saint Petersburg, Russia.

Introduction

Rev. Dr. Robert Bruce, the second moderator of the Church of Scotland, was so slow to enter his pulpit at Saint Giles one Sunday morning that the elders sent a young boy to check on him. The lad reported that Dr. Bruce was talking to someone. When asked how he knew that, the boy explained that he heard Dr. Bruce say, "I will not go out there unless you go with me."

I grew up in churches like that, and "Jesus was a part of our family," just as Corrie Ten Boom said about Jesus' involvement in her family. We were God conscious, which was wonderful when we walked with Him (but a conscious curse when we did not). From the New Testament to Dr. Bruce in the 1500s, to the Ten Booms in the 1940s, to the present, the supernatural continues to be an unmistakable reality in the lives of those who follow Jesus Christ as God and Lord. Here are some stories and reflections about how and why that happens.

"There are things which a man is afraid to tell even to himself, and every decent man has a number of such things stored away in his mind." So says Fyodor Dostoyevsky, the Russian novelist and journalist who was either Christian or the best non-Christian I have ever encountered. Perhaps we have not lived long enough to be aware of the truth he spoke. But sooner or later we must admit, at least to ourselves, that as God assures us in the Bible, "The heart is desperately wicked." Some of us have consciences seared with a hot iron, so we can dismiss both Dostoyevsky and the Bible as bogus. In those cases, the Holy Spirit may never convict individuals of their sin and the need to repent and follow Jesus. Who can say for sure?

But we who have come to accept Christ as God and Lord still need radical repentance daily. Salvation does not lift us to a higher moral level where we no longer sin, but it gives us the Holy Spirit to guide us, to comfort us when we do the will of God and to convict us of our sins when we do our own will. As Christians we must battle our own inclinations to sin, no matter what Democrats or Republicans or foreigners do. Even if we are no longer attracted to the grosser sins, we find ourselves battling more refined sins.

We may have to struggle against the sense of entitlement, for example, long after our teenage years have passed. No doubt Dostoyevsky had to fight the desire to be more respected, for his house was modest compared to that of the poet Pushkin, although to me Dostoyevsky was far more profound in his understanding of the personality than Pushkin was.

Dostoyevsky said, "If there is no God, everything is permissible." Then it is merely tradition that makes something right or wrong, or some articulate person with clout. But if God exists, and I am certain he does, then his revelation of truth is to be studied and obeyed.

King David prayed that God would cleanse him from hidden faults (sins he was not aware of within himself). Sometimes we can hide our evil intent until it produces harmful actions. God stands ready to forgive us and to cleanse us from our sins—both hidden and exposed.

I frankly do not know how Dostoyevsky stood with God. It is clear that he loved his children and was devastated when his three-year-old son died. He would stand for hours looking at a painting of Mary and Jesus at his last house in Saint Petersburg. I am sure he respected God, and he probably loved him. It is too late to mourn for Dostoyevsky if he did not.

But we do live, and we are responsible to follow Jesus Christ as God and Lord. Let us be completely open and honest about ourselves with him, and let us ask him to cleanse us from all unrighteousness daily. In 1 John 1:9 (ESV) we read, "if we confess our sins, he is faithful and just to forgive us our sins and to cleanse us from all unrighteousness.

Coakley

I just saw the name Coakley on the side of a truck in New York City, and it took me back to my Tennessee childhood. According to many, mine was a deprived childhood. That said, we were fortunate not to see liars or thieves or wife beaters or pedophile singers as role models. No, we looked up to Rev. Ray Coakley as my favorite preacher and Rev. Johnny Sauceman as my brother Darvin's favorite preacher. I doubt that these two great men could even pronounce the names of cars (such as Lamborghinis and Porsches) I see all around me now.

As an adult, in retrospect, I no longer idolize the reverends because I am certain that their hearts were "desperately wicked," as is the case with everyone who ever lives, except for Jesus Christ. But I am also certain that whatever their besetting sins or just occasional sins, by the time they stepped into the pulpit, they were walking humbly with Jesus Christ, because the fire fell. We knew that we were on holy ground and in the presence of the God of the universe. Even as little children we knew that (which is a good reason to keep children listening to worthwhile sermons).

I would like to be able to say that I continued to keep the important things important, but I did not. I never idolized Porsches or other luxury items, but I definitely looked for worth and value apart from walking humbly with the risen Jesus Christ. "All we like sheep have gone astray; we have turned—every one—to his own way; and the LORD has laid on him the iniquity of us all." Isaiah 53:6 (ESV)

Since my childhood I have been privileged to know several Godly ministers and laity in different countries. I do not idolize them, but I value and respect them highly. Like I do in these individuals, I like to think that some little boy or girl will see Jesus Christ reflected clearly in our lives. Whether pastors or teachers or next-door neighbors, some are trying to take advantage of children for their own pleasure or status or for some other selfish gain. Who will influence children not for any personal gain but for the glory of Jesus Christ and for the children's benefit?

Jaded

I live in the richest part of what is arguably the richest city in the world. New Yorkers are famous for being jaded. Nothing much impresses them because they have seen about everything. Over 300 languages are spoken here, and thirty-eight percent of the city's residents were born in another country. Many of the rest are from other states. Although I love the Great Smoky Mountains of Tennessee more, I do love it here.

I understand more clearly now why Jesus says it is easier for a camel to go through the eye of a needle than for a rich man to enter heaven. More money gives one the ability to keep searching for satisfaction with new restaurants, new houses, or new wives, etc. My wife and I sometimes watch the TV show *House Hunters International*. We see people picking out exotic locations worldwide, and they often gush about how they would enjoy watching a particular beach/mountain/urban scene forever. But I am sure that for most, boredom soon sets in.

When I left my home in rural east Tennessee (and by the way, it is always "east" and never "eastern" to generations born there) for university in Knoxville, Tennessee, I thought I had died and gone to heaven. Beautiful women, friends, money, work, and even classes were interesting, for the most part. But I was soon shocked because I found myself bored or jaded. I tried Montreal, Amsterdam, Paris, and other cities, but they, too, became routine. As Saint Augustine wrote, "Our hearts are restless until we find our rest in Thee."

Ecclesiastes 1:2 teaches that all "is vanity and a striving after wind." So said King Solomon, who was rich, had hundreds of wives, and oversaw great building projects. And so multi-billion-dollar building projects are all around me in the Hudson Yards section of Manhattan. Around Wall Street I overhear people discussing losing$5 million here and gaining $35 million dollars there.

But to avoid being jaded, we must touch our extremely finite minds to the infinite mind of God, in faith and obedience. Jesus says, "I am the way, and the truth, and the life" (John 14:6). Supernatural peace and joy and meaning and purpose come through him, no matter how much or how little money, status, or health we have. We may still have loneliness or other troubles, but we are promised an abundant life when we follow the prince of peace.

Solzhenitsyn

Alexander Solzhenitsyn was a man dedicated to truth. He was one of the great Russian writers. He died in August, 2008, at the age of 89. It is quite remarkable that so many who suffered semi starvation in Russian or Nazi prison camps have actually lived into old age. Bad governments make good writers, and terrible governments produce great writers. Russian writers have thrived.

As a young man Solzhenitsyn was an idealist who supported the communists and an army officer decorated for bravery while fighting the Germans. But he was sent to a concentration camp when he criticized Stalin in a letter to a friend. There he met several who had been supernaturally converted to follow Jesus Christ as God and Lord. Through them, Solzhenitsyn did the same.

When his accounts of horrible prison conditions were published, the communists accused him of being a traitor trying to court favor with the

West. He countered that he wrote so that his own people would know the truth about their history. He was exiled in 1974 and lived in Vermont for twenty years. There he finished *The Gulag Archipelago Volume 2* and *The Gulag Archipelago Volume 3* about a string of prisons in the Soviet Union.

He won a Nobel Prize in Literature and was invited to speak at a Harvard commencement. His love for truth got him as much opposition from the Harvard culture as he had received from the communist culture. In Russia he attacked communists for not allowing freedom and liberty, and the Americans cheered him. In the USA he deplored media freedom that allows/promotes violence, crime, and pornography.

Of course, the Harvard faculty and students then (and now) were almost completely immune to violence. That is because they sent their children to private schools and lived in gated communities or other rich enclaves and hired poor people to kill other poor folks who tried to rob or otherwise harm them. For example, ex-presidential contender Hillary Clinton was openly against average citizens having guns to protect them from thugs while she employed bodyguards with guns to protect her from thugs.

Solzhenitsyn was criticized by much of the American media because he was against laws that allowed evil to flourish in this country. Drunken drivers, for example, are permitted to keep their cars and to harm others. They are protected by legislators who are supported by alcohol companies. Violence is glorified and victims are often portrayed as deserving whatever they get, particularly TV shows and films like *The Godfather*. Society gets more coarse and vulgar, with much disrespect shown to males/females/parents/children (listen near a playground to confirm this). Divorce is prevalent, as documented by divorce statistics. Meanwhile truth dies when individuals try to rationalize what the Bible calls evil, whether in the Russia of Solzhenitsyn, in the USA, or any other country.

"So what?" some will ask. Well, only someone whose life is not based on truth would ask that. Jesus claims to be truth and calls all to base our lives on him and his teachings. The Holy Spirit lives within each Christian in order to remind us how to live. His truth prompts us to be for whatever the Bible calls good and against whatever the Bible calls harmful or evil. Glance at the Bible once in a while if you want to know specifics.

For Solzhenitsyn, as for all Christians, right and wrong and good and evil really exist. Christianity is based on truth, and those who follow Jesus do so not to get happy or rich or to have an easy life but because he is truth. He suffered because he spoke and lived the truth.

Are our lives based on truth or fiction? Are we willing to consciously pray to know and to follow truth, wherever that leads us? Someone said that if you speak the truth, you had better be funny or people will kill you. Perhaps they will just torture you in a prison as Solzhenitsyn experienced. By living in truth, we may suffer negative consequences, but I hope we know it is worth it.

These are accounts of people throughout history who knew what Solzhenitsyn was talking about and who experience God on a deep level. It may be in a dilapidated shack or in a magnificent cathedral, but wherever people humble themselves before the God of the universe, he comes down in power. May that happen to you the reader; for the first time or more deeply.

Marriage

I thought of marriage a few times in my early twenties, but I met no one I wanted to marry, so marriage remained an abstract idea. At age twenty-five, I rededicated my life to Jesus Christ and began to search for a wife. I attended Bible studies ably led by Chuck Anderton in Knoxville, Tennessee. The concept of a wife began to appeal to me more and more. After a while he justifiably remarked that I and another guy named Bob needed to quit asking women in the Bible study to go out because they then stayed away!

I prayed as sincerely as I knew how, "God, please show me the woman you want me to marry." I wanted nothing dramatic, only to meet a person soon in a park, grocery store, etc. One day, in the midst of that prayer, I saw her face in a vision, and I was certain it was from God. I was stunned because she was very beautiful and looked Swedish. The view was straight on, and I was unable to tell the color of her eyes or hair. I distinctly remember that she looked sad. Nevertheless, I was very thankful to God and much encouraged.

As the years dragged on, I left Tennessee for seminary in Boston, worked in Canada, and continued my career. I always remembered the vision and her face, but for five, ten, fifteen, twenty years, I assumed I had taken a wrong turn somewhere and perhaps missed her. I dated others. One day I picked up a magazine of 500 beautiful Russian woman looking for love, reasoning that there were surely some Christians among them.

The most stunning of them had two children, and I was about to pass, since it is difficult enough to have a good relationship with one person. Then I read under her picture, "Wants to meet a man who has God in his heart." I later discovered the translator actually added that caption!

I wrote, and we met in Russia. The photo was a side shot, but as soon as I saw her I was certain that she was the one I had seen in the vision 25 years earlier. She had also seen me, about two years before we met—not in a vision ... but in a dream.

May you also "pray through" on important matters until you know the mind of God and feel his supernatural peace.

Chariots of Fire

The first time I was kicked out of a pastorate was a huge letdown (the second time was somewhat easier). I can laugh about it now, but it certainly was not funny at the time. Afterwards, I relocated about a mile away in downtown Montreal because the presbytery allowed me to stay in a seminary student dorm there. I led Bible studies among some students, and only God knows if I made any positive difference in their lives.

By the mercy of God, several of us then saw the film *Chariots of Fire*, about a Godly Scot, Eric Liddell, who won a gold medal in the 1924 Olympics held in Paris. As his sister harangued him about missing Bible studies and other pursuits she thought he should be doing, Eric answered that God made him fast, and he had to run, because "When I run, I feel [his] pleasure." Another powerful part of the film was just before a race, in a category for which Eric had not practiced. An American runner handed Eric a piece of paper with words from 1 Samuel 2:30, "... for those who honor me I will honor ...." I was overwhelmed then by the love of God when I heard that great promise, because I knew the Holy Spirit was applying those words to me. Tears streamed down my face in that dark theater because I was certain I felt the pleasure of God when I preached. Yet my future in that field looked extremely bleak. I had no idea if I should try to stay in the ministry in Canada, return to Tennessee, or to go to another place to explore another field of work. That line in that movie fortified me to keep on looking for another church.

I found a welcoming congregation in Toronto, and from all the outward evidence, it was my most productive pastorate. I had tried to be a good pastor at my first congregation, but I failed in many ways. By the time I found out that several congregants hated me before they even met me, I wished that many of them would go to hell. I am not proud of that. Instead, I am bragging on the God who showed great and seriously undeserved mercy to me.

I cannot agree with the great French singer Edith Piaf, who sang, "I regret nothing." I regret a lot. Looking back, I see the truth of Romans 8:28. "And we know that for those who love God all things work together for good,[a] for those who are called according to his purpose."

That promise is for those who are kicked out of pastorates, legitimately or not, for the sick and lonely, for those who have relatively honest and kind governments, and for those who have evil criminals over them. We just need to repent of our sins, love the Triune God, and then the pleasant as well as the unpleasant will work together for our good.

Does Christian revival equal pious emotionalism that ignores justice?

Historic Christian revivals do include justice. I had such revivals growing up in east Tennessee. We were farmers/laborers. We were concerned with holiness, or “walking with God.” We watched the rich get richer and more distant from God, with few exceptions. Luke 12:48 proclaims, “Everyone to whom much was given, of him much will be required....” This is from the Bible not a Communist manifesto! So private faith, when it is really from God, cares about justice in society. There is no contradiction between personal holiness and justice on a larger scale.

Jonathan Edwards, who was the catalyst for the first great revival or awakening in this country, was for treating all with respect and for fair wages for all workers. He did not court the favor of the rich nor did he hate them. He said, “Some men shew a love to others as to their outward man, they are liberal of their worldly substance, and often give to the poor; but have no love to, or concern for the souls of men.

Others pretend a great love to men's souls, who are not compassionate and charitable towards their bodies. The making a great shew of love, pity, and distress for souls, costs them nothing; but in order to show mercy to men's bodies, they must part with money out of their pockets. But a true Christian love to our brethren, extends both to their souls and bodies." He says we cannot deny help to the undeserving since that would clash with God's gift to us who are undeserving and with his command to love even our enemies.

John Wesley preached repentance and the need for all to follow Jesus as Lord. He also supported fair prices, a living wage, and honest, healthy employment for all. The Quakers and Wesley and Wilberforce preached the need for salvation, and at the same time opposed slavery. John Newton was a converted captain of a slave ship who wrote the hymn “Amazing Grace.” It’s lyrics sing, “Amazing grace/How sweet the sound/That saved a wretch like me./I once was lost but now I’m found/Was blind but now I see." Christian revival brings life again to a person.

Evangelism brings life to the person for the first time. As Christians are revived we, ourselves, become holy, and then we encourage justice as far as possible. Just how and what methods are best to use, are determined when we depend on the Holy Spirit of the Bible.

The Holy Spirit is considered the red-headed stepchild of the Trinity.

The Book of Judges says everyone did what was right in his own eyes. But even a dictatorship is preferable to anarchy, where there is no law and, therefore, no one is safe. When a person says, "Anything goes," the meaning is usually that the Holy Spirit should be ignored. The Holy Spirit was the inspirer of the Bible, which at times contradicts the feelings and logic of each one of us. Christians understand the sentiment to ignore the Holy Spirit, because the Bible offends us as much if not more than it does those who are not Christian.

But if we can do what the Bible clearly teaches not to do and still feel great, the Holy Spirit is not part of our lives. Evan Roberts, who spearheaded the great revival of 1904-1905 in Wales, taught that God calls us not only to avoid sin, but also to avoid what is doubtful. Read 1 Corinthians 6 and its list of behaviors that characterize one who is *not* a Christian. If you have grave doubts that you can learn, accept, and adhere to these rules, you know neither English nor Greek. The original Greek words are much more direct and blunt about drunkenness, sexual behavior, etc. I have been guilty of some of the sins listed, yet I was convicted by the Holy Spirit when I followed those human, natural inclinations. We are not naturally disposed to do all of the same sins, but we are all attracted to at least some of the sins listed in 1 Corinthians 6.

God is separate and distinct from his creatures (us). He calls us to love and to obey him, the Triune God, and to be holy. This is the exact opposite of the attitude, "Anything goes." But how can we know if God the Holy Spirit is really with us and directing us? The Holy Spirit inspired the Bible and never leads us contrary to the Bible. Admittedly, some passages are murkier than others, so we should build our lives on what is clear, and especially when the teachings are repeated in both Old and New Testaments. Christians have great freedom to do all that is best for us, as well as the freedom to avoid what is sinful and harmful for us. That is not always crystal clear in all circumstances. The Bible is a guide, and we must depend on the Holy Spirit to lead us, specifically when choices have to be made.

All of us have made some wrong choices. But the only difference between a Christian and one who is not Christian is that the Holy Spirit is with the Christian. We have the ability and the desire to honor Jesus Christ in what we are and in what we do, although we may still choose evil any time we desire. If we falter, the Holy Spirit will convict us and make us miserable until we repent. Also he gives us joy and peace and fellowship with God the Father and God the eternal son Jesus Christ when we depend daily on the Holy Spirit to guide us. Christianity is first, last, and foremost, an encounter with the supernatural, the Triune God. The Holy Spirit is the point man, or the way we are contacted and stay in contact with God, if we approach him at all.

Who is the Holy Spirit/Holy Ghost, and do all people have this spiritual entity?

Part 1

Again, Christianity is first, last, and foremost, an encounter with the supernatural. God is eternally in three persons: the Father, Son Jesus Christ, and the Holy Spirit. These three compose the Trinity. They are the same in essence and being, and co-equal, but have different functions. Saint Patrick of Ireland used the clover to teach that God is in three modes. So many are turned off by the institutional church because it has so often "a form of godliness, denying the power thereof, (2 Timothy 3:5)" as the apostle Paul described the situation. Someone remarked that if the Holy Spirit left the world, most churches would continue exactly as they are, and I am convinced that is true, unfortunately.

Many grew up in churches and either walked the aisles and made a commitment to Jesus or made quieter professions of faith in church classes, at home, or elsewhere. Regardless, the profession was in vain or was empty unless the person was drawn supernaturally by the Holy Spirit to worship Jesus Christ as God. I cringe when I hear hymns declaring how we are one in spirit, or how there is a unified spirit in the service, meaning a strong implication is that everyone in the church building is automatically filled with the Holy Spirit. It is no wonder that Christianity is dismissed as fake and shallow by so many who were taught that they had the Holy Spirit, when often that was not the case at all!

1 Corinthians 12:3 commands, "...no one can say 'Jesus is Lord' except in the Holy Spirit." In other words, a person can make many professions of faith and can join many churches, but until the Holy Spirit prompts and draws a person to make a commitment to Jesus Christ as God, one is left with only an empty form of Godliness—a vain pretense.

The Holy Spirit is God, as Acts 5:3-4 clearly teaches, and is therefore not just a wind or idea, as some anti-Christian groups claim. In these verses Peter said that an individual lied to the Holy Ghost (the word ghost is from the German *geist* while the word spirit is from the Latin, meaning exactly the same). The lie was furthermore said not to a human being but to God. Also, the Holy Spirit is a person. He comforts (John 14:16, 26,

16:7-11) and has intelligence. He has will (Romans 8::16, Acts 16:7, 1 Corinthians 121) and has affections (Isaiah 63:10, Ephesians 4:30). We are not to grieve the Holy Spirit, and 1 Thessalonians 5:19 warns us not to quench the spirit.

The Holy Spirit is the sanctifier who communicates to Christians. He teaches (John 14:26) and testifies to Jesus Christ (John 15:26). He guides, shows us things to come, and always glorifies Jesus Christ (John 16:13-14). If one claims to have a spirit that does not glorify Jesus Christ, the person may be telling the truth. But he or she definitely will not have the *Holy* Spirit and should be aware that the alternatives are demons.

Does everyone have the Holy Spirit? No, the Holy Spirit is given only to those who obey Jesus Christ as God (Acts 5:32). Furthermore, Jude adds that some are devoid of the Spirit (Jude 19). The Spirit spoke to Peter (Acts 10:19) and he is witness to us (Hebrews 10:15). The anointing of the Spirit abides in you (Christians) and teaches, according to 1 John 2:27: The conscience of the Christian bears witness in the Holy Spirit (Romans 9:1). Every person has a conscience, which is a compilation of societal rules and family traditions, and even a God-given sense of what is right and wrong. But the Christian has the Holy Spirit to inform and to guide the conscience in specific ways, often in ways that are against our own values and hopes, as well as those of society.

Part 2

As a spiritual entity co-equal with God the Father and God the eternal Son, Jesus Christ, the Holy Spirit is a person who comforts, convicts, has intelligence, and has affections. Paul made the point that his preaching and speaking was in demonstration of the spirit and of power (1 Corinthians 44, 13). Under the influence of the Holy Spirit, Paul taught that the kingdom of God is not in word but in power (1 Corinthians 4:20). In other words, we can say everything directly from the Bible and have correct theology or understanding of God, and still not *know* God.

If the power of the Holy Spirit is not an unmistakable part of our lives, we have not known anything about the kingdom of God, nor have we ever entered it! That is not to say we always have that conscious union with God and strong sense of his presence. David and others lamented the seeming absence of God when he did not reveal himself for periods of time. Yet true Christians (and pre-Christians like David who had the Holy Spirit and was never left by the Holy Spirit), are comforted when we honor Jesus Christ and condemned when we do not obey his teachings. By the way, I have heard some say that when Paul taught about sexuality, for example, we are not to obey since Jesus did not get so specific. We cannot legitimately separate the teachings of Jesus and Paul, since the Holy Spirit is God, and the Holy Spirit guided Paul as he wrote specific instructions for church situations that did not exist when Jesus was walking among us. There is never a wedge between Jesus and the Holy Spirit and God the Father, for they are the same in essence and being!

When someone speaks of having union with the risen Jesus Christ, it will seem like an illusion until we personally have been supernaturally drawn into such a union also. Church hymns seem ridiculous when they talk about experiences we cannot imagine. Ministers need to emphasize over and over that the promises of the Bible and hymns do not apply to every listener or reader but only to those who have been drawn from the kingdom of darkness into the kingdom of Jesus Christ. As the New Testament was being written until the present, many who had never been converted rose to leadership in churches and used the church only as a means of making money or of gaining status and attention. Such individuals do not need Christian revival but Christian conversion.

Much to my chagrin and that of other Christians, the Holy Spirit does not always lead us in ways we want to go. If you claim to be Christian and have never experienced God saying no to your hopes and plans, I am sure you are deceived and are not Christian at all. We all have very limited understanding of our situations as well as hearts that "are desperately wicked," therefore, it is impossible to always be praised by God when we plan or hope for particular things to happen. The Bible promises that God's ways are much higher than our ways and often very different.

Paul, for example, crossed many mountains and faced dangerous obstacles in order to preach the gospel in a section of what is now modern Turkey. But Acts 15:7 records that he was forbidden by the Holy Spirit to preach there, and when he tried to go into Bythinia, the Spirit also forbade that! Since that happened to Paul when he was in the center of the will of God, how much more likely is that to happen to us as we go about our plans? We are to stop and to pray for repentance and guidance. We should read the Bible so often that we know the mind of Christ in general ways and then pray that the Holy Spirit guides us in specific ways. The Holy Spirit is a great comfort, even when he warns us not to proceed in a particular direction. That is because he wants only what is best for us and will guide us into ways that are better for us and for others, also, when we sincerely want that to happen. Sometimes I feel I am salt without flavor.

Luke 14:34-35 teaches, "Salt is good, but if salt has lost its taste, how shall its saltiness be restored? It is of no use either for the soil or for the manure pile. It is thrown away. He who has ears to hear, let him hear." So spoke Jesus. At another place he said that his followers are "the salt of the earth." Salt not only adds good taste to many foods, but it preserves. In other words, society rots unless we who are Christians are salt with the flavor of Jesus Christ.

When we see rot in our society, we can blame the political parties, criminals (sometimes these are the same people), our spouses or children or neighbors. But as the old song teaches, "It is not my sister or my brother, but it's me, O Lord, standing in the need of prayer." We can stand for Godliness as far as we know, still be salt that has flavor, and not see results in positive ways. I am somewhat cheered by the observation of John Owens, the great puritan writer on the Holy Spirit, who said it is possible to be close to God and not to be aware of that fact. But we should be very careful not to think we are close when we are not.

How can we who are Christian be made salt again? What can we do but search our hearts, and better yet, ask God to search our hearts to see if there is any wicked way in us and to lead us in the way everlasting? I do pray that as sincerely as I know how. I pray to be more sincere, if possible, when I pray that way. Is my prayer answered? Sometimes I am confident that it is heard and answered. At other times I am doubtful, for often I see no change in my life or in the lives of others for whom I pray.

I pray for deeper and deeper layers of repentance and guidance. I would like to sense the Holy Spirit coming in power to cleanse and to purify in unmistakable ways. That has happened before, so I know it can happen again and again. At the same time, I can find no place in the Bible that promises that when we pray for holiness, it will always come in dramatic ways. It will come to the Christian who really wants it, I am sure. "Draw near to God and He will draw near to you," is a command and promise from God (James 4:8). But to draw near is not always the same as coming unmistakably into his presence every time we humble ourselves before him.

"The just shall live by faith." (1 Corinthians 13)

When we are right with God, we are to live by faith in his promises for those who do love him. Therefore we are not to live by our feelings or logic, but in the revealed truth of the Bible. When the Holy Spirit deems it fit and appropriate to anoint his truth with his clear presence, I am glad, as is every Christian who ever lived. But sometimes we are to follow God in the dark, relatively speaking. "Who among you fears the Lord, and obeys the word of his servant? Let him who walks in the dark and has no light, trust in the name of the Lord, and rely on his God." Sometimes I do that. Sometimes I do not. But I am much better off when I do, and then I am salt to anyone around me, to add good flavor and to preserve Godliness in this culture.

One hymn says, "Revive us again, fill each heart with thy love, may our souls be rekindled with fire from above." We either need to be saved/converted for the first time, or revived from time to time with fire from above.

Christian revival means Christians quit taking a little bit of materialism ... hedonism ... American culture ... eastern mysticism ... Gnosticism ... , and base our lives on the God of the universe. "You have hewn cisterns that will not hold water," warned the Old Testament prophet. We make mistakes (sins) in our twenties and spend the rest of our lives paying for them (STDs, abortions, financial disasters). But Christian revival means to repent and to turn to the risen Jesus Christ for our hopes and plans.

I also did the opposite of that for several years, just as you did or are doing now. God can use our past, no matter how we messed it up. But I am convinced that when we build on Godly and positive actions and thoughts, we will have better impact on others and a more fulfilling life for ourselves. Revival for me came not because I am smarter or better than others, but because several car wrecks got me thinking that I was heading in the wrong direction. I knew that already, but I needed some disaster to get me to turn around.

The Bible says those God loves he chastises or disciplines, and without that we are illegitimate and not really children of God at all. So when we a bump in the road, I hope that instead of whining we go to the Lord in prayer and get God's perspective. David did that many times. We read that he inquired of the Lord before he undertook any important action (though he did neglect to ask God's opinion before he committed adultery with Bathsheba and then have her husband murdered).

Do we sincerely do go to him in prayer before making decisions? Or do we plough ahead, relying on our or our friends' opinions? That is tempting to do after only a nod to God. Frankly, I do not fast and pray as much as I did in the past, and I am not convinced that I am better off. But I am not in anguish very often over my sins and those of my fellow Americans. The Bible says in Psalm 30:5, "Weeping may tarry for the night, but joy comes with the morning."

We want the joy without the weeping, but that is impossible except in a shallow and trivial way. When we draw near to God, he draws near to us. We can be sure that has never happened to us unless we have caught a glimpse of the holiness of God and how far we are from being holy ourselves. In other words, if we have ever really come into the presence of God, we have been traumatized by the consciousness of our sins. That leads to either hostility and resentment towards God, or a brokenness before God (revival).

Dr. Mounger wrote a little booklet about the heart being the home of Christ. He encouraged us to search each room of our hearts, as we would houses. Then we are to look for anything and everything that would not honor Jesus Christ. We may not have two or three spouses or significant others in our houses/hearts, but if we are honest, we will regularly find some selfishness, desire for revenge, or other traits that hinder us from being in the center of the will of God. God says in the book of Revelation that if we are lukewarm, he will spue us out of his mouth. May God help us to have deeper and deeper layers of repentance and to take out the little bits that keep us from walking humbly with the risen Jesus Christ.

All Christians are sometimes offended because God calls us according to *his* purposes (not ours).

Where would you place yourself on an optimist vs. pessimist scale? I am a pessimist by nature, but when I trust Romans 8:28 I am an optimist! The verse promises that all things work together for good for those who love God. When we are certain that we love God, that promise brings great comfort. We have the assurance that his love and power remove the evil from all circumstances that we must face. Every circumstance then becomes a method of molding us into the image of Jesus Christ. So, when we receive criticism that is just, we are then not too arrogant to listen and to improve.

And when we hear unjust criticism (or what we just perceive as being unfair remarks), we can listen and still have the confidence to keep living Godly and productive lives. Our lives may or may not be productive in the eyes of society, but when we love God we live for his praise, and not for the praise of others. Oswald Chambers wrote, "Many are devoted to causes (political parties or denominations) and so few are devoted to Jesus Christ." But whether we are for or against a cause or particular ideas, the important thing in life is to be devoted to Jesus Christ, through whom all things were created and who has all power in heaven and in earth.

Then nothing will be able to separate us from the love of God when Jesus Christ is our Lord, says the Holy Spirit in Romans 8:39: Paul, through whom the Holy Spirit spoke, has the certainty that he is one of those who loves God and follows Jesus as Lord. John Calvin says that he knows that, not by special revelation, but by a perception common to all the Godly. Whatever happened in the past or will happen in the future, there is no luck or chance or accident. God reigns, and our task is to align ourselves with the will of God and to seek His glory in all circumstances we enter. Sooner or later, what the world regards as harmful, is an advantage to the Christian. No, I do not always see that either!

From a human perspective, we make things happen (or not). But from God's perspective, God sets one up and brings another one down. Psalm 23:1 says, "The Lord is my shepherd." When the Lord of the universe really is our shepherd, we shall not want or lack any good thing.

That is the promise of God, and we are to trust his Word when it conflicts with our feelings or logic! We who are Christian, are called by God according to his purposes and not according to our purposes. That offends every Christian sooner or later. Dr. James Dobson said his father was a very gifted artist, who was deeply disappointed when he sensed that God was calling him to preach. Finally, near the end of his high school when he was impressed by the Holy Spirit to make a decision to preach, he turned his face up in an act of defiance and said, "It is too great a price and I won't pay it." Just then his Godly mother came into the room; she noticed his ashen face and inquired about what was wrong. When he told her, she thought he was just being emotional, and she began to pray.

As she prayed, suddenly she stopped in mid-sentence and said, "I don't understand it. Something is wrong." For seven years her son did not hear the voice of God again. If you have never heard the voice of God for the first time, you will probably think that is not possible, and that she was faking or delusional. But for the Christian who has heard God speak, it is devastating not to somehow sense his guidance and comfort clearly, at least sometimes. He rededicated his life to Jesus Christ, became an evangelist, and later the head of an art department in a college. When we love God, he causes even the detours we take to work together for our good. That is because of his great promise in Romans 8:28, that all things work together for good for those who love God. That promise includes all that has happened in the past, all that is going on right now, and all that will happen in the future. What peace and joy that verse gives to the Christian who trusts it. I am amazed at the difference it makes in my own life when I do trust that verse over my doubts and fears and troubles!

One of the ancestors of Dr. James Dobson was promised supernaturally that all of his descendants would be saved (converted) down through the fourth generation. He was not only promised that nothing would be able to separate him from the love of God, but even that nothing would be able to separate his descendants from the love of God in Jesus Christ either. Through being drawn by the Holy Spirit to love Jesus Christ and then giving our lives to him, we need never to fear the past or present or future. The Godly soul stands and thrives on the inward testimony of the Holy Spirit based on the Bible, and not on external supports.

When we are self-righteous, it is offensive to know that our righteousness is as filthy rags to God.

I only recently discovered that when the very Godly Duncan Campbell held great revivals where thousands were converted to Jesus Christ (and with evidence of changed lives), he was opposed not only by liberals but by conservative churches that broke away from the Church of Scotland. The so-called free churches were concerned about what they perceived as a drift away from historic Christianity by the main church body there. Yet when the main church group welcomed a true work of God, those who considered themselves more pure and more doctrinally correct were bypassed in their dead orthodoxy, and their children for the most part were never converted. A dear lady in my congregation in Montreal was present in those days, and belonged to one of the free churches, yet never showed any concern or interest in the things of God.

Many who objected to the sins of the Roman Catholic Church with the bloody Crusades and the Inquisition, etc., formed Protestant denominations that then proceeded to murder about as many innocent people, all in the name of Jesus Christ who died to save the very ones being slaughtered by those who fancied themselves to be his followers. Prayer sessions often turn into gripe sessions against those of different theological persuasions, instead of meetings to meet with God for his forgiveness and guidance.

Undoubtedly such individuals do have many sins that need repentance. But we miss a great work of God in our own lives when we compare ourselves favorably to those we consider to be more liberal/conservative. We can always see others to the left or to the right of ourselves. And it is easy to see their sins, because it feeds our pride and arrogance to feel that at least we are not as bad as some other person or group.

But God says that even the most conservative, orthodox, historically Christian person or congregation or denomination, has righteousness that is as filthy rags in his sight. This sounds unduly harsh when we are self-righteous, but God says it is the contrite/repentant heart that he will not despise- all others he does despise! This is true even when we know and affirm truth with our minds. To give intellectual assent is important, but never enough to approach God. He must take the initiative and call us, and then once drawn by the Holy Spirit we can respond with faith and obedience—not before.

Neither I nor you nor any other person or group is immune from the human inclination to avoid the first word of the gospel- repent. But only through repentance can anyone become friends with the God of the universe. Then only by praying for deeper and deeper layers of repentance can we have his words in due season, with his attitudes, in order to walk with God and also to encourage others in his direction. This is the most worthwhile and fulfilling life possible for anyone. Does that mean we will have great success as Duncan Campbell had? Perhaps and perhaps not. Isaiah and Jeremiah were very Godly prophets, yet God told them not to worry about whether anyone would believe their message or not- God promised them that others would not!

The Israelites had the law and the prophets, and yet Isaiah foretold that only a remnant of them would ever be friends with God. We have media pastors and all kinds of creative and technological and expensive methods to proclaim what God says. Yet Barna research shows that fewer and fewer young people in the USA are being converted to love and obey Jesus Christ. The exceptions see someone like Duncan Campbell, who preached in the power of the Holy Spirit. He was unconcerned about being considered Calvinist or Arminian, but proclaimed both the power and sovereignty of God, and our responsibility to respond to the gospel. With a holy life he told of the great mercy and love of God, and also of God's great hatred of the sin that so harms us. When we get a glimpse of the love and justice of God, we are convicted of our sins and our need for the Savior, Jesus Christ. If we imagine ourselves to be pure love and pure justice, we will cause our children and others we love to gag when we point them to Jesus Christ. Instead, let us point others to Jesus Christ who is full of grace and truth, and not to ourselves, so full of the opposite, at best!

"Blessed are the pure in heart for they shall see God." I don't know about you, but sometimes I have trouble seeing God. Sometimes he seems very distant and seems to have forgotten about me. I know verses to the contrary for those who are friends with Jesus Christ, but I am stating a factual situation. If you have times like that, so did King David, who was called a man after God's own heart! God promised though the prophet Samuel that David would be king, but before he was crowned, enemies carried off his family and the families of his men. Then his own soldiers blamed him for their misfortune and spoke of stoning him. It was at that time that David strengthened himself in the Lord his God, but for a while instead of seeing God at work, David saw only his friends who had turned on him to kill him!

Luke 24:16 says "Their eyes were kept from recognizing him." This refers to the disciples who walked towards Emmaus and were joined by Jesus on their journey. They talked of how they "had hoped" in Jesus, but at the crucifixion had lost hope. These were not pagans or those who were being entertained by the news of his demise, but his friends!

I am one of those friends of Jesus who can say many times that I have lost hope in his goodness. It is difficult to speak of that to others for it means to admit that we have pride and arrogance when we know the Bible and its great promises for his followers. But if we pretend to be better than King David, we will be hypocrites in addition to embracing the above mentioned sins! Any times we are sad and depressed or mad and impatient at others, we lose hope in the love of God for us, and that he reigns and really, no kidding, causes all things to work together for our good (Romans 8:28),

On the other hand, we see God in the slow driver ahead of us, in the days and nights of loneliness, in the blocked plans for work or" blocked productivity," when we keep faith in his promises that he reigns and is love. Those two traits of God were emphasized so much by the Presbyterian churches, that I knew I belonged in that branch. Hymns such as "O Love That Will Not Let Me Go" by the blind Presbyterian minister George Mathison, spoke to me deeply. I am not implying that the power of God and love of God is always held in balance by that group, or that when it was, I was trusting in those attributes of God as I should have been, or that one cannot find those teachings in other branches of Christianity, but the Presbyterian mix worked for me and still does. I could give several examples of recognizing God throughout my ministry where my eyes were opened to see God clearly at work. I could also speak of many years where, as with the disciples in Luke 24:16, my eyes were kept from recognizing him. I can honestly say that I was at least as dedicated to God and as intelligent, etc., during the times of darkness as I was when God was accomplishing things through me clearly.

The Dutch Christian Corrie Ten Boom and her sister Betsy were in a German concentration camp because they helped hide Jews from the Nazis. While in their prison Betsy recognized God even then, for at that time her heart was more pure than Corrie's. Corrie griped and complained and wanted revenge on her torturers, but Betsy was much more forgiving and peaceful, and died in the camp. Only later did Corrie have her eyes opened to see the purpose of God and his plans for her life. David, the two disciples on the road to Emmaus, Corrie, I, and you, sooner or later have times when God does not fit our logic or feelings, and our eyes are "kept from recognizing him." May God have mercy on us then, so that we continue to follow the Lord by faith instead of by sight/logic/feelings!

Politics

Republicans and Democrats both have elements that embrace and reject the teachings of the Holy Spirit as laid down in the Bible. Republicans emphasize that "those who do not work should not eat, as the Bible teaches, and they encourage individual responsibility and the accumulation of wealth. They tend to try to conserve the past mores and since the older the individual, the more likely that person is to be honest, that is sometimes a plus. Republicans tout family values in the sense of protecting male-female marriages, the norm since the Bible teaches that a man (singular) shall leave his parents and cling to his wife (singular). Also, a Republican made it four times easier to open a business here than in the European Union!

On the downside from a Christian perspective, Republicans tend to favor big business so much that labor or environmental concerns may be ignored. I recall that the multimillionaire Adriana Huffington was running for the Republican nomination for governor of California, and she got huffy when a reporter asked her why she paid only $800 in taxes the previous year. Instead of answering that very legitimate question she merely complained about the question. Surely no one who cares a whit about fairness is for laws that allow her and many others in her financial category to pay fewer taxes than poor people do.

On the other hand, Democrats generally teach where much is given much is required (a variation of an often-quoted passage in the Bible). They have supported the poor and working classes with Medicare and social security. Immigrants historically entered the USA at the lowest rungs of society and gravitated to the Democrats, joining racist southern agrarian landowners against northern industrialists (big business). When I was a social worker in a hospital I visited a dying Pentecostal minister, who was full of the Holy Spirit unmistakably, and almost as devoted to the fiery labor leader John L. Lewis. This Democratic concern for the downtrodden coal miners and poor caused blacks to largely abandon the historic party of Abraham Lincoln for the Democrats. Just as few white evangelical Christians vote Democratic, few evangelical black Christians vote Republican. Abortion, feminism, and homosexuality have also found more acceptance in the Democratic Party as a result of the emphasis on individual rights.

So, from a Christian point of view, the Republicans seem to be more concerned about personal morality while the Democrats seem more interested in public morality. But the Bible teaches us to be holy and righteous and also concerned about justice and mercy in all areas of life. Are Christians assimilating, or having much impact on either party? I am convinced that neither party deserves to be seen as the party of God, but I hope that Christians in each camp encourage and support people of integrity and fairness.

Even good people once elected sometimes lose their ethical attitudes and behavior, and sometimes scoundrels convert and take the high moral ground while in office. So, it is difficult to really know the candidates except through the lenses of the media, and even if we really do get to know them, they may radically change once in power. I hope we support justice and mercy and pray to walk humbly with God enough so that we will recognize it when politicians embrace it. We have no good reason to bash rich or poor, business or labor, but we are all to work for a fair and just society. All segments of society are to be treated with respect and compassion when different interests compete. We are commanded to pray for our president, senators, and congress whether we voted for them or not. When we are righteous then our prayers will benefit them more than if we had not prayed for them, as we ask God to guide and to encourage them in his ways. Our prayers also help us to defang some of our arrogant and bitter attitudes when we lift up our elected representatives to God. The high moral ground may seem much simpler when we are not privy to all the facts, so when we pray for others, it helps to deepen humility within us. How much better it is for whichever side is in power to have a Godly and respectful and peaceful electorate, instead of one that does not care what pleases God, but practices rudeness and even violence. This is because God tells us in Proverbs 14:34 "Righteousness exalts a nation, but sin is a reproach to any people.

"The line dividing good and evil cuts through the heart of every human being."

So said Alexander Solzhenitsyn, after his imprisonment. He had documented the cruel and evil behavior of the guards and the communist officials in Russia. He himself was made a prisoner after he wrote to a friend saying critical remarks about Stalin. He was completely disillusioned about the communism he had previously supported, when he saw the lies that were told just in order to get the thousands of slave laborers necessary to build the cities and to mine and to build up the Soviet empire.

His book *The Gulag*, gives clear and precise stories of heroism among the prisoners and stories of brutality and cowardice by the guards and others responsible for running the terrorism machine. But in the midst of all that, Solzhenitsyn met dedicated Christians and became one himself. Then the Holy Spirit allowed him to see that he was also guilty of sin. As an officer he had a sense of entitlement, and he expected his orderly/servant to treat him with deference. He insisted on rights that were denied to others who had lesser rank and saw that he was full of pride also. He repented and walked with God, and blessed his prison walls for breaking down his arrogance until he was able to seek and to find the truth, Agan, in John 14:6, Jesus said. "I am the way, and the truth, and the life." Without his trauma, he would not have seen his need for God.

Without many car wrecks I would not have seen my need to follow Jesus Christ either. God was merciful, yet sometimes his mercy seems severe when we are comfort and pleasure seeking, instead of seeking first the kingdom of God. "Seek ye first the kingdom of God, and his righteousness, and all these things will be added to you," the Bible promises. All things that we need, in other words, will then be granted to us. Perhaps we do not need the relationship we are now in, or the job we have, or the wealth we have accumulated, or the health we so value. Solzhenitsyn did not need the status he had as an army officer. Although he did not join in the rapes and murders of German women once the Russian army crossed the German border, avenging the German tortures and murders (they had a policy of murdering twenty-five percent of each village and town they entered in order to terrify the survivors), he saw his own sins and his need to find forgiveness and to make peace with God.

He saw that although he might be better than some people, he had no hope of being friends with God unless he cast himself upon the mercy of God as a sinner, and prayed, "God have mercy on me a sinner." The most upright and socially acceptable person still has, the Bible says, righteousness that is as filthy rags in the sight of God (Isaiah 64:6). In our eyes perhaps, another person is better than Hitler or Stalin or someone else we know. But no one can boast in the presence of God, when we really do come into his presence in a Godly church service, for example. God is holy and perfect, and his perfection and holiness makes even the most Godly of us cry out for mercy and forgiveness, when and if he ever, has made his presence known to us truly. When the holy John, who was exiled to the isle of Patmos, came into the presence of God, he did not prance around bragging about how wonderful he was. No, the Bible quotes him as saying, "I fell at his feet as though dead." If something similar does not happen at your church, you are not going to church- but a social club.

Since I was single until age fifty, I understand how difficult it is to wait for God, and how tempting it is to be involved with someone without "praying through" until we have clear peace and guidance from God. I dated some who were wonderful Christians, but others I had no business dating at all, and I almost married two of them! I had misgivings, but after many years of increasing loneliness I grew desperate and hoped for the best. I had no peace from God so I did keep praying and took a vacation to be with Christian friends and returned completely convinced that I should break it off. The second near disaster was averted only because the woman showed her fangs not long before the marriage.

At that time, I had pastored for over fifteen years, I was praying and reading the Bible regularly, and was walking with God as closely as I knew how. And still I was close to catastrophe two different times. That is scary!

According to Barna research, only ten percent of Christians pray about whom to marry, where to work or to live. But I am sure that a very small percentage of those people pray until they are certain that God wants them to marry a particular individual or not. This is incredibly important, because with our unique abilities and limitations and experiences, the next best person for us is far inferior to the very best person God has for us. In this situation the quote by Oswald Chambers is especially true when he says, "The good is always the enemy of the best."

A good friend who had warned me that the first woman I almost married was not right for me (God bless him), later spoke excitedly about someone he met, and the only good thing he could say was how beautiful her legs were. This was a good man, not a womanizer, and always spoke and acted respectfully towards women. I met her only after the marriage and saw no evidence that she was for him at all, but much evidence that she was not best for him. I had left that area and had no possibility of giving advice, but it is so important to get the prayers and counsel of Godly friends before making a very important decision such as marriage. Otherwise, we either ruin our lives or settle for a faint shadow of the great plans God has for us. How terrible it would be to always know that we had married out of his will, as many have deliberately done.

The most educated and brilliant among us have very limited wisdom and charm, and never enough to marry or even to date without the permission of the Holy Spirit, who is the point man for the Trinity. I do not like to think that I am easily swayed by my feelings, but I saw clearly that I would have destroyed myself except for the great mercy of God. So it is not enough to lift up a few sincere prayers for protection and guidance as we make dating and marriage choices. God wants us to know his will-not guess it, and especially when the decision has so many far reaching consequences. 1 Samuel 25:3: "... Abigail was discerning and beautiful , but the man was harsh and badly behaved." Her marriage was almost certainly arranged for her in that culture, but we have the possibility and therefore the responsibility to "pray through" until we know for sure that God has arranged our marriage.

Christian work habits?

Are we teaching and practicing good work habits? A few years ago, forty-six percent of Americans under age forty-five bought Japanese cars. Was this because they were not patriotic? No, it was because at least some of them read *Consumer Report Magazine*, which showed of fifty-four car models with below average performance, fifty-three were American. Does quality work matter to God? According to the Bible, it does.

Colossians 3:23 says, "Whatever you do, work heartily, as for the Lord and not for men (your employers). Some have advertised themselves to be Christian in order to be hired, and then did substandard work. But carpenters are to do their best when they build houses, or when we teach, or deliver pizza. Management is to respect employees and to provide safe and positive environments and fair wages. Employees are then to do quality work, even when it makes slackers look bad.

Christians are to be especially honest and hard-working, whether we get more money or applause or not, because we are promised by God that he rewards us when we work for his glory in the midst of any task. Our American prosperity tempts us to spoil our children rotten, to raise them to think they are entitled to wealth without earning it, and to be handed everything easily. But individual responsibility is very important to stress, instead of measuring in our minds how much we think others owe us. Every breath is a gift from God, and he gives people in the USA usually many more advantages than in other countries where people are at least as Godly, hard-working, honest, and intelligent. I hope these facts bring thanksgiving within us, instead of pride and arrogance.

The Russian writer Solzhenitsyn noted that the West (those countries west of Russia) has human rights, "but man's sense of responsibility to God and society grew dimmer and dimmer." Those who believe that God is only an abstract projection of our own hopes have no awe of a personal God, and may see verses encouraging honest and wholehearted work to be either management propaganda or musings of neurotic employees.

Although false guilt can exist from family or societal expectations, the Bible teaches that God has revealed right and wrong to us. It is right to use our abilities for honest and positive work to honor God, to make a more peaceful and just society, in addition to supporting ourselves. The alternative is to pursue meaningless pleasure and irresponsibly at the expense of others!

George Washington said, "Let us with caution indulge the supposition that morality can be maintained without religion. Whatever may be conceded to the influence of refined education on minds ... reason and experience both forbid us to expect that national morality can prevail in exclusion of religious principles." Hitler proved that Washington was right, for he won over the great German universities long before he influenced the masses. As we can testify about ourselves, our neighbors and spouses, education just makes a person more refined, and certainly not better. Or as C.S. Lewis would put it, education just makes a person a more clever devil.

Our second president, John Adams wrote, "We have no government armed with power capable of contending with human passions unbridled by morality and religion ... Our Constitution was made only for a moral and religious people. It is wholly inadequate to the government of any other." Are we still a moral and religious people? I may be the wrong person to answer that question, since my umbrella was stolen at Walmart shortly before writing this article. But a George Barna study found that 57 percent of evangelical youth do not believe in an absolute standard of truth. Therefore, even when truth is preached and taught as being real and clear and unchanging, what the Bible calls sin is considered okay when the individual wants to make an exception for pleasure or materialism.

In the not too distant past, those who did what the Bible calls wrong admitted they were wrong (for the most part) and did what they wanted to do anyway. But now the whole notion of truth is outdated for many, even within churches that theologically teach truth. Several are outraged at the very notion that anyone can know truth at all. Jesus said, "The truth will set you free," yet many prefer to stay in bondage to fables or feelings. Dr. Wayne Greene, a Los Angeles Jungian psychologist, feels that a clear break between good and evil is not something we want our children to learn these days. It is relatively easy to make such pronouncements from a rich suburb or a gated community where crime is very rare. But I suspect that every single victim of crime prefers that the criminal had made "a clear break between good and evil," and that individuals choose good (honesty, kindness, unselfishness, and so on). When we rationalize and excuse harmful behavior in ourselves and in others, often this evil continues to develop to logical consequences when consciences become seared as with a hot iron. Finally, some are able to shoot innocent children to death, or harm others who stand in the way of greed and other sins, when internal restraints against evil behavior are removed by our acceptance of the rules of the world.

Memorial Day tradition

On Memorial Day each year, our family joined mom's extended family to decorate the graves at Saint James Lutheran Church in Greene County, Tennessee. I felt very welcome, and respect Lutherans highly because of those times. Finally, mom felt guilty for neglecting dad's family so she asked him if he would like to go to decorate the graves of his people on that day. He answered, "Why? No, they would not know anything about it."

Most of the flower arrangements or the details in homes result from female preferences. Guys, on the other hand, usually prefer the practical and fewer frills. I do not think one approach is better or more loving than another way. Men tend to think an emphasis on the fancy and ornate is trivial and impractical, while women tend to think that the spartan and austere is cold and less cozy.

My dad never put his arm around my shoulder or told me that he loved me, yet I never doubted that he loved me. I did not sense my mom's love more because she was more demonstrative since both showed love in different ways. Dad did things with me and enjoyed my company, and encouraged independence. Mom concerned herself more over losses and troubles to indicate her support. Children need to be affirmed from different angles, and that is one reason God hates divorce.

Cultures also express love in different ways. Africans often resent questions about their children, while Europeans regard such questions as methods to establish rapport. Northern Europeans sometimes seem cold and aloof to Southern Europeans while northerners consider their southern neighbors sometimes too emotional and shallow. In the USA, southerners can choose to describe the speech of northerners as precise, or harsh. Northerners can choose to characterize the speech of southerners as soft, or lazy. In other words we can choose to appreciate our differences or insult one another!

My parents loved their own parents equally as much, I think. I am glad they didn't criticize each other for different ways of expressing their love. Let us pray to be full of grace and truth as Jesus was (John 1:14). Then when others do not show us love as we show love because they are a different gender or race or culture, I hope we pray for them and treat them as we want to be treated.

In the first place, they may have the best of intentions towards us. Several times a person has told me of how another person appreciates me, when I had no idea that was true. I have had the opposite happen too! But even when we know someone doesn't appreciate us, we are still to try to express the love of God to them in ways they can recognize and accept. I know from experience that is not always possible. But especially for those who are close to us, we are responsible to keep looking for ways to encourage them and to build them up. If flowers are meaningful to you, let the other person know. If flowers are not important to a person who is significant to you, try to find out what is. Then if it is possible and ethical, do it!

Playboys or Godly men?

Are our men becoming playboys or Godly? In 2011 only thirty-seven percent of the college graduates in the USA were male. The good news is that women are studying more and accomplishing more, and I for one applaud that. But the bad news is that men seem to be increasingly irresponsible. The average man in his twenties spends four hours a day playing video games. We all need to unwind at times, but to me this seems excessive.

So why are many females making great progress while so many males are shirking responsibilities? Hugh Hefner and his ilk have encouraged men to be playboys. Of course, they could not be that way unless women gave consent to be play girls. But much worse than that, many churches teach men to treat women as playthings to be discarded when they get tired of them.

A Presbyterian minister friend in Toronto dumped his wife and children and remarried and moved to another church. He was evangelical and highly respected across Canada. I met both women, and from a human point of view, it was nearly impossible to say he was wrong, because the new wife was far better looking and much friendlier.

But since God says that he hates divorce, at least in the churches, I am convinced that his view should trump our feelings or logic. I understand that it is normally not easy in this kind of situation, and in many other ones either. But he and we are responsible to do the right thing-to be faithful to a spouse and children, even when we prefer to be a playboy.

Men who have considered themselves historic Christians in the past have for the most part shouldered the responsibility to confront evil—not to make excuses for it—in ourselves first of all, then in our families. We have not only tried to protect our sons and daughters from society, but have tried to protect society from our sons and daughters also. I know there needs to be a balance between nurture and toughness to do what is right (which I have certainly have not always done), but the balance seems skewed towards nurturing what the Bible calls selfishness and ungodliness many times.

The head of a Christian organization recently advised a caller who wanted to date, to first of all divorce his wife who has Alzheimer's disease. The co-host objected that Christians vow to stay married until death. He replied that Alzheimer's is a form of death. By his reckoning, the loss of beauty or income or ability to hike the Great Smoky Mts with me could qualify as a form of death. Thankfully, even many pagans have more compassion than to be a playboy in such terrible conditions.

On a much more positive note, Dr. McQuilken, the president of a Christian college in Columbia, SC, realized that his wife who developed Alzheimer's needed him more and more. He resigned in order to spend time with her. He said they loved each other, she needed him now more than ever, and was much more peaceful when he was with her. He considered it an honor to get to spend time with her, and to take care of her. He is a person of good character, and a Godly example for us all (especially if you are looking for a spouse).

May God deliver us from playboys within or outside the church (and the females who enable them), who live for selfish materialism or pleasure. None of us are immune from the charms of irresponsibility, but may God help us to be more open to the highest form of existence—to be acting justly, loving mercy, and walking humbly with the risen Jesus Christ.

Put God above nation or ethnic group.

A retired newspaper editor told me this story when he learned I had worked in Toronto. Just after the Sun Sphere in Knoxville, Tennessee, was shattered by gunshots, he was in Toronto riding in a taxi. He had mentioned to the driver that he was from Knoxville, and he later remarked how beautiful a certain glass building was. The taxi driver said it was too bad that we could not have nice glass buildings in Tennessee. Well, we are not all trigger-happy savages. But relative to Canada, I admit that we are very violent.

There are one hundred times more murders in the USA than in Canada. Yes we do have ten times more people, but that is still a ratio of ten murders for every one committed in Canada. Why is that? I have two theories to explain the difference. The first one is that the USA was born in violence. The revolution that overthrew the yoke of Great Britain also encouraged a contempt for authority that continued as the colonists pushed west. Often the biggest bully became the law, whereas in Canada settlers normally continued to respect authority. Canada was settled by almost exactly the same ethnic stock, but they never overthrew their government. I know many of the founding fathers were dedicated Christians, and perhaps they did the right thing. But the fact is, that our nation was formed by bloodshed while Canada was not. Their history of westward expansion is relatively boring because it was considerably more peaceful.

Another huge factor in the fierceness here compared to Canada, is the introduction of slavery. Colonialists in Jamestown, Virginia, were approached by a Spanish slaver who wanted to trade slaves for food, and the practice first took root in this country. Slavery brutalized master and slave alike. It was an evil institution. Some Christians recognized it as such and fought it , while some treated others as they did not want to be treated themselves, thus completely contradicting the Bible. Abraham Lincoln spoke eloquently when he said, “As I would not be a slave, so I would not be a master.”

Canada has its own problems, but the legacy of revolution and slavery are not among them. They have achieved a free and prosperous country without either event. “O, we are not that violent,” I protested to a Canadian friend who was appalled at the level of viciousness. Then he told me of driving down I-75 near Atlanta when he noticed suddenly a man in a car beside him, pointing a gun at him. He said he assumed he had cut him off in traffic unintentionally. He sped up and finally lost him at an exit (I confess that I proceeded to tell him some stories much more gruesome than that just to shock him).

May God give us the gift to see ourselves not only as others see us, but as God himself sees us. I love my country as much as anyone, but God says that all nations are as nothing before him. So I hope we are friends with the Triune God and put him first in our lives, above any national or ethnic pretentiousness.

Spiritual seekers find boredom or awe in church?

The church is one of the last places spiritual seekers will go for spirituality. Why do so many who have an earnest desire to experience God not even consider going to a church? If you have been to several churches you already know the answer.

One of the pastors who preceded me would abruptly end a meeting of the leaders of the congregation if it interfered with his hockey game. It is common to hear conversations before and after church about anything but salvation or holiness. Even in a church setting it is a struggle to get our minds on the things of God and how to honor him. Yet at the same time there is an increased consciousness of the unseen world outside the church buildings by those who never darken the door of a church.

Do you think it is possible that those who claim to be friends with the creator might develop at least a vague interest in the supernatural? If so, you would think they would be curious enough to discuss what God is doing in our lives and how to join with him!

We need to take seriously the criticisms of so many spiritual searchers that they do not see Christians involved in any kind of spiritual quest such as prayer meetings or Bible studies or social involvement. Their case is sometimes overstated, but it is rare for church members to miss meals for fasting or sports events in order to grow in favor with God. American Christianity tends to be a mile wide and an inch deep, many outsiders have noted. Even Christians/church members interested in spiritual growth sometimes see churches as caught in the grip of rationalism and enlightenment banalities, and much look elsewhere for substance.

Episcopalian priest and futurist Richard Kew States, "Western believers are for the first time in approximately 70 generations being challenged to live in a culture that has cast itself adrift from the predominance of Christian ideas and values." Nazi Germany and Soviet Russia being exceptions, European culture has been deeply influenced to at least give lip service to Christian concepts of justice and mercy. Now we are more nearly like the generation into which Christianity was born. When the Holy Spirit is an unmistakable reality in the lives of churchgoers, and the pagans will see the same kind of explosive growth as the early followers of Jesus Christ saw.

Where are the churches like those in the book of Acts, where Ananias and Sapphira were struck dead by God (Acts 5) because they pretended to be more holy than they really were, in order to get more status? Do we elevate such people to leadership in our congregations, or is the Holy Spirit so free to reign that the awe of the Lord Jesus restrains such individuals in our midst? What are you doing to help move your congregation from a mere social club (when that is the case) to a place where the Triune God of the universe is sought and found and followed? Social and political and personal justice then flow from people who love what God loves, hates what God hates, and who consider important what he calls important.

I understand that rejection of universal truth claims does provide some comfort for an increasing multi-culturalism in the USA and Canada and Europe. After all, history shows us that truth claims have been used to oppress and persecute segments of the population that did not share the values of the dominant group in a society. So it is logical that many would welcome views that promise spirituality with no restraint on our selfish instincts.

At the same time, Jesus Christ claims that he is eternal God with all power in heaven and in earth and the judge of all people. I and all of his other followers can be justly criticized for many sins of omission and commission. But no one who knows the life of Jesus Christ has any legitimate complaints about him. When we live to honor him, his presence and power fills our churches. Then the result for the spiritual seeker is not boredom but awe!

The 1800 Revival

By the year 1800, the effects of the Great Awakening/Revival of 1735-1740 had almost vanished in the USA. There were no Christians at Yale, which was formed at least in part because Harvard had forsaken historic Christianity. Princeton was more evangelical, yet only two students there even claimed to be Christian. The rest put on plays that mocked Christianity, burned Bibles, and were admirers of the French atheist Voltaire.

If you murdered someone in the northeast or Virginia and did not want to get caught, all you had to do was to travel to Kentucky or Tennessee and blend in with the wild masses. In these areas there were no court cases for years at a time. Oh, there were a few law abiding folks; some had a pitched gun battle with outlaw elements in Kentucky, but lost!

However the grandson of Jonathan Edwards, the main catalyst for the 1735 revival (and later president of Princeton), became president of Yale. His name was Timothy Dwight, a devout Christian of integrity and courage. His preaching influenced many students to begin to follow Jesus Christ as God and Lord.

Holy Ghost revival spread throughout the country, and Methodist minister Peter Cartwright was one of the main leaders in Kentucky. Thousands were brought into the kingdom of God (including the parents of Abraham Lincoln), with visible changes in behavior for the better.

Meanwhile in the White House, President Thomas Jefferson published a Bible with the supernatural references to Jesus deleted, he had children by one slave and brought friends over to rape some of the others. So the revival did not convert everyone, yet still, huge numbers of Americans began to act justly, to love mercy, and to walk humbly with the risen Jesus Christ. But as far as I know, revival has never happened throughout history without Christians first of all being convicted of our own sins, and our need to draw closer to God.

When asked how I am, I normally respond, "Better than I deserve"(yes I probably got it from the financial expert Dave Ramsey). I do not always feel that way, but as a Christian I am sure I did nothing to deserve salvation or being kept by God when I chose to raise hell, and I have many more benefits from family and country that I absolutely did nothing to deserve. Yet many who go to church will argue with me, and claim that they deserve much more. Unfortunately, that is a sense of entitlement that dogs all Americans, Christian or not.

Christians, however, know that Jesus died as a substitute for our sins when we were unlovely and enemies of the cross. Our only logical response should be great gratitude, not, "Give me some more." I know many of us are walking on the edge of a financial cliff, and whether it is a problem of our own making or not, this or some other problem tends to occupy our highest thoughts. But Jesus says, "Seek first the kingdom of God and his righteousness, and all these things will be added to you."

I have trouble believing that all the time too. If I have money I do not have a spouse, if I have money and a spouse I am sick, or someone is out to get me, or some other difficulties are around. That is true for all people almost all the time, so we can all give excuses for not seeking first the kingdom of God and his righteousness.

What is your excuse? What is my excuse? What keeps us from humbling ourselves before the mighty hand of God and pleading for revival in ourselves firstly, and then in our land? Are we waiting for a better spouse, or better health or a better financial situation? Then this is another god to us, and we disobey the first commandment, which says, "You shall have no other gods before me."

As far as I know, we have never had a more hypocritical president than Thomas Jefferson. So no matter who is in the White House (or in the primary residence of your country), we never have reason to despair over the state of Christianity in our nation. It is not a political problem anyway, but it is the problem of those of us who call ourselves Christians if the nation where we live does not experience an outpouring of the Holy Spirit in power. Second Chronicles 7:14 "If my people who are called by my name, humble themselves and pray and seek my face, and turn from their wicked ways, then will I hear from heaven and will forgive their sin and heal their land."

We can depend on that to take place! Research shows that couples argue about money more than anything else. But the money and heated discussions on how it is to be spent, only points out the basic selfishness of human nature. When a couple rages at each other over whether to pay money for more clothes or more toys, more trips to the beach or the mountains, something deeper is at stake. Money is not the problem but the love of money is. We all need money for food, clothes and shelter. But how fancy must our food and clothes and shelter be? The answer is much if we are selfish and greedy and like to show off. But to be precise, that desire is never a need but only a want.

A TV program recently spoke of greed being the foundation of capitalism. That is perhaps true, and harmful when it is without regulation, but I am sure that greed permeates any system. That is because our hearts are naturally geared towards our own "well-being," even when others are hurt by our ambition. That is why it is so important for us to pray to let God define our "well-being." When it is well with our soul, when we walk with God, we have peace and joy with him and with anyone else who is walking with God.

Certainly, it is important to have our family walking with God, even if no one else we know does that. Families and friends can and should see any crisis, economic or otherwise, as a very important opportunity to encourage each other in all possible ethical ways. This may mean to cheer us on in a very difficult and ill-fitting job, or to encourage the search for more compatible work. But whatever else encouraging each other means, it will include praying for and with each other, to know and to do the will of Jesus Christ. Only four percent of Christian couples pray together regularly, so the vast majority are missing a key ingredient of a Godly and mutually edifying marriage.

Sincere prayer for repentance and guidance will result in more patience and kindness within us, and will kill or at least suppress the desire to look down on others who have less and to be jealous towards those who have more. Thinking Christianly, whether we have a great or terrible economic situation, means to consider important what God says is important, and to consider unimportant what he judges as trivial. "Be content," says a Bible verse above a photo of two little Amish girls clutching some homemade dolls. Well, I am sure they must also fight the universal human desire for more and more things. But if we have love from God and our family and friends, we are rich in what matters most. We all realize that sooner or later, but some do not discover it until we have amassed money and have separated ourselves from God and family and friends. But when we have love and respect, I hope we appreciate it and do not take it for granted.

And if we feel we do not have love or respect, ever or for only short periods of time, then we are still called to grow in grace or favor with God anyway. Sometime difficulty, financial or otherwise, is a shortcut to the grace of God. We are all called to get our worth and value from being friends with Jesus Christ, and nothing else. That is not natural or easy for me to do, or for you or for anyone else in the world either! When we think we are walking with God, we are often just depending on our money or job or family for status. Or we feel worthless because we have no money or job or family. Either extreme keeps us from the peace Jesus offers to those who love and obey him in pleasant or unpleasant circumstances.

"All is vanity," God spoke through Solomon. A German billionaire who committed suicide recently evidently agreed. Many of those who knew him undoubtedly envied him for his work, his house, cars, tailored suits, etc. But instead of envying someone, let us be thankful if the Holy Spirit has drawn us to follow Jesus Christ, and then love and obey him daily. He said the foxes have holes but the Son of man (referring to himself) has nowhere to lay his head. Do we really feel that we deserve better than the one through whom all things were made, and for whom all things were made? Yes, we do think that. May God forgive us and have mercy on us.

Klan leader preaches in a black church (after his conversion to Jesus Christ)

USA Today reported that a high ranking Ku Klux Klan leader in Texas was in the habit of calling a black preacher, with threats to kill him, among other insults. But one day he called and his tone was radically changed for the better. The Klansman informed the preacher that he had become a Christian, and furthermore, God had called him to preach. The minister invited him to preach the next Sunday at his church. When the Klansman asked for directions, he was told that he should know, for he had burned the church down (three times if I remember correctly).

That was one church service I would like to have attended! I wonder if the pastor told anyone in advance who was coming to preach, for he could have packed it to the gills if he did. Or perhaps it would have been a more powerful bombshell if he had just announced that a Klan leader who had threatened to kill him and had burned their church was now about to speak. Either way, I suspect it will be a service that will be long remembered by those who were there.

The Klansman had a clear change of heart, as any one does who is truly converted to Jesus Christ. Then the cross becomes an object of respect instead of a symbol of hatred, as in the photo by the article. Klansmen who really follow the cross of Jesus Christ repent of their sins and treat others as they would like to be treated, regardless of color or status or any other trait. True love means to encourage others to do what honors Jesus Christ and to avoid whatever does not honor Jesus Christ/the Triune God, who inspired the Bible.

But after the Klansman repented and had to ask for forgiveness, then the church members had a big problem. They then had to forgive him, if they had any hope of walking with God, for God says if you do not forgive others then I will not forgive you. They had to work hard to rebuild the church this evil guy had burnt, and had no doubt been hurt by his influence when they looked for jobs or tried to live in peace normally. When I am wronged, I prefer the person get on TV or in a newspaper or on the internet and say what a terrible person he was and how wonderful I was, and how terrible it was that I was wronged. But that is pride and arrogance speaking. We are to forgive even when the offender is unrepentant. That is because our relationship with God is at stake, and we are to walk with God, no matter what others do or do not do.

There have been many examples throughout history of very evil people coming to Christ, and becoming a new creation. And we are right to be glad every time that happens. But Klansmen are not the only ones who need to repent, since the Bible says that all have sinned and come short of the glory of God. Furthermore, God says that even our righteousness is as filthy rags in his sight. That offends those of us who have not murdered or followed Hitler or Stalin or Charles Manson, etc. But we all have either open or secret sins that are unholy and need to be forsaken in order to walk with God. So let us pray to be thankful that God accepts not only the Klansmen and the racists from all races, the mean and the lazy and the unkind, but us also, and calls on everyone to repent and to follow Jesus Christ as Lord.

Work and our sense of worth

What do you do? Men especially tend to get our sense of worth from our work, historically. But I have met several immigrants in Tennessee who were medical doctors and other highly educated professionals who deliverer pizza, wait on tables, and do other menial work. Increasingly, such low paying jobs are also being filled by Americans who are highly educated. Predictions are that such low status and low paying jobs are to increase in the USA, while white collar work will decrease.

I am convinced that higher education is very valuable even if the person has to dig ditches to survive. We need to know how others thought throughout history in order to understand our own culture, and especially to know God's perspective. His perspective often comes to us through people in other cultures and times in history untainted by our own warped culture. They had pressure to conform to their cultures and when we know that, we see our own times more objectively. But as stepping stones to financial success, higher education has more and more limited value in the USA. As a matter of fact, many are being suckered into paying for education now that cannot deliver promises of better jobs, especially with less respected institutions.

Our sense of worth and value cannot legitimately be based on what we do for a living. We may have a high status job today and lose it tomorrow because of the economy or sickness or other things out of our control. Actually, God is in control. He sets one up and brings another one down, says the Holy Spirit. We tend not to believe that when all seems well, and arrogance causes us to take credit for everything. Yet the Bible says all we have we received, so therefore we should be thankful and to use our gifts and abilities to honor Jesus Christ. We can do that in any work, or we can honor the devil in any work.

The Bible says that the people followed worthless things, and became worthless themselves. I remember how warped my values became as I got degrees and advanced in professional jobs. I cared less and less for the things of God, or to honor Jesus Christ at all. Even after I rededicated my life to Jesus Christ, I had to undo many years of selfish and culturally warped thinking. I had restarted in the right direction, but had to throw out much baggage that was heavy weights in my effort to run a good race for God.

When we remember that all we have we received from God, and that he opens and shuts doors, that will keep us from pride when we have great jobs and money and status, and it will rescue us from depression when we have the opposite. Many in the world are at least as intelligent as Americans and work just as hard, yet have much lower standards of living (although the playing field is becoming more even). And many of these I have met and am certain that they are at least as close to God as any American is. How do we measure success?

Whether we are up or down in the eyes of others, I hope that we go to the good Lord and walk with him for our worth and value. Sometimes I do that. Sometimes I do not. I know to do that in theory, but I must repent much for I get arrogant when I am up and depressed when I am down, if I wander the least bit away from dependence on God for my worth and value. If you are human, then you must face the same temptations. God have mercy on all of us.

A statue of responsibility on the west coast to balance the statue of liberty on the east coast

An immigrant to New York City was overjoyed at the freedoms and liberties available in the USA, represented by the statue of liberty. But soon he was upset at the selfishness and sense of entitlement that we as Americans have. Seventy percent of the lawyers in the world are in the USA, to help us defend our rights. But what about our responsibilities? Canada (happy Canada Day, July 1) has nationalized medicine to care for the sick there (I and my parishioners benefited much) and the murder rate is one hundred times more in the USA. Yet we have many more attending church as a percentage of the total population.

"It may be the devil or it may be the Lord, but you're gonna have to serve somebody," sang Bob Dylan. Going to church does not make one a Christian any more than going into a garage makes one a car. One must add fenders and replace a heart with a motor, etc., as someone pointed out. Putting up a statue of responsibility has no more power to change lives than the statue of liberty. It gives a good feeling for a while, and little more. So many songs and writings very eloquently describe problems, but they remain, until the heart is changed. Tears may flow and resolutions may get made. But when restraints are not internal, then we must have prison or tyranny to keep our baser instincts from devouring us.

The French revolution of 1789 and the Russian revolution of 1917 unleashed freedom for the masses, but then millions were murdered. In both countries, the church leadership existed to honor the kings instead of the king of kings; Jesus Christ. Meanwhile, Godly priests were for the most part, banished to the countryside in both countries. The very same days the Russian revolution began, the top Russian Orthodox priests were meeting in Moscow to argue over what colors of robes to use in the ceremonies. But freedom in a Godly sense would mean that the rich in those countries and in this country would use their wealth to establish fair wages, support education, health care, and would use their influence to push for fair taxes.

"Proclaim liberty throughout the land to all its inhabitants." This verse from Leviticus 25:10 is inscribed on the Liberty Bell in Philadelphia.

But where liberty is not restrained by Godly internal restraints, we have chaos and lawlessness where no one is safe. "We have no government armed in power capable of contending with human passions unbridled by morality and religion ... Our constitution was made only for a moral and religious people. It is wholly inadequate for the government of any other." So said our second president, John Adams. He did not need to specify then what religion he meant for all knew clearly it was Christianity, and if one reads his writings, it is unmistakably that.

"There are two freedoms: the false, where man is free to do what he likes; the true, where he is free to do what he ought." Charles Kingsley. If we value our freedoms, and I hope we do, then we must remember that they are established on the freedom to worship God, to act justly and to love mercy, and to walk humbly with him, as he requires. We should not be free to harm others, to be selfish and to allow our greed to rip over our fellow countrymen and women. Where do we draw the line? We have more church goers than Canada, but from living and working in both countries, I am convinced that they had more Godly people with influence in government in their country. As an American I am not proud of that.

What I am proud of is people like the man from Bean Station, Tennessee, I talked with this week. He values preaching in the power of the Holy Spirit, for he saw his granddaughter saved recently. He spoke of being told by God to say something to a new person who moved into his neighborhood, and after many delays he did. Both were encouraged by his obedience to God. God of the Bible always balances liberty and responsibility well when we humble ourselves enough to know and to obey him. We will have revival in our land when we do.

A professor at the University of North Carolina just published a book that teaches that the problem of suffering drove him from being a fundamentalist, evangelical Christian to an agnostic. It was not just his own pain that bothered him, but the anguish of others. He looked at the standard defenses of God for allowing such torture and rejected them. I understand how he can do that. If we say people suffer because they do wrong, we can always see innocents who have as many or worse difficulties. My mother was very Godly, yet her cancer was as terrible as the concentration camps of the Nazis it seemed. If we claim that suffering is redemptive, we can see many who get bitter when they are deprived of happiness and who attack those who had nothing to do with their situations caused by mean parents/neighbors, etc. Also natural disasters kill millions, presumably the righteous along with the unrighteous. Certainly, dictators of nations as well as individual criminals cause evil that their victims did nothing to deserve.

The problem of pain and God resurfaces in every generation, for as Ecclesiastes 1:9 declares, "There is nothing new under the sun." The English publisher Malcolm Muggeridge added that there is nothing new, only old things happening to new people. And the prophet Job observed that the little ones of the wicked dance about with few cares while the righteous suffer.

The fact is that no one has more than a smattering of insight as to why anyone has suffering or joy, or whether we deserve either. Another fact is that all of us are dying, and after we die I do not think it will matter to us a great deal whether we were murdered or a tree fell on us or we died "of old age." And although the professor said he went from being Christian to agnostic (not knowing whether God exists or not) because he was bothered by suffering (everyone who ever lived can say the same) does not make his analysis a true view of reality. From the Augustinian/Calvinistic view of salvation, which I hold both by theology and experience, once one is Christian one cannot take oneself out of that state even by suicide. So I am convinced that he was either never really a Christian and that he gave merely an emotional or intellectual assent to God, or that he really is Christian who is deeply struggling with how God can be both loving and all powerful and still allow suffering. To many, God is either loving and weak, or all powerful and mean to let people have pain. If we are honest, all Christians have these thoughts from time to time, that if God were truly good he would fit our logic and feelings in difficult situations.

But the Bible teaches that God is both all-powerful and perfect love, and this teaching is offensive to everyone sooner or later. Certainly, it has been to me in my relatively minor suffering. Especially at these times I look at the cross. Christianity is not a set of myths or fairy tales but is rooted in history that truly happened. Jesus was murdered and bodily rose from the dead. He suffered for our sins, the completely innocent dying for the completely guilty. When we are drawn by the Holy Spirit to accept his offer of salvation, we become his followers and then the same spirit begins to dwell within us, to confirm and comfort us when we honor Jesus and to convict us when we do not (mainly through the Bible and never in contradiction to the Bible). When we suffer (as people of every religion and no religion do) we can draw near to God or rebel by beginning to trust our own opinion of what should happen and when. I have done that more than a few times. But the Holy Spirit remains within us to give us peace when we keep on obeying and worshipping Jesus Christ, and ask for forgiveness when we lapse. Ultimately and sometimes the only way we can be sure that God loves us in particular circumstances is because God died on the cross for us.

Janissaries

The Janissaries were elite soldiers of the Ottoman Empire, which originated in Turkey. As the empire spread Islam across the Balkans, the Christian nations that were there were defeated many times. Leading in the front lines were the Janissaries. They were the captured children of Christians, who were raised as slaves. After being forced to learn the Turkish language and customs, as well as Islam, at first they were basically bodyguards for the sultans. Over the years thousands were taken captives, and led the battle charges, many times against their own parents and other relatives.

Dr. James Kennedy made the point that although Christian children are rarely taken captive by Muslims now, they are often captured by the culture and turn against their parents. Materialism and hedonism charm all of us to some extent, even without the threat of outside violence. Some may object that the parents were not really Christian but were just churchgoers. Others may claim justification for abandoning Christianity because their parents were hypocritical and not worthy of emulation. No doubt that is true in some cases.

At other times, however, Godly and devout Christians had children who were still captured by the culture, and who turned away from the Christian faith. I was in that category. I saw the New Testament lived out by my parents, and by preachers who preached in the power of the Holy Spirit. Yet even after all that and supernatural conversion, I still turned against the faith of my parents and my own faith. Unlike the Janissaries, I freely chose to embrace a foreign culture that did not think Christianly.

Why? By the time I went to university, Christianity was no longer considered cool by most educated and well off folks in the USA. Instead, it was seen by them to be weak and not relevant, and the realm of simpletons. When I did check out churches near the university campus, God was not there. So the non-Christian world view seemed to be more powerful and more glamorous. The hedonism and materialism seemed to overwhelm all but ignorant hicks.

The Ottoman Empire later imposed a tax of one out of a number of boys in their conquered regions. As word got back of some Janissaries rising to fame and status in the empire, several parents competed to sacrifice their sons. Many Christian parents today do the same- not to a sultan, but on the altar of hedonism or materialism. Instead I hope we encourage others to follow the one who says, "I am the way, and the truth, and the life" (John 14:6). We may or may not have fame or status when we do that. But we will have peace with the God of the universe.

Near death experiences of some relatives

"Well, boys, come on over home." My father related that he and some others were talking with his uncle Dave Guinn of Greene County, Tennessee, when he uttered these words. He was sitting in a chair, slumped his head over, and then breathed his last. What a great way to die! He was surrounded by friends, and was a positive witness for Jesus Christ to the end. They knew he had lived a holy life, and they saw he died well also.

"The best is yet to come," my father was fond of saying. He was speaking of heaven, which awaits every follower of Jesus Christ. He had never read or heard of Corrie Ten Boom, who along with her family protected Jews from the Nazis in the Netherlands and were murdered for their kindness, but she had the same exact words to encourage Christians. That is a statement of fact and not a sentimental one. The Bible promises that eyes have not seen nor have ears heard of the glories of heaven. So it will be much better than we can imagine, and the hot country will be much worse than anyone can imagine.

My paternal grandfather died when I was a few months old, and was a holy man by all accounts I have heard. He was in a coma for several days before he died, but at the end revived and spoke to some of his children. But they had died much earlier, and he had conversations with them. Then he died himself.

Death is a curse word in our American culture, and now the term sex has replaced it. Explicit discussions of that subject abound. When someone dies, they are spoken of as "passing on. "But that is what you do to give a baton to another runner in a relay race, and it does not convey the finality of what really happens to a person. I am not suggesting that we return to a time when we gather the family around the corpse in the casket and take photos, but such photos are much more edifying than a lot of photos taken in our time!

It may sound morose, but most ministers prefer funerals to weddings, myself included. I appreciate weddings, with the change to encourage patience and kindness and forgiveness (1 Corinthians 13). But we all know it is easier to get a divorce than to rise from the dead. So at funerals, people are usually much more open to thoughts of eternity and things of ultimate importance.

"Also, he has put eternity into man's heart," says the writer of Ecclesiastes. For uncle Dave Guinn, that meant the best was yet to be. For aunt Millie, from another part of the family, eternity in her heart meant the worst was yet to be. As she lay dying, she screamed for those around her to pull her feet out of the flames. Was it a delusion as her immediate family interpreted her anguish? Don't bet your life on it.

1 Corinthians 13

1 Corinthians 13 is the great chapter from the Bible on love. The word translated charity or love means to seek the highest good of the other person without expecting a reward. The chapter spells out how to love in very clear and practical ways. To have a good marriage or even a decent friendship, we must have love.

Charity is long suffering, or in other words, true love is patient. This means we must put up with more guff and difficulties than we prefer. Love is kind. To be kind is to want to encourage the other person. We must ask from time to time if we can help the other and how can we do that. When they see we are sincere they will begin to tell us, and our relationship is deepened. To be kind also means to pray that God help us to desire to uplift the other, and that we ask God to help us to seek and to find ways to do that.

Love is not envious. So we do not want the gifts or abilities of our spouse or someone else, but we pray to identify and to develop our own so that others can benefit from our friendship. Love is not boastful, for the Bible teaches us that all we have received comes from God. He gave us the ability to make money or to be strong or creative, so we should never brag, but encourage our spouse and anyone else around us to reach their highest potential also.

Love is not arrogant or proud. We are kept from these sins when we understand and trust the Bible when it says God is the one who opens and closes doors (Revelation 3). We are to try to understand our purpose specifically and individually instead of being condescending towards others who lack our resources.

Love is not rude. So we do not make sarcastic remarks or insulting put downs when we love as God commands. These are marks of hatred instead of love By the way, social research shows that it takes from five to twenty positive words to overcome the effect of one negative word. So it is much better to keep quiet than to insult our spouse or anyone else!

Love does not insist on its own way. We do not selfishly try to go on vacation only where we want to go, or to spend the money on ourselves, for example. Let us pray to be more concerned about the needs (or even wants) of others around us.

Love is not irritable. When we seek the highest good of the other person we are not crabby, cranky, grouchy, touchy, or easily provoked, in other words. Instead of assuming the worst and or carrying a chip on our shoulder, let us assume the best when there are several ways to interpret something. It is very unfortunate when we have learned distrust in the past and automatically think our spouse or others we meet have the same characteristics. They may be better or worse, but we need to seek their highest good calmly, nevertheless.

Love is not resentful. We do not carry a grudge because the other person did something we oppose, or did not do something we proposed. We deal with problems when we are Christian in order to please Jesus Christ and to encourage others in ways that are best, not to gain status or comfort or some other advantage. As Dr. Lewis Smedes at Fuller Seminary pointed out, when we carry a grudge we feel superior towards the person we feel has wronged us, but the loving response is to forgive all real or imagined sins. Christians can forgive because we know Christ has forgiven our sins. Therefore Christians have the motivation and the power to forgive others their relatively minor sins against us!

Love does not rejoice in wrongdoing but rejoices in what is right. We know what is wrong because the Bible teaches us what is wrong, and we know what is right because the Bible teaches us what is right. Other kinds of love are mentioned in the Bible (family, erotic/romantic, friendship). But agape, or the kind of love in this chapter is commanded. When we depend on the lawgiver who gave the law, we have the ability to carry it out.

Beauty will save the world.

No, not that kind of beauty. Prince Mishkin, the Christlike character whom Dostoyevsky had uttered that phrase, was undone by the beautiful woman he adored. "By nature, men desire the beautiful," said Saint Basil the Great. Chattanooga, Tennessee, turned a dumpy downtown into a gorgeous waterfront area, and I applaud that. We all prefer beauty to ugliness in any area of life. And beauty is mentioned favorably in the Bible, with Sara, Rebecca, and Rachel, for example, and the eye pleasing city and temple Solomon built.

But the Bible also declares that a beautiful woman without discretion is like a ring in a pigs snout, and when the stunningly magnificent church of Saint Basil in Moscow was built, Ivan the Terrible had the eyes of the architect put out when he was asked if he could build another one like it, and answered in the affirmative. Psalms 90:17 says, "Let the beauty of the Lord our God be upon us." That kind of beauty is commanded for all of us. Only the liars and the unkind and the resentful, fail to appreciate the beauty of honesty, kindness and forgiveness. In other words, all of us at some point prefer the ugliness of sin.

That is because sin wraps itself in shallow beauty, even as the devil seems to be an angel of light, and passes himself off as good to us. When we choose not to study the Bible enough to recognize good from evil, we are seduced by this inferior beauty that destroys us. American advertising is by far the best in the world to put lipstick on a pig, and to make us swoon with greed and selfishness for things. When we are not saturated with the Word of God/the Bible, we are led to believe that we need more stuff to have worth and value. So the average house size has doubled in the last twenty years, and we feel we need more and more and more, to have a beautiful life.

I like a photograph I have of two Amish girls playing with a simple doll. Above them is the Bible verse, "Keep your life free from love of money, and be content with what you have." I am certain that they struggle with that verse also, but they seem to have a better start than most of us. Yet we can simplify, and still not have the beauty of the Lord upon us.

"For to me, to live is Christ," said Saint Paul. Tamika, in the Jane Adams Hull House in Chicago, had been homeless and abused. But at a birthday party she sang the song “Amazing Grace” with great power and grace. When asked about how she could do that, she replied, "If I could not sing I would have to take drugs. Because drugs kill the pain, but beauty is bigger than the pain."

Dostoyevsky also said, "The Holy Spirit is the direct seizure, the grasping of beauty." No one can deny that who has come into the presence of God unmistakably, and has had the Holy Spirit fill us with his power. At such times we do have the anointing and a glimpse of the beauty of the Lord God. By repenting of our sins and by throwing ourselves upon the mercy of the God of the universe, this is possible. May God help us not to settle for a lesser beauty.

Prophets and pastors

When I pastored I tried to get the people on God's side, whether they were on my side or not. I would have had an easier ride if I had been more needy of the affirmation of others (as I was told and I do not doubt). I think my examples of pastors while growing up in east Tennessee were normally introverts as I was, and not as socially skilled as those who attracted large crowds. I think they were more prophets than pastors, as I saw and still see myself to be.

Prophets either predict the future or proclaim the word of God clearly for the present. They are extremely popular and dearly loved when they predict money or comfort coming our way, or that God approves of whatever we are doing at a particular time. And sometimes God does indeed give us comfort and confirmation of something pleasant that will happen. My mother and two others affirmed that I would be married many years before that happened. They and I were convinced that they spoke under the influence of God, and I appreciated the news. I also prayed through myself, and got a vision of my wife twenty-five years before we met (and she saw me in a dream two years before we met).

On the other hand, the prophet Jeremiah told people that they must repent or face the destruction of Israel. He was mocked and hated for his loving concern and truth telling. The prophet Micaiah stood alone against 400 false prophets to warn King Ahab that he would lose the battle of Ramoth Gilead and indeed die in that battle. He was persecuted and imprisoned while the fake prophets predicted victory, and lied.

I think loneliness is the common trait for all true prophets because the brooding and the time alone with God is necessary in order to hear clearly from the Lord. The most common trait needed for a pastor is perhaps good social interaction in addition to being a God called preacher and pastor. They need backbone and courage also, in order to balance out the need for the approval of others. Prophets, on the other hand, often should be more sensitive of the needs of others and more sympathetic.

I am sure I did not do a great job in this area. I like to think that the more we are shaped like a hammer (that breaks the rocks in pieces, says

God of his word when preached in power), the less we can be a container or a saw. But I am sure I could still be more kind and understanding and still be prophetic!

Psalms 19:12 says, "Who can discern his errors? Declare me innocent from secret faults." Which of us can be aware of our sins sometimes for they are hidden even from ourselves, in other words? The faults and sins of pastors and prophets are often not recognized, as are the different ones of parents and children and lawyers and farmers and politicians ... We all see clearly only the most open and commonly disliked sins such as murder and robbery. We all need the fire of the Holy Spirit to burn up the dross, the parts of us that are a hinderance to being in the center of the will of God. Holy Spirit, convict us of all sin, open and secret, and confirm us in what best honors Jesus Christ. Amen.

Is it okay for people of different religions to marry each other?

It is fine when neither has a commitment to their respective religions. For mere churchgoers, it is no problem to marry a non-churchgoer. Recently Chelsea Clinton, whose father is Baptist and whose mother is Methodist, married a Jewish man. I have no way to even guess whether she is supernaturally converted to Jesus Christ or not, which is the only way anyone becomes Christian. Otherwise we must count Hitler and Stalin and Mussolini as Christian since they were baptized as infants.

But I do know that if she or anyone else is Christian and marries a non-Christian, they will have radically different goals. "For to me, to live is Christ," said Saint Paul. That means not only to be kind and honest, which is no conflict among people of good will with any or no religion, but it means to pray and to live to honor Jesus Christ as the name above all names. When we are sincerely following Jesus as Lord, that will bring different ways of bringing up children, and always praying and desiring that they have friendship with the God of the universe and eternal life with him.

Occasionally I hear of a Christian marrying one who is not Christian, with hope of changing that person later. But that is not the right thing to do. It is not fair to the unbeliever to expect them to change later. When we marry, it should be to the person we love and respect as they are, not for what the spouse may become!

Also, when we marry someone of a different religion, there is no strong belief there or it would not take place in the first place. But often later one becomes much more attached to their religion. When I began dating, I was Christian but not a dedicated one at all, and on first glance I fit in very well with those who were not, with males as well as females. I would not let myself get close for I knew I was saved/supernaturally converted, and at some time I planned to revert to a close fellowship with God. I knew that would create a huge distance between me and anyone else I married who did not have that relationship. Since I was also called to preach the gospel of Jesus Christ, I knew that would add much more difficulty to a marriage with a person who was not only Christian, but a very dedicated one.

Often people of different religions marry and one gets more dedicated to a religion later. I knew a family in Toronto where the wife was a churchgoer and the husband was Muslim. He later became more serious about his religion and they divorced, and had much bickering regarding how to raise the son in one religion or the other.

"Do not be unequally yoked," says the Holy Spirit. As with oxen ploughing, when we are unevenly matched in religion, this adds problems even those of the same bent must face. What joy and peace to be able to pray together to know and to do the will of God, the Triune God the Father, God the eternal Son Jesus Christ, and God the Holy Spirit. Also when demonic attacks come, as they do to those of no faith or to those of other faiths, it is great calm and confidence to serve the God of the universe together, and to know that "he who is in you is greater than he who is in the world," says the Holy Spirit to those who love and obey Jesus Christ.

It's football time in Tennessee

I said to the University of Florida football fan that I hoped she was treated well while she was in Tennessee, and she replied that was almost always the case, but once some students from the University of Tennessee took little packets of ketchup and dripped it on them as they were leaving the stadium. I replied that was not good, and told her of how my high school was integrated, and people predicted some fights, and indeed some fights broke out. But I noticed that the same whites who fought with a few blacks were the same people who were fighting with other whites before the blacks came. So she could be sure that those same Tennessee fans were rude and hateful to other Tennesseans before the Florida fans arrived!

I am always puzzled about coworkers and neighbors who had much interaction with someone who does a terrible crime, and they always say how nice the person was. Well, if one just talks about UT football or the weather or some other trivial matter, it would be hard to know if the person who works besides us is a wonderful person or a mass murderer. I think of the guy who murdered many, called himself the BTK (bind, torture, kill) guy, and was finally discovered as a leader in a church after bragging to the police about his crimes and they were able to trace the calls to a computer in the church. Was he involved in a Bible study where they repented of their sins and prayed to understand and apply the Bible? Was he ever asked to pray in public, as Christian churches in the Soviet Union did when they wanted to know if a communist informer was in their midst? If not, why was he allowed to rise to leadership in a congregation? That is an example of letting the fox guard the henhouse!

But what about our families- are we reading the Bible and praying with our spouse and children in order to understand what God wants us to be and to do, and then pray to be and to do that? I seriously doubt that the students who dumped ketchup on our guests had just come from Bible studies with parents or friends where they were encouraged to treat others as they want to be treated. No, I am convinced they were taught to have a "good self-image," which translates into pride and arrogance. Such a view will cause us to see other teams, nationalities, ethnic or social groups as inferior people to be mocked or used, or in extreme cases, to be bound, tortured, and killed.

I notice that when parents let their children sass them and say rude things and create mayhem in public, most women smile and chuckle at such antics. I doubt they would be so amused if they understood that these same kids will be the ones who break into their homes ten to fifteen years later to rob or to do other harm. No one who has lived in a college dorm with other students could possibly be shocked at any atrocity committed, for guys in such a setting are very open with disrespectful attitudes towards anyone weaker.

It is very important to get people interacting with truth-the truth of the Bible that is a standard above all cultural and individual standards. It says to love God and to love your neighbor, and the whole Bible is basically a commentary on what that means. If we are not good to our Tennessee spouse/child/neighbor/dog, we are not going to be good to those from other states or countries. If the family of the BTK guy claimed that he was a good guy, they are very far from the Biblical definition of good! And if the ketchup drippers are defended by their families and friends, they would be in a long line of those who encourage rudeness and disrespect. But I hope we join the line of those who look for rudeness and disrespect within ourselves first of all, who repent, and who pick ourselves up again to follow Jesus Christ.

Preaching in the power of the Holy Spirit

When I asked if his pastor preaches in the power of the Holy Spirit, he acted as if I had asked his personality profile or world view. So he answered that he is a good man, with practical sermons. But how can anyone know if the pastor is a good man unless God is with him unmistakably? He may say good words and act wonderfully in public and be the opposite in private. I dated a woman at the University of Tennessee whose father was a pastor and who beat his wife very much. He probably did not speak of doing that in the pulpit.

Furthermore, the man who ignored my question implied that it is impractical to emphasize the spiritual. No, it is impractical to stress the emotional or just our opinions without hearing from God before and as we speak. Preaching with the anointing or power of the Holy Spirit is very practical, for God speaks to us clearly and deeply and shows us what we are doing right and what we are doing wrong. We want to know that only unless we are determined to keep on doing the opposite of whatever pleases Jesus Christ. God has all knowledge and understanding of any person and circumstance, so it is not logical to not want to have his words spoken in church services.

Those who are converted to follow Jesus as God, called to preach, and who repent much and pray for his guidance, do preach under his direction. I am very sad that such historic Christian preaching is so rarely heard or understood when it is written about. Our opinions or melodious voice may impress some, but they will help only in very shallow and trivial ways. How very important it is to have the very words of God when we speak in his name.

1 Corinthians 4:20 says, "For the kingdom of God does not consist in talk but in power." Words are very important, but even good words will be inappropriate and will have little impact unless they are birthed by the Holy Spirit and delivered by those who are broken, repenting, and walking in the light of Jesus Christ. I heard Dr. Stephen Olford preach at Park Street Church in Boston, and God was clearly with him. About 300 gave their lives to Jesus Christ that day, one was a person I had been talking to about conversion. When he was on the radio, I would always quit switching stations and listen, for his words were always very powerful and positive for me. How did he know they would be that way?

He had no way of knowing that I would listen, but he was under the influence of the Holy Spirit. May God forgive us for daring to ever preach without getting our message from him. And yes, I have needed and asked his forgiveness for doing that. Have you also?

Every man/woman did what was right in his/her own eyes.

So says the last verse in the Book of Judges. The Israelites had murdered each other and had done many other sins, much as our society today has done. But instead of focusing on the sins of those outside the church, we as Christians need to make sure that verse does not apply to us! It is so easy for even very Godly people to quench the Holy Spirit and to depend on our own experience or charm or education to make decisions. But this is rebellion, and the Bible says rebellion is the same as divination/witchcraft.

George Verwer is the head of Operation Mobilization, which sends ships to different ports of the world for the purpose of evangelism. Once in India they distributed 100,000 tracts in a city and had no response at all. They were so disappointed that they fasted and prayed. God led them to another place, and with his methods they then saw several repent and give their lives to Jesus Christ. Now they could have fasted and prayed just as sincerely and not have seen any results at all, but at least they would have had peace that God was with them.

God does not promise that we will always see great results when he goes with us, but he does promise that his presence will go with those who desire it. Moses was grieved when God did not want to go with them. Are we? Do we know the difference when the presence of God is with us, and when we are just doing what is right in our own eyes?

It is so easy to drift into our own selfish concerns and ways of doing things. Long before we murder or steal or do other crimes, we began to get cold towards the things of God, and lukewarm toward wanting to be in the presence of God. But we must desire the giver more than the gifts in order to please Jesus Christ. We are to desire to love and to honor him instead of to seek honor for ourselves in terms of results or status or glory because we saw many converted or raised much money or built universities, etc.

I remember going into the pulpit in Toronto and I planned to nail someone to the wall. I have no idea now who it was or what the situation was, but I was convinced that that person needed to be straightened out. I looked up and the person was not there that Sunday. I was so convicted by the Holy Spirit for such wrong. The individual may or may not have needed to change, but I am sure that I was not the person to move them in that direction; at least not that morning in that place. I still grieve because I had the opportunity to preach the gospel under the power of the Holy Spirit, and that morning I wasted my time and that of the congregation on doing what was right in my own eyes.

I related that to my cousin and she told me that her father, Rev. Lofton Marshall, invited another minister to preach to his congregation, and the sermon was to the deacons. The minister preached about how they should repent and straighten up. When he finished, her father said that would have been a good message if any deacons had been there. I know the preacher that Sunday was normally a very Godly person, but he also missed hearing from God on that occasion!

We cannot fight the corruption of ourselves or our society with dead orthodoxy. In other words it is not enough to know the truth of Jesus Christ and to understand it, as important as that is. We must also humble ourselves before the good Lord, and pray to be doing what is right in his eyes and not in our own eyes. That is easy to say and hard to do. But the hard decisions to follow God daily brings justice and mercy in balance, otherwise we get harsh instead of firm and weak instead of gentle.

An altered state of consciousness

Country music singers often lament through lyrics of drunken loneliness. I understand why most want an alternative reality because normal life can be stale or depressing. Drugs and alcohol do bring us an altered state of consciousness, and sometimes that may be superior to our present conditions. As a boy I never doubted that an alternative reality existed-for God was unmistakably real in our church services. God anointed the sermons that were preached. The Holy Spirit was plainly in the church services, as those who were not Christians were converted to become followers of Jesus Christ, and those who were already followers became more dedicated to him.

I recall the Rev. Tom Maples of Knoxville, Tennessee, who would preach and testify at our church, who was so full of the Holy Spirit that the power seemed to overflow and run out his shoes. He had the habit of preaching and at the same time shaking hands with several who were in the front rows. As a boy of about ten or eleven, I remember vividly that one time he shook my hand while he was preaching, and it seemed that lightening passed between us. He stood there for quite a while as the Holy Spirit witnessed to the both of us that he was with us, and was pleased with us deeply. I pray that happen for us and for those we love. That is an alternative reality with no bad side effects!

And yet only a few short years later I had drifted into a coldness towards God, and had much more interest in things that I knew did not please God. I never doubted my salvation nor my experiences with God, but I had become lukewarm, as the Bible phrases it. I had grown up in rural east Tennessee, and had listened to WBZ Boston radio, etc., and had caught a glimpse of the larger world, and I imagined how superior that would be to my own. My father refused to buy a TV, to protect us from more evil, and he did manage to curb our greed a bit by that kindness.

The first time I was in Montreal, I remember seeing a woman dancing in a second floor apartment building, near McGill University, and I wanted to be a part of that lifestyle that seemed so marvelous. I dated a model there, and I seemed to have gone so much farther than my background. After returning to study at the University of Tennessee, I avoided any connection with my Godly past. I hoped that I could enter a higher alternative reality with whatever my friends and other cool people were doing.

But I was wrong. I entered a much lower alternative reality. As Saint Augustine noted around 400 A.D., "Our heart is restless until we find our rest in thee (the Triune God)." Must all Christians go through this search for greener pastures until we find that all is bleak and barren apart from love and obedience to Jesus Christ? I hope and pray not. Even the church often offers a false gospel- that prosperity is Godliness or anti Biblical sexual behavior is Godly, etc. "Come let us return to the Lord," the prophet pleads, but that will not happen until revival comes.

As I lived in world class cities in different continents, I saw the highest alternative reality is walking with God. We can do that anywhere and in any circumstances. Even the most simple and mundane life has eternal significance when we live for Jesus Christ, since he reigns and therefore there are no random acts. When we love the God of the universe, he promises that all things work together for good. So we have meaning and purpose as we walk with him. May he grant that altered state of consciousness to us, either for the first time or more deeply.

Some try to gut Christianity of the supernatural elements such as the virgin birth or the resurrection, supposedly to make it more acceptable to "modern" minds. The thinking is that our generation is smarter than those that preceded us, less gullible, and therefore not able to swallow the supernatural parts of the Bible, and can accept only the stories urging us to be nice. So angels and anything else recorded as miraculous is rejected as nonsense, by those who are in this category.

But these same folks often encourage us to accept the ethical teachings of those they think are either liars or deluded lunatics. But that is not logical at all! If God exists, why does it seem incredible that he can do whatever he wants? What kind of God must fit into our logic or experiences before we worship him? Only a God of our own creation, a human construct or illusion would exist then. Such thinking is in reality only a call to worship ourselves, a common enough event throughout history.

Matthew 1 and Luke 1 and 2 record the birth of Jesus Christ. Matthew 1:3 quotes Isaiah 7:14, which says, "Behold, the virgin shall conceive and bear a son ..." The angel Gabriel told Mary she was favored, and she would be with child by the Holy Spirit. So although they had not had sex, Mary told Joseph her fiancé, that she was pregnant. I imagine she added not to worry, because it was by the Holy Spirit. Can you imagine the atmosphere? The woman he loved and trusted had told him that she was pregnant, although not by him or by any man, but by the Holy Spirit! Was he a gullible and naive person because he was not modern? That was not the case at all. We know his character, because instead of ranting and raving and causing her great harm, Matthew 1:19 tells us, "Her husband, Joseph, being a just man and unwilling to put her to shame, resolved to divorce her quietly." What made him change his mind? What convinced him that Mary was telling the truth? Probably the only thing that would make any of us change our minds in such a situation- God spoke to him (this happens over and over in the Old and New Testament). Matthew 1:20 "But as he considered these things, an angel of the Lord appeared to him in a dream, saying, 'Joseph ... do not fear to take Mary as your wife, for that which is conceived in her is from the Holy Spirit.'"

Your God is too small and an extension of your imagination, if you do not believe that God has all power in heaven and in earth; can and does communicate with those he created. He chose to be born as one of us, eternal God through the virgin birth, and yet human son of mankind through his earthly mother. As the old Latin carol says, "O come let us adore Him, Christ the Lord."

"John is still alive in the Maine woods."

I was given that information by a guy after I preached a sermon in Portland, Maine. I answered, "That is interesting (it is always interesting to have crazy people in the congregation)." I had just preached on John 21:19-23: Jesus said that Peter would have a violent death by which he would glorify God, and said, "Follow me." Peter had noticed John and quite naturally had asked Jesus what would happen to John. Jesus had answered that IF it was his will that he remained until he returned, what was that to him, and had added, "Follow me." John records that some spread the rumor that John would not die, but of course he did die, since Jesus was speaking hypothetically.

Unfortunately, the parishioner who informed me that John was still alive nearby, had ignored those words of Jesus, and had missed the whole point of the story. Jesus said (as I did my best to explain in the sermon) that Peter was not to worry about what would or would not happen to John, but to focus on following Jesus. It was none of his business if John had an easier life than Peter because Peter was to follow Jesus in the midst of the plans that God had for Peter.

All Christians are like Peter sometimes and wonder why we must be sick when others are well, or why our children do not live nearby, or why others who clearly do not have our wonderful traits are treated better in some ways.

A mother recently told my wife that their little girl had been given three weeks to three years to live. God have mercy on them. I am sure they are tempted to look at healthy children and to ask why they could not see their daughter graduate, marry, produce grandchildren, etc. Psalms say we are to offer to God a sacrifice of thanksgiving. To be thankful to God we must sacrifice self-pity, resentment, or jealousy at times, in order to worship God and to serve him. We must sacrifice our own analysis of a situation, our own educated guess about how our lives should progress, in order to follow Jesus Christ wholeheartedly and obediently.

What prevents you and me from doing that today? Few of us are suffering as much as the parents of the little girl who is predicted by the doctors to die shortly, so our objections to following Jesus are more shallow and trivial.

Peter was crucified upside down, and John was boiled in oil. He survived, and was the only one of the twelve disciples who died a natural death (yet the boiling in oil could have been more painful than dying as Peter did). The Bible promises that “all who desire to live a godly life in Christ Jesus will be prosecuted.” So if we are not suffering persecution at least occasionally for the sake of Jesus, we need to ask ourselves if we really, “live Godly in Christ Jesus.”

Someone asked C. S. Lewis if Christianity makes a person happy. He answered that, unfortunately, the happiest person he had met was an old guy who was completely selfish and not Christian at all! Those who lie, steal, manipulate to get power and status, or cut down their competition, may get the girl or the job, and may indeed be happy. But when we have been supernaturally converted to follow Jesus Christ as God and Lord, we quit comparing ourselves unfavorably to others and our highest goal is to follow Jesus.

Beware of wolves in sheep's clothing.

"As I Lay Dying" had its lead singer hauled off to jail for six years in 2014: Tim Lambesis was found guilty of hiring a hit man to murder his ex-wife. His band had pretended to be Christian, as they admitted, in order to keep selling records in the Christian market. Mr. Lambesis estimated that only about one in ten bands he knew in that market are really Christian. Given their words and attitudes, which sounds about accurate to me. It is sad to read that many fans would come up to them after a concert and request prayer. The band would say that they did not pray in public, but were okay with the fan praying.

Can we recognize the wolves when they are dressed in sheep's clothing? Do we compare their words and attitudes with what the Bible teaches? Please study the Bible, pray to understand and then to apply what we read. It is at least billions of times better than the next best book. The more truth we know, the less we will be taken in by fakes.

Flash and glamour has charmed not only the young, but those in every generation. A retired gentleman told me recently that good preachers entertain. I replied that no, they preach in the power of the Holy Spirit. Then if that is not fascinating, we value the trivial at best, and the demonic at worst.

I suspect that the music group, "As I Lay Dying," was entertaining enough to make a living for a while. Talent does lift one above the crowd. But the Scottish minister Robert Murray M'Cheyne said, "God blesses great love for him more than great talent." The blessing will mean great peace from God, whether it means loads of cash or not.

When I was a boy I remember an old couple in upper east Tennessee named John and Margie. His eyelashes were ingrown so much that he was in constant pain and almost blind, but he was a calm and gentle Christian of peace. She was more animated, of course. She would often sing the Easter hymn, "Were You there when they Crucified my Lord?" She sang just barely better than I can sing, but she tried to honor her Lord Jesus Christ. No fans ever came up to her after a song and asked her to pray for them. That is too bad, because she walked with God. Therefore according to James 5:16, her prayers were powerful and effective.

Do we teach our children to recognize the one out of ten so called Christian bands that are Christian? Such a band will say a good word about Jesus Christ when possible, and will think and act Christianly. Not one of us does that always, but when we really are Christian we will repent and again try to follow Jesus Christ. Matthew 7:15-16 says, “Beware of false prophets, who come to you in sheep’s clothing but inwardly are ravenous wolves. You will recognize them by their fruits."

The sermon "Sinners in the hands of an angry God," by Edwards, is repulsive to many today, with its clear call for repentance to gain heaven and to avoid hell. But we do not know how much of the sermon was heard by the original congregation in Enfield, CT. This is because during the sermon the listeners rioted and he could not finish! So the sermon was difficult for many to hear in the 1700's also.

If that or similar opposition has not happened to us when we preached, we need to ask ourselves if we are truly preaching and living the gospel. The same person who wrote 1 Corinthians 13 (Love is patient, kind, not crabby, ...) and emphasized the love and beauty of God also had revivals and riots! Acts 14 records Paul preaching in Iconium, with converts and threats of death. The same happened in Lystra, where Paul was stoned. In Acts 16, Paul preached in Philippi, had converts to Jesus Christ, and was flogged because those abusing a slave girl lost their income through Paul. Acts 17 records Paul making converts again at Thessaloniki, and ruffians formed a mob and tried to murder him. Acts 18 tells us that also happened at Corinth, with success and also opposition. Acts 19 lets us know that in the city of Ephesus that pattern was repeated, and in Acts 21, Jerusalem also was witness to the same work of God and similar opposition by Satan.

Not one of us can claim to be more brilliant than Paul or Edwards, so it was not their low intelligence or naivete that got them into trouble for the reviving of Christians or getting non-Christians converted. They walked with God, so it was not their obnoxiousness either. But it takes repentance and holiness to bring the power of God in to our words and messages. Paul, Jonathan Edwards, Moody, Spurgeon, Evan Roberts, Duncan Campbell, and others have had that in their lives and ministries. Do we?

The Holy Spirit was exaggerating?

"Indeed, all who desire to live a godly life in Christ Jesus will be persecuted." Either the Holy Spirit was exaggerating when those words came through Paul, or he misspoke, or we are not living very Godly in Christ Jesus. I say this because we in the USA are not seeing revival or Christianity or persecution either. I know we cannot pray aloud in schools anymore, but we Christians took prayer out of the churches first (except for proud and self-righteous pontificating, for the most part).

Paul, Edwards, and others who preach historic Christianity have been called "unloving" by some. But it is not really being loving unless we not only point others to what is good and holy, but also warn folks to turn from what is evil/harmful/unholy. We are not doing that very well, but we do very well at making excuses about why we do not. May God convict each of us because we Christians hinder Godly revival which he wants this country to have!

Critics think not, and that God is an ogre if the Bible is true when it says that God sent his son to die on the cross as a substitute for our sins. They consider their definition of what is loving to be higher than the teachings of love found in the Bible. Holiness is a joke for such folks, and sin is something they never admit to doing. Therefore the divorce is always the fault (not sin) of the other person, the robbery they did was justified, and the revenge was appropriate also.

But God hates sin so much, his justice demanded that it be punished. All have sinned, so all must be punished, and severely, since God is holy and cannot stand sin at all. How could God remain perfect and holy without condemning his human creatures to the utmost? Only the perfect Jesus Christ could be the perfect sacrifice, as God required in the Old Testament; the lamb without blemish, the one slain from before the foundation of the world. Only that would satisfy the justice of God, and at the same time allow his love to reach us, sinful humanity.

So Jesus on the cross became the lamb that was slain: he took our sins upon himself. God the Father poured out his wrath against sin on the person of his son, God the eternal Son Jesus Christ, so that through faith in him we can escape the justice our sins deserve. Thus the mercy of God is allowed to reach us only through the one who became sin for our sakes. We were not made one with God when that happened, so the atonement does not mean we became at one with God. No, the atonement means that Jesus atoned for our sins, took our place, and through his love we can escape the punishment our sins deserve, which is eternal death or hell. But the free gift must be accepted for it to become a reality in our lives!

Sentimentality about the loving Jesus does no one any good unless we accept by faith that Jesus was crucified for our sakes. It was our menace and rebellion against God that caused a loving God the Father, to offer his own son to suffer, die, and rise again for us. "With his wounds we are healed," says the prophet Isaiah about Jesus, long before Jesus added flesh to be born as a baby on earth. Could God have saved us/delivered us from the consequences of sin, by an easier way? Could he not have fit our notions of what is loving and easier in order to benefit mankind without the blood? I do not doubt that he could have done that, but I am convinced that God did what is best, given his perfect love.

The old hymn asks, "What can wash away my sin?" (its title) and answers, "Nothing but the blood of Jesus. What can make me whole again? Nothing but the blood of Jesus." Whether we spiritualize communion (as Quakers and Salvation Army do) or see it as the literal blood and body of Jesus (as Orthodox and Catholics do) or see it as symbolic (as Presbyterians, Baptists, and Methodists normally do), Christians accept that Jesus was slain and that his blood was shed for us, on the cross. Frankly, neither I nor anyone else has more than an elementary understanding of why God could not have arranged for our salvation in an easier way than crucifixion of his son.

Part of that puzzlement is, I am sure, because our concept of sin is so shallow. We have such a low regard for the holiness of God, that to do what the Bible calls sin, seems trivial to us. Therefore the penalty for sin should also be shallow, according to this line of thinking. I include myself in this category on some days, I am sorry to say. Even we who are Christians fall into "the cultured despisers of Christianity" group unless we remain careful to think Christianly.

Saint Patrick

Patrick was a boy of sixteen when he was captured by Irish raiders and taken from his home in Britain. He was made a slave, and was an isolated shepherd. Lonely and afraid, he turned to his religion for solace and became a devout Christian. In his Confessions, Patrick wrote, "At 16:.. in a strange land, the Lord opened my unbelieving eyes, and I was converted." According to his writings, after six years, God spoke to him in a dream and commanded him to leave Ireland. So he escaped his captors and walked nearly 200 miles from county Mayo to the east coast of Ireland. There he convinced some sailors to accept him as a passenger, and returned to his home.

Later, an angel in a dream told him to return to Ireland as a missionary for Jesus Christ, As he put it, "to dwell in the midst of barbarians ... for the love of God." In his Confessions, he referred to Romans 8:28" ... for those who love God all things work together for good." He affirmed, "Whatever happens to me, whether pleasant or distasteful, I accept, giving thanks to God who never disappoints." So he returned and made a huge impact for Christ in his adopted homeland. It is said that he used the shamrock to teach them the idea of the Trinity, and that the powerful Irish symbol, the sun (which is seldom seen there because of all the rain), he had incorporated into the cross to constitute the Celtic cross. The following is a translation of the hymn, I bind unto myself today, which is attributed to Saint Patrick, and is found in the hymnal of the Presbyterian Church in Canada. We would do well to pray this for ourselves!

"I bind unto myself today the strong Name of the Trinity, By invocation of the same, the Three in One, and One in Three. I bind this day to me forever, by power of faith, Christ's Incarnation; His baptism in the Jordan river; His death on Cross for my salvation; His bursting from the spiced tomb; His riding up the heavenly way; His coming at the day of doom: I bind unto myself today. I bind unto myself today the power of God to hold and lead, His eye to watch, His might to stay, His ear to hearken to my need, The wisdom of my God to teach, His hand to guide, His shield to ward, The word of God to give me speech, His heavenly host to be my guard. Christ be with me, Christ within me, Christ behind me, Christ before me, Christ beside me, Christ to win me, Christ to comfort and restore me, Christ beneath me, Christ above me, Christ in quiet, Christ in danger, Christ in hearts of all that love me, Christ in mouth of friend and stranger. I bind unto myself the Name, the strong Name of the Trinity; By invocation of the same, The Three in One, and One in Three, Of whom all nature hath creation, Eternal Father, Spirit, Word. Praise to the Lord of my salvation: Salvation is of Christ the Lord."—Saint Patrick, 372-466

He died on March 17, 466: Since the universal church did not break into west/Latin/Roman Catholic- east/Greek/Orthodox, until 1054, and there were claims that the Irish church was independent and was subsumed into the Catholic church later, both Protestants and Catholics claim Saint Patrick as their own. It is safe to say that no Protestant or Catholic who followed the God of Saint Patrick murdered each other over the last 400 years in Ireland. Several unconverted church members on both sides lived for political or financial gain, and did violence to their neighbors there. And to be more accurate, undoubtedly several backslidden Christians joined in the evil on both sides of the religious fence. Meanwhile, Protestants and Catholics who did and do love and obey the risen Jesus Christ, follow his teachings and example, even as Saint Patrick did.

Those with the highest self-esteem are in prison or should be?

On the other hand, God declares in Isaiah 66:2, "This is the one I esteem: he who is humble and contrite in spirit, and trembles at my word." But when we steal the money of others as Madoff of New York City and Dennis Bolze of Gatlinburg, Tennessee, and countless others have done, God is very far from us. So skip the books on how to achieve a high self-esteem, for such folks feel they deserve to take revenge on others, and have a sense of entitlement which prods them to rape or murder or loot ,and otherwise rip over others. A high sense of self-esteem allows us to take advantage of others so that we benefit from our greed and selfishness.

But the higher esteem we have of God, the more we live to honor him and the less glory we seek for ourselves. Then we get our sense of worth and value from living for Jesus Christ, and not looking to lord it over others financially or mentally or emotionally, etc. The Bible says all we have we received from God, and when we admit this, we have joy and thankfulness instead of pride. But high self-esteem makes us feel that we deserve the favor of God. "Why did God not let me marry that person/get that job/avoid losing my shirt in Dubai/ad nauseum?" That is the whine of those who have a sense of entitlement because of pride and arrogance.

The Bible never speaks of how great it is to have a high self-image or how terrible it is to have a low self-image, not because the psychology there is deficient, but because God's thoughts are much higher than ours. He teaches us to deny our self, pick up our cross, and follow him for the most joyful and fulfilling life possible. We may or may not have money, love, status, health, and other things valued by everyday people. But for the Christian who walks with God, "The joy of the Lord is my strength," is not an empty slogan. No, I do not always walk closely with God either, and what gives joy to God is not always my strength, as a result.

So one can object, "If a high self-image is wrong, then should we see ourselves as miserable sinners and go around repenting all the time?" Well, if we do not, we will have a much more miserable life, a trivial one, with shallow meaning and purpose. "Life is a bitch-then you die," so said one of the more caustic bumper stickers. It takes a while to discover that, if one has money, love, beauty, and health, as King Solomon had. But he did conclude that his stables of women and horses and glorious buildings and fame and his great self-image was joyless, as he turned his back on God. "All is vanity," he admitted. But nothing is empty and insignificant when we walk with the risen Christ. He causes everything to work together for our good as we humbly follow him.

My widowed mother

My widowed mother dated a guy who, upon her death, informed me that I would miss her prayers. He was a leader in a church, an arrogant and difficult person, so I put no confidence in what he said. From earlier incidents I knew that he was intending to discourage me. But it did get me thinking, and my doubts of the truth of what he said were confirmed when I read a passage about David in the Old Testament. God was tired of the Israelites several times and wanted to destroy them. But he showed them favor and forgave them. Why? Different times God said he spared Israel because of his righteous servant David. But what struck me was the fact that David was already long dead when God showed more kindness to the Israelites because of David. Therefore the prayers of David, who was called "a man after God's own heart," were powerful and effective even after his death. 2 Chronicles 21:7 teaches, "Yet the Lord was not willing to destroy the house of David (Israel) because of the covenant that he had made with David."

So the intended result of the guy who had been dating my mother was harmful. But the outcome was good. I understood the providence of God much better and appreciated it more than I would have if he had not tried to depress me! Because of him I understand and am joyful about the fact that when I live a Godly life my prayers benefit those I pray for more than if I had not prayed, even after I die! I am sure that I am not always righteous enough to qualify for the statement in James 5:16 (the prayers of the righteous are powerful and effective), but I am sure that at least sometimes I am in that category.

The brothers of Joseph in Genesis sold him into slavery, suffered a famine, and went to get grain from Egypt. Meanwhile Joseph had risen to be the governor there, finally revealed who he was to them, and forgave them. After his father died, the brothers were afraid that Joseph would then take revenge on them. But he said in Genesis 50:20 "As for you, you meant evil against me, but God meant it for good." So many lives were saved as a result of his obedience to God, and even as a result of their disobedience! So Joseph reassured them that they were safe.

Do we have that kind of trust in God when others try to harm us? If they fail it is quite easy to forgive and to trust God. But if they cause us to lose a job or health or family, it is much more difficult to take the attitude of Joseph. We may object that Joseph was elevated after the brothers sold him into slavery, while we are suffering terribly. But so did Joseph; for many years he was in prison with no term limits and no one on the outside who could or would help him.

But God rescued him through his interpretation of dreams for Pharaoh. Not only did he interpret dreams, but after spending many years in jail through no fault of his own, he was not bitter. That is a much more impressive miracle to me than the fact that he could understand dreams! Pharaoh was also deeply impressed, so much that he made Joseph the governor over all of Egypt. I am sure he would not have done that if Joseph had been merely an interpreter of dreams, and yet bitter and resentful!

When people try and even succeed in wronging us, do we pout and plot revenge? Do we feel sorry for ourselves and lose our trust that God is in control and means it for good when we love and obey him? Probably even Joseph lost that trust from time to time over the years he spent in captivity. But if so, he pulled out of that funk by trusting the love and power of God. "If God is for us, who can be against us?" The Holy Spirit asks that through Paul in the book of Romans. Are we for him? "... everyone who loves the Father loves whoever has been born of him," Jesus said. When that happens, we can trust that all things work together for our good. Do I always do that? I would add lying to my sins if I said yes. But I do pray to trust that promise more, so that God will be honored, and also so I will be more pleasant to be around (with more patience and kindness and less panic and whining).

People between the ages of 25-50 in this country have seen their earnings plummet over the last ten years, and that was before the recession hit. Even many who make good money are wiped out and bankrupted by major illnesses in the USA. If you have ever been to a big city you may have noticed that the largest buildings are often those of insurance companies (John Hancock in Boston, for example). Look at those buildings and the salaries of their executives, and then tell me with a straight face that our health insurance system is good and fair! Only someone who is relatively rich or knows nothing of the health care systems in other first world countries can say so!

I worked in Canada for ten years and had church members in hospitals dying of cancer and having assorted other ailments. Not once did I hear anyone complain about the health care system there. When I was sick I was very well cared for also, as were older Canadians I quizzed about their system as late as last year. And when I worked in the Netherlands, I and all others had excellent health care, while that country spends one half as much per person as we do in the USA. We can learn from them if we will, instead of promoting policies that make us closer and closer to a third-world country where all but a few are poor, while the rich must put up strong walls around their houses for protection. I much prefer that we keep a country where fences are for decorative purposes, or to keep the dogs in or the cows out!

I do not have health insurance, for I must choose between eating food and that. I may be healthy for a while longer, but if I do not eat I will be sick soon for sure. Over 60 percent of house foreclosures in this country are because of medical bills, and several of these people even had health insurance. So when you see advertisements, always ask yourself who will benefit from the ad and who will lose if we follow that advice.

"Everyone to whom much was given, of him much will be required," says the Holy Spirit (Luke 12:48) who inspired the Bible. Yet recently I saw photos of people from this area happy as they demonstrated in Washington for "fair taxes." I happen to know that some are owners of companies, can stay in fancy hotels and eat out there, and have excellent health care. Yet they consider it unfair for the richer to pay more taxes, as in Europe or Canada. Actually that happened in this country until the 1950's, but since then taxes have become more regressive for the most part.

I understand and accept that creativity and hard work should be rewarded- the Bible says those who do not work should not eat (unless unable to work). But the point is how much is fair and reasonable? The Old Testament commands that all debts be forgiven every seven years! So God always has been and always will be for justice and mercy. Yet sometimes they seem to contradict each other, don't they?

Someone in this area who worked happily and effectively and honestly for nineteen years (and was off two days sick during that time), showed up and was told to leave for good in two hours. All those who worked there were fired and replaced by younger workers. I suppose one could argue it was mercy for the new hires, but to be just it seems that only the lazy or incompetent ones should be replaced. And perhaps the owner would claim that happened. "What does the Lord require of you, but to do justice, to love kindness, and to walk humbly with your God?" Whether in a personal or national context, we will not balance justice and mercy well unless we walk humbly with God. He knows when we call for "justice" or "mercy" to cover our sins, or for selfish reasons of comfort or status or greed. God knows none of us are humble in his sight for very long periods of time. May God help us to humble ourselves before him for the first time or more deeply, and to pray that he help us to combine justice and mercy well in our personal lives, and in the life of this nation.

Ghost tours

Ghost tours are advertised in various cities, and as I flip through channels it seems that hauntings and mediums are more popular than ever. How can we think Christianly about such matters? Do ghosts really exist? Well, the King James Version of the Bible mentions the Holy Ghost several times. The Greek word pneuma is translated ghost from the German and spirit from the Latin, but mean the same. If we say we are Christian we have no choice but to believe in the spirit world, since the Bible says, "God is Spirit, and those who worship him must worship in spirit and in truth."

The Holy Ghost/Holy Spirit is the third person of the trinity, who has intellect, will, feelings, and who communicates to humans (see John 16, Acts 13 and 16...). If one is merely a church member that may sound foreign, but no one is a follower of Jesus Christ without being drawn to him by the Holy Spirit, and then accepting that supernatural call. In addition to the Holy Spirit, the Bible clearly and repeatedly teaches that other spiritual entities exist. They are called evil or unclean spirits.

Jesus and his followers cast them out of humans who were being possessed by them in the gospels and the book of Acts. And no, they did not mistake evil spirits for other sicknesses, for these were mentioned also. That practice has been largely taken over by quacks, as with all other areas of the Christian church at times throughout history. But the Roman Catholic and Orthodox churches have clear procedures still for dealing with such matters. Some Protestants also cast out demons by Biblical means also.

But most of the interest in ghosts/spirits seems to be in old houses where people get creepy feelings or see unexplained appearances or are chocked by unseen forces. The Bible is quite silent about such matters except to mention "familiar spirits." In my opinion, when such occurrences happen, then some demon that was associated with an individual while he or she lived may be hanging around a house and hassling occupants or visitors. But the only spirit I want around me is the Holy Spirit. If I get impatient or start to take revenge or to do anything else the Bible he inspired says not to do, I sense his conviction and displeasure. I much prefer that than to being spooked or harassed by an evil force.

So it is curious and somewhat amusing to me when I hear of people paying to be scared on tours or trips through houses. When I want to get the hell scared out of me, I just go to a church where the preaching is in the power of the Holy Spirit. Then sins in my life get pinpointed and I sense the importance of repentance and cleansing. But if I hang out with evil spirits/ghosts/demons, I fail to see how that benefits me or anyone else (or if you consider it fake then the same logic holds). As C.S. Lewis noted, it seems good to avoid extremes about considering spirits too much or too little. Sometimes I am tempted to pray, "Lord Holy Spirit," in addition to praying Lord God my Father or Lord Jesus Christ. But I am kept from doing that since there is no precedent in the Bible or church history. After all, the Holy Spirit exists to honor Jesus Christ and to bring attention to him! May God help us to go and do likewise.

All Christians believe in the supernatural, because the Bible says "God is Spirit, and those who worship him must worship in spirit and in truth." Furthermore, the Bible says no one can claim, "'Jesus is Lord' except in the Holy Spirit (1 Corinthians 12:3)." But what are we to think when we read reports of ghosts in houses? Are they always tales told by drunks, or the nervous, or immature children?

There is the possibility that cruel relatives are just trying to scare children or the faint hearted, or that an overactive imagination is at work. Boogertown Road was named that, not because of mucus in the nose but by people who heard the wind whistle through the area, and it reminded them of a "booger" or "haint" or ghost. But I was raised by Godly parents, and there was absolutely no hint of haunted houses in my background. So I was surprised to find belief in those happenings when I pastored my first congregation.

It was in Montreal, and I counted over twenty languages spoken in the church (not including my southern accent which most considered a separate language). More cultures were represented than languages in that location. So I learned that what most Americans consider strange supernatural events, are routine for those from third world settings. For example, one Asian group would ask me to come and to bless their homes before they moved into them. That was certainly a new concept for me, but I knew Roman Catholic and Anglican communions did that as a normal routine. As I searched the Bible I was convinced that it was valid to do so, so I did.

When I pastored in another city, a very Godly Portuguese member of the congregation told me about moving to a new place where she sensed the presence of God strongly. She knew nothing about the previous occupant until she began to receive mail addressed to the person, who was with the Salvation Army. The prayers of that person had saturated the apartment and their effects lingered after my friend had moved in. Actually I had the opposite happen to me when I moved to that city, because the previous tenant had "held hands with the devil," as the singer Bono phrased it.

When I moved back to the United States, I bought and renovated a house built in 1838, near Morristown, Tennessee. It was used as headquarters by Confederate General James Longstreet during the Civil War. Before I moved in I invited a Christian friend to accompany me as we prayed in each room that Jesus Christ would be honored, and commanded evil spirits to leave in the name of Jesus. It was like talking to a wall until we reached the attic. Then both of us sensed the presence of evil. I prayed the same prayer I had prayed downstairs, and it was peaceful. When I returned to check about a week later, the attic was as normal as possible.

The Morristown newspaper reported the story and a woman approached me and told of the problems in her house with ghosts, and asked me to do the same in her house. I politely declined and explained that I did it only to have peace in my own residence. I told her what I did, and explained that any dedicated Christian can do the same.

The Knoxville News Sentinel related how a theater group using the Bijou building downtown had noticed a ghost there. A church later rented the place for a while, and ran the ghost off. When the theater group returned they complained because the ghost was cast out by the Christians. "Ghost" seems cute to many, maybe because of "Casper the Friendly Ghost" comic books. "Spirit" sounds more dreadful, but the words mean the same. Ghost is from a German root word, and spirit is from the Latin. Both terms refer to a presence without a body. As an educated person, of course when folks talk of ghosts or spirits in places, I look for other explanations first. But as a Christian the supernatural is unmistakable to me (as with all Christians). Therefore I do not automatically rule out the possibility that as the Holy Spirit moves and touches and indwells people, so do other spirits or ghosts.

When I first saw him, he was in a medical clinic, sitting with his back towards me, with only a glimpse of his profile. I remember being struck by him. He was about eighty, wearing suspenders, with an unusual calm and peaceful demeanor, and with great dignity. As a social worker I later visited him and recognized him as the same person when he was admitted to the hospital for cancer.

Rev. John McReynolds

I was not at all looking for God. But when I entered his room, the Holy Spirit filled the place with his presence. It was an awesome place because of Rev. John McReynolds. And I was surprised, because of the gentleness with which God was drawing me back to him. For several years before that encounter, the only interaction with God I had was one of dread. I was hammered by guilt and by the anger of God when I sensed his presence at all during those years. But now in this hospital room, I realized the love of God again and how sincere his welcome was.

I said nothing about any of this to the patient, for I was still not open to even talk about God. So instead, he spoke of mining coal underground since he was eight years old, working sixteen hours a day for fifty cents a day. The labor leader John Lewis was next to Jesus Christ to him, because he fought for and won better conditions for the miners. It is a sin that the coal companies were so greedy and so uncaring towards their workers. For the most part, there was no trace of Christian influence amongst them. The owners helped build some big churches in Pittsburg and other large northern cities, but they were the kind described in the Bible as "having an appearance of godliness, but denying its power." The Holy Spirit adds these words about such churches, "Avoid such people."

On the other hand, people like John McReynolds walked with God and encouraged others to do so also. The last time I visited him during his second stay in the hospital, again we discussed several topics but nothing about God. But finally he looked at me from his bed and said, "I believe you will be a preacher someday." I knew that God was calling me to do that since I was a teenager, and was determined not to go in that direction. I had discussed that topic with no one at all. So when he said that, I was so stunned that I started to cry and walked out of the room, not being able to say a word because of the shock.

I never saw him again, but heard that he died soon afterwards. When I meet someone from that area (Wise and Coburn, Virginia) I tell them that story when I have the chance. He had a profound and positive influence on me. I am sorry I had no opportunity to tell him, but by my reaction at our last meeting, I am sure his insight from God was confirmed to him. He was very close to God, and faced death with great peace.

What kind of impact do we have on others? Will it come to light that we were good in public and a devil at home? Or is what others see is what they get? Jesus Christ was the only perfect person who ever lived, and the rest of us need to repent and to ask forgiveness a lot. Otherwise we will never draw near to the God John McReynolds knew and loved and obeyed.

It is a serious thing.

"It is a serious thing to live in a society of possible gods and goddesses, to remember that the dullest most uninteresting person you can talk to may one day be a creature, which, if you saw it now, you would be strongly tempted to worship, or else a horror and a corruption such as you now meet, if at all, only in a nightmare." British professor C. S. Lewis was a thoroughgoing supernaturalist, which is why he could say such a thing. According to the Bible, the individual has infinitely more value and worth than any nation or culture, whether for much better or for much worse, depending on our acceptance or rejection of Jesus Christ as God and our Lord.

Those of you who saw the movie "Chariots of Fire," may remember the runner Eric Liddel as he read from Isaiah 40:17 "All nations before Him are as nothing; and they are counted to Him as less than nothing, and vanity." (KJV) Yes, that includes the USA and Israel also. But that is the opposite of what most and perhaps all nations teach, as the politicians try to cover themselves in glory. "Nations, cultures, arts, civilizations- these are mortal and their life is to ours as the life of a gnat," as C. S. Lewis puts it. We live forever in joy that is far above what we can imagine, or in torment which is far below what we can imagine; forever.

Each individual has so much worth and value because God created us and gave us life, and the freedom to choose him or to reject him. Jesus, who is co eternal and co-equal with God the Father, loved us so much that he died on the cross as a substitute for our sins. He asks us to consciously love and obey him. We have purpose and meaning in life because our choices really do matter, not just for this life but for eternity. I hope that we remember that the person we help or hurt, marry or otherwise befriend, will have everlasting horror or everlasting splendor. So we are much more positive than we appear to be, or we are more negative than we appear to be- now and eternally.

Healthy relationships are characterized by respect and mutual care. Support and encouragement should be the norm from spouse to spouse, friend to friend, child to adult and adult to child. By the way, few children realize the power they have to encourage also. When they express interest in an adult and listen, that is as healthy as an adult doing the same for them.

I hope we give children as well as other adults freedom to have their own opinions without put-downs or sarcasm from us! In Godly and positive relationships, this is true. Also, freedom to have other friends is very important, for not one of us can meet the needs of another person totally. Freedom to make mistakes without yelling or screaming at others (or accepting it from others) is essential for an environment reflecting Jesus Christ. We want others to be patient with us, so doing unto others as we would have them to do unto us applies to our relationships, if anywhere.

Trust is also vital for good relationships. We cannot enjoy being with another person if we wonder if they are unfaithful or not, or otherwise calling good evil and evil good. Honesty is necessary for a relationship to thrive. If we do need to correct, we are to do so with humility and love, and to keep on being truthful. Journalist Helen Rowland said, "Telling lies is a fault in a boy, an art in a lover, an accomplishment in a bachelor, and second-nature in a married man." I am sorry that was her experience, and very glad that others do not have that to live with.

In the best of relationships, there is responsibility for self, and not blaming and self-justification. Jesus asks in Matthew 7:3 "Why do you see the speck that is in your brother's eye, but do not notice the log that is in your own eye?" Answer: Pride and arrogance. May God help us all to pray to be more irritated at our own sins than the sins of our spouse or child or parent or friend!

Freedom of movement is an outgrowth of trust and support in a good bond. Jealousy is excluded in a mutually respectful relationship—a rare enough situation and impossible when one is unfaithful. Sooner or later such deceit will bite us. Shared decision making is also important, except in the case of very young children. It is interesting to see parents let children who cannot yet walk pick out their shoes or other clothes. Later they can and should, with restraints on cost. But where to vacation or how to spend money should be mutual decisions among adults. Personal property and privacy and "no" is respected in any healthy bonds also.

How important it is to know that home is a place where we are never attacked with violence. Instead, I hope that home is a safe haven, where we know we are heard and can speak with peace and listen in peace. If sexual abuse has occurred, I hope and pray you become a survivor. That is never the will of God for anyone, and women who put up with that and refuse to protect their daughters or sons, have already lost the love and respect of their husbands. The only thing worthwhile to lose is the love and respect of the children when they prefer to overlook evil for the sake of money or comfort from a husband or lover.

Emotional safety is also necessary for a relationship to be Godly. When we pray for words in due season that heal and comfort and encourage- this excludes ranting, harsh condescending tones or sarcasm. Perhaps we do that and are unaware of it. Ask our spouse or friend or child or parent to make sure we do have kind and encouraging words, and pray for forgiveness to God when we do not have them, and then ask forgiveness from anyone in our house or extended family.

Captive to the culture

Evangelical churches in the future in the USA will be more captive to the culture than liberal ones, noted author Os Guinness was told by a professor at Cambridge about 30 years ago. My guess is that they are just about tied for such a dubious honor! Many churches/ministers gutted the supernatural claims from their Bibles, following the lead of such theologians as Rudolph Bultmann. He claimed that the parts of the Bible that taught the bodily resurrection of Jesus Christ, that God speaks to people, etc., are too offensive for moderns to accept. Evangelical/conservative Christians were right to be dismissive of such attacks on historic Christianity and the Bible.

Instead, with few exceptions, evangelicals championed the doctrine of the Bible and the early church leaders, but without caring whether we had words that were for that time and place, and spoken under the influence of the Holy Spirit. How do I know that? It is because I have seen such dead orthodoxy, that often any and all interest in Christianity was killed in the minds of those who attended such churches. They are justifiably repulsed by "Christians" who advertise that name on their company logo and do shoddy work, and who go to church and have multiple divorces, when those who do not even attend church have been married once and are faithful to their spouses.

Politicians pandering to the conservatives advocate protecting "family values," and I wonder which of their three or four families they dumped that they are talking about! Newt Gingrich, for example, committed adultery with his present wife while married to his third one. Yet he was hosted by a national evangelical radio talk show about his latest book on how Godly the founders of the USA were. No doubt that is largely true.

My ancestors, John and Abigail Adams, for example, had one of the greatest love stories in history, as we know from their collected letters and outside testimonies. Yes, I know they were Unitarian, but they both loved Jesus Christ as God. Abigail wrote to their son John Quincy, that she would prefer to know that he had drowned in a storm at sea than to hear that he had abandoned his Christian faith. They left a Godly heritage. Can the children of this darling of American evangelicals (or our children) say the same?

Evangelicals, for the most part, have also substituted "excitement" and flamboyance and strutting, for humble dependence on God during church services and in home settings. While criticizing liberal/mainline churches for dry membership classes that produce fake Christians, they often emotionally appeal to people to come to Jesus, promising a powerful puppet in the sky that we can manipulate. But no one can come to me unless they are drawn by God the Father, Jesus taught in the gospel of John. Nor can anyone say with sincerity that Jesus is Lord/boss/ruler of my life, except by the drawing of the Holy Spirit (1 Corinthians 12:3). This can happen through church membership classes or alter calls or at a quiet and private place, or not at all by these methods. What is important is that we are drawn supernaturally to Jesus Christ, and then respond with faith and obedience to him.

I hope we are not trying to be liberal or conservative to fit our personal or cultural biases, but that we pray to be historic Christians. Jonathan Edwards, the president of Princeton and the main catalyst for the Great Awakening/Revival of the 1740's, wrote often of his sense of vileness before almighty God, and his sense of ongoing repentance. When was the last time you heard a minister talk like that? I will give you a hint- it is the last time you saw true Godly revival break out!

As a descendant of presidents John Adams and John Quincy Adams, and John Sevier, the first governor of Tennessee, I am predisposed to speak English. I also prefer to see it and to hear it (although Sevier's ancestors spoke Basque and French, and my own family, the Marshalls, spoke the Gaelic a long time ago). We all exist more comfortably in our own culture, and have huge disadvantages when we are surrounded by another culture and language. As millions pour across the southern border of the USA, Spanish is fast becoming the majority language in more and more locations in this country.

Furthermore, I and many Americans have almost been bankrupted by medical bills, while illegal and not a few legal immigrants get free medical care. A Russian fake minister and his wife in Sevier County got free care recently, for example, making untrue claims on their web site and raking in money from over 400 well-meaning and naive Americans who support them. But do not hold your breath waiting for the border to close, for if it did not when only two or three million illegals were here, it is ridiculous to expect it to close when twelve million are here along with over twenty million of their relatives. Republicans wanted them here for cheap labor and to depress wages for their workers, and Democrats wanted them here to collect more votes.

But how should we think Christianly about this matter? If you want clear words about how important the USA is to God, in its present or future form, here they are. "Behold, the nations are like a drop from a bucket, and are accounted as the dust on the scales. All the nations are as nothing before him, they are accounted by him as less than nothing and emptiness," says the Lord God through the prophet Isaiah in Isaiah 40:15,17: So wave the flag and get sentimental if you wish, but do not dare to claim God's approval when you do!

God's view of the nations extends to Israel, France, as well as to this and all other countries in the world! Will we be concerned to "protect our American way of life?" Or is there anyone who values God's point of view? Only the individual has eternal significance to God: not this nation or any other nation or language spoken. Acts 17:26 says, "And he made from one man every nation of mankind to live on all the face of the earth, having determined allotted periods and the boundaries of their dwelling place." In other words, from a human point of view, we or our ancestors chose to live in this country, but from God's perspective, he inspired everyone who is here in the USA, to be here.

Why? Acts 17:27 says, "that they should seek God, and perhaps feel their way toward him and find him." Will those who come here legally or illegally find God through us, or will they find crabby and inhospitable people who sneer and complain loudly when we hear another language or see other customs introduced? Will we who claim to value the Bible as the Word of God let the Holy Spirit who inspired the Bible, be our guide? Or will we choose to be led by our fears and prejudices and discomfort over hearing other languages? Will we fly the American flag above the Christian flag in our hearts? Will we be bitter to find that our language or ethnic group has been outnumbered? Or will we pray to welcome all people with love and respect?

I am sure it does not bother God at all when my color or language is surpassed by other colors or languages. I pray that we consider important what God considers important, and trivial what God considers trivial. I am sure that I do not always do that, but I am more and more convicted of sin by the Holy Spirit when I do not. I am not called by God to advance the glory of blue eyed or brown eyed people, or those who call God "Gott," or "Bog" or "Deus." I am called, as all people are, to glorify Jesus Christ as God. To do that I must first of all repent- and repeatedly repent, of any and all allegiances that compete with him, whether national or linguistic or racial or whatever. Then I am to ask God the Holy Spirit how to best honor and glorify Jesus Christ by my words, attitudes, and actions.

Syncretism

It is called syncretism when a religion is mixed with elements of a culture that opposes it. Each society tries to mold Christianity into its image, and the USA is no exception. The Bible teaches that we are helpless on our own and must rely on God (Psalm 37:40), but 81 percent of Americans believe that the Bible helps those who help themselves, according to Barna research. The Bible teaches that Jesus alone is the Savior of mankind, and we must come to him in trust and obedience and worship. Yet 38 percent of Americans say all religions teach the same lessons, so what religion you follow does not really matter. So only American culture keeps such folks in church, instead of union with the supernatural, the risen Christ.

The Bible teaches that we are blessed to be a blessing to others, but 72 percent of Americans think we are blessed by God so we can enjoy life as much as possible. One can see the selfish cultural norm struggle with the Biblical commands! The Biblical view is that the most important thing we can do is to love God with all our heart, soul, mind, and strength (Matthew 22:37). But the American view is that the most important thing in life is taking care of family (not at all a bad goal, but not the primary one according to the Bible, and with few baby boomers having children, that goal is increasingly irrelevant to such folks). Deuteronomy 6:5 tells us that the primary purpose of life is to love God completely, but the American idea is that the primary purpose of life is enjoyment and fulfillment (grab all the gusto).

While the Bible teaches that there is only one God who can justify people (Romans 3:30), 53 percent of all Americans believe all people pray to the same God or spirit, no matter what name they use. So to the majority, the name Jesus Christ is just a symbol, instead of a person who lived in history and rose from the dead and calls all to worship and obey him as God. Although the Bible teaches clearly and repeatedly that Satan is real, powerful, and evil (1 Peter 5:9), 60 percent of Americans feel Satan is merely a symbol for evil. Thus supernatural elements of the Bible regarding God or Satan are trivialized and joked about or ignored altogether unless they fit into American prejudices.

The Biblical teaching is that no one is righteous in God's eyes, and salvation is by the grace of God (Matthew 19:16-30, Romans 3:10, Acts

4:12), is being undermined by 55 percent of Americans who believe that people earn a place in heaven by being good or by doing enough good things for others. Certainly, the Bible teaches that we should do good works, but as thankfulness for salvation and never in order to earn friendship with God. Many Americans also believe in complete opposition to the Bible, that Jesus committed sins, that the Holy Spirit is not God, that Jesus did not rise from the dead and return to earth physically, that whatever works for you is what is true, and that there are some sins that even God cannot forgive. We can choose whether to live the Bible and to pass the truth of it to those we love, or to pass on American dreams and culture that are often at odds with the Bible.

If I were a sadist or masochist, I would not disagree. But God requires us to act justly, to love mercy, and to walk humbly with him (Micah 6:8). When we do this, we do not treat others like garbage, and we wish to be treated with respect. Others may or not respect us when we are holy and walking with God. But then we are neither attracted to such people, nor do we wish evil to be done by them or to them.

In fact, when we are abused, as we all experience at some time on some level, with dishonesty or slander, etc., if we walk with God we must forgive them. When Jesus is our Lord and Savior, we agree with him in everything, and therefore honor his words, "Father, forgive them, for they know not what they do." So we do not have sweet dreams of getting revenge. Well, actually, we might, but need to repent when we have them.

Beautiful music and a beautiful face can make most of us turn our backs on what is good and holy, and therefore what is best for all people. I do not recall ever wanting to be abused by anyone, but I am sure I have wanted to use others for my own selfish reasons on occasions. That is a form of abuse, and I hope and pray that is a thing of the past. Anyway, calling such contemplations or dreams "sweet" is not acceptable from the point of view of the Holy Spirit.

But it is impossible for me to identify with those who want to be abused. On November 20, 2009, *The Los Angeles Times* reported that a man was arrested after a policeman overheard him offering a boy $31 to spit in his face! Easier to understand are those women (and some men) who accept abuse in exchange for money, either as prostitutes or as wives/husbands. Many stay with a husband who beats or browbeats or who even sexually abuses a child, in order to keep a lifestyle higher than she could have as a waitress or clerk or even as a professional. Greedy dreams fuel such selfishness, and root out repentance and holiness, without which no one will see the Lord (except as an enemy). May God help us all to respect ourselves and others, as made in the image of God and therefore with great eternal worth and value.

Rotary Club in drag or a Godly church?

I was a Rotarian. I met wonderful people there, and I highly respect the good work they do. But I am convinced that a Godly church is very different. The Rotary clubs basically take in civic minded, pleasant and responsible and caring folks, and encourage them to enhance their lives and the community where they live. So do Rotary clubs in drag, that pass for Christian churches. At such clubs, generally upright and moral people have sermonettes instead of sermons, and *prayerettes* instead of prayers. Members are wont to complain that prayers are not allowed in schools when they do not have them in their churches. They go to what they call church in order to enhance their lives, and to add refinement to social graces, to improve their speaking abilities or to make business or social contacts. There is nothing inherently wrong about that, and I favor that in real Rotary clubs.

But a real church is radically different "My house shall be called a house of prayer," Jesus said. In other words, it is a place where people listen to God, get his views and attitudes, and his perspectives from the Bible. And then we also get discernment on how to apply those in our daily lives. A Godly church is a place where we come into the presence of God unmistakably, and where even children know that God is there in power. It is a place where people are dragged by the Holy Spirit from the power of Satan into the kingdom of light. It is where there is an awe of God. It is where we turn from sin through conversion, or through Christians already converted being convicted of lukewarmness and of not being holy.

A Godly church is where a good word is always spoken of Jesus Christ, and where people sincerely try to live for him also. It is where the Bible is preached in power-where words are anointed for that time and place.

Therefore, the preacher in such a setting is one who humbly walks with the living God/the risen Jesus Christ. It is a place where people go to meet with God and to commune with him much more than the minister or the singers or any mere human who might be there. It is a fellowship where we give up all words and thoughts and attitudes and actions that do not please God, and where we pray to keep only those that do honor God.

A Godly church is where God is so unmistakably there that those in the congregation either repent and turn to God for the first time or more deeply, or they have such terror that they either leave or are afraid to join the congregation, as in the book of Acts. If you did not have this awesome and unmistakably presence of God when you went to a church on Sundays, you went to a Rotary club in drag! Someday I hope you go to a Godly church, or even a real Rotary club. Just do not hang out at a Rotary club in drag, or you may mistake that for historic Christianity!

He came the first time as a baby but will return as the judge of all.

Christ has died, Christ is risen, Christ will come again—that is the historic message of Christianity. John 17:5 says, "Father, glorify me in your own presence with the glory that I had with you before the world existed." The eternal God added human flesh and became a baby, while he continues to be God. That was the first advent or appearance of Jesus on earth. Over 300 passages in the Bible state that Jesus will come again, and this is called the second advent. Christians disagree on the particulars of how he will arrive or the chronology of events at that time, but no one who claims to be a historic Christian disputes all those verses. Both those living at that time and those who have died previously- every eye shall see him when he returns.

He came the first time as a helpless infant, but he is coming back as the judge of all people. "Not in that poor lowly stable with the oxen standing by, we shall see him, but in heaven, sat at God's right hand on high," teaches one of the Christmas carols. Mark 13:26 states, "Then they will see the son of man (born of Mary so he was both God and man) coming in clouds with great power."

It is more sentimental and comforting for all to focus on the baby Jesus, although songs such as "Santa Claus is Comin' (In a Boogie Woogie Choo Choo Train)," and "Sock It To Me Santa" try to divert us even from that level of contemplation! So church goers have our heads full of trivial nonsense as we enter the doors, often to sit for more shallow entertainment to follow once we are inside. But whether heaven Jesus will usher in will be one foot off the ground, billions of miles away, or in a totally unimagined dimension, I do not care. The same Jesus Christ who walked the earth will be there. Those who choose not to walk with him here on earth will not be forced to be with him in heaven, for Jesus is a gentleman who respects our wishes.

It is very difficult for those in rich and peaceful countries to look forward to the second coming of Jesus Christ. Instead, it is natural to see heaven as being right here. I share that problem sometimes, as do other Christians also. I do not wish more hardships for myself or for anyone else (except sometimes for those who have wronged me, and for that attitude I need to keep on repenting). But if the material world is all that is, and if love and hatred and joy and sorrow only evolved with no creator, then all is random. So then there is no meaning or purpose for life at all.

But if there is a creator, then we should examine competing claims. I have done this, and I encourage all to look closely at the life, teachings of Jesus about himself and to us, and I hope you consider the crucifixion and resurrection of Jesus and the evidence for that (see earlier article on the resurrection). I also suggest you find a church where the minister has been supernaturally converted, instead of diving into a seminary to avoid the draft or to sway weak and silly women (or similar men).

Thanksgiving to God is unnatural

We are more prone to thank our parents or "our lucky stars" than to thank God for anything. It is unnatural, so the Bible commands us to do so. Psalm 50:14 says, "Offer to God a sacrifice of thanksgiving." We must indeed sacrifice very much, in order to give God credit for anything. When life is difficult, then we must sacrifice self-pity and resentment before we thank God in the midst of our troubles. After all, the Bible teaches that God has all power. Therefore, he could have stopped the thief or murderer with a bolt of lightning. He could have given us more abilities, or more favor in the eyes of the person we wanted to marry, or the person who fired us. As God turned the heart of King Cyrus to allow the Jews to return to Israel after seventy years of captivity in Babylon (as the Bible predicted would happen), so he turns the hearts of others to love and respect us or not. But when we suffer rejection of loss, it is natural to feel sorry for ourselves, and not to feel like thanking God at all.

So when life is easy and full of joy and peace and prosperity, are we more likely then to be truly thankful to God? Absolutely not! Then we are tempted to take all the credit for ourselves. We are then prone to be smug and arrogant, and to look down on those who do not "deserve" what we have achieved. So we must sacrifice pride to thank God when life is pleasant. As a matter of fact, we are much more likely to thank God in poverty than in prosperity, in sickness than in health, as Tolstoy and many others have noted.

We may sing "Now thank we all our God" and other songs of gratitude and preach and speak of how thankful we are to God. But are we really? Perhaps. When we have deeply thankful hearts toward God, our attitudes are transformed. Then we humbly accept whatever God sends to us in terms of gain or loss, and pleasant as well as unpleasant circumstances. No, I do not always do that either. I also find myself thinking that I deserve much more pleasant situations and fewer unpleasant ones.

But the Bible teaches that God reigns, and that he molds each of us by unique circumstances he allows us to enter. What draws me closer to God may drive you farther away, and vice versa. That fact is easy to accept when we seem to have life by the tail, but extremely difficult to embrace when God brings suffering into our life. And if we see Satan behind our troubles, so what, for God has all power!

In the church of Rev. Harry Ironsides in Philadelphia, the assistant pastor and his wife were having a baby. Rev. Ironsides and the congregation were joyful and kept inquiring about the progress. Finally the father announced that the child was born, but was severely handicapped. Ironsides answered with this quote from Exodus 4:11 "Who gives speech to mortals? Who makes them mute or deaf, seeing or blind? Is it not I, the Lord?" The context (it is good to know the context before we quote a passage from the Bible or any other book) is that God had chosen Moses to lead the people of Israel, and Moses had objected with the excuse that he was slow of speech.

I thought of that passage when my wife announced recently to me that she thought she was pregnant. I was fearful that the fact that I was thinking of that passage might mean that our child would be severely damaged in some way. But I prayed to keep being thankful to God, no matter what happened or did not happen (a test showed that she is not pregnant).

I am for thanksgiving—in theory.

I am all for thanksgiving—in theory. But sometimes, it is so unnatural that I sulk and complain, and I remain in a funk, unless I consciously remember a great song that goes like this: "Count your blessings, name them one by one. Count your blessings, see what God has done. Count your many blessings, name them one by one. And it will surprise you what the Lord has done." I must literally begin naming some of my many benefits in order to beat the gloom back at times. For example, I deliberately thank God for having peace with him, for my family, health, food, clothes, shelter, two dogs and a cat, beautiful nature around me, and for nobody shooting at me.

Helen Keller, who is on the back of the Alabama quarter, was both blind and deaf. Yet she could write, "I thank God for my handicaps. For through them, I have found myself, my work, and my God." We can all be thankful not only for our abilities, but also for our limitations, as Helen was. But it is so tempting to always be comparing ourselves with others who have more money or health or status or something else that we value. May God help us to value our present circumstances, and to grow in the midst of them now.

"... give thanks in all circumstance; for this is the will of God in Christ Jesus for you," teaches the Holy Spirit. Since I wrecked a truck in New Jersey, I make about one fifth of the money I made then, and for me that is a significant hit. But that is money I do not need, since God has promised to supply all our needs! Also, neither I nor anyone else was hurt badly. I no longer go to sleep while driving, as one half of all truck drivers admitted doing during research. I got to return to this beautiful area to live where I love. So I am thankful for all these facts (although remaining thankful for making far less money is an ongoing struggle).

Also, I am thankful for the great promises in the Bible for those who love and obey Jesus Christ, as I do sometimes. Then the promises that all things work together for good apply to me. So even setbacks and less money and sickness, as well as all the pleasant circumstances, work together for good. No, I do not feel that any more than you do at times, but we can choose to base our lives on the Bible or not, and no other book has the credibility it has.

I am probably among the ten people in the USA who love country music the least, but a song by Garth Brooks got my admiration. It seems he was rejected by a girl in his high school, attended a class reunion, saw her, and returned home to write the song, "Thank God for Unanswered Prayers." Ruth Graham, wife of evangelist Billy Graham, related that if God had answered all her prayers, she would have married the wrong man about ten times. When we love and obey God and trust his promises, every day is Thanksgiving Day. We all enjoy being around thankful folks more than crabby and resentful ones—I need to remember that truth applies to me too. And may God help us to have the attitude of the first secretary of the United Nations, Dag Hammarskjold, who said, "For all that has been, thank you. For all that shall be, yes!"

The first Thanksgiving Day

Thanksgiving Day was begun by the Pilgrims, who landed November 11, 1620, in what is now Plymouth, Massachusetts. Why did they come? Instead of swapping theories, we know because they left a record. According to them, "Having undertaken for the glory of God and the advancement of the Christian faith and honor of our king and country, a voyage to plant the first colony..."

During the first winter, forty-seven (about half) of them perished. Thirteen out of eighteen wives died. The remainder almost starved to death. But aided by Squanto (who had earlier learned English as a captive and became a Christian, by the way) and other Indians who befriended them, they hunted and fished and began to plant crops as soon as possible.

In 1621, Governor William Bradford declared a day of public thanksgiving to God. It was held in October (in Canada, it is still in October). Indians brought deer and turkey. They taught the Pilgrims to make pudding out of cornmeal and maple syrup and introduced them to popcorn. The new settlers provided carrots, cabbages, onions, and cucumbers, and made pies of blueberries, apples, and cherries. Foot races and wrestling matches were held, and Thanksgiving was extended over three days.

Soon afterwards, new immigrants came from England without supplies. So the resources of the Pilgrims were stretched to the limits over the winter of 1621-1622: As a matter of fact, for a while, they were all reduced to a ration of five kernels of corn each. Miraculously, no one starved.

The next fall they had plenty of food, and they celebrated Thanksgiving again. But the first course that was served featured an empty place with five kernels of corn. If we have a family, we may want to begin the practice of first giving five kernels of corn on an empty plate to each person, to remind us of the sacrifices our spiritual ancestors made to take the gospel of Jesus Christ to this country.

Governor Bradford wrote, "As one small candle may light a thousand, so the light kindled here hath shone unto many, yea in some sort to our whole nation ... we have noted these things so that you may see their worth and not negligently lose what your fathers have obtained with so much hardship." Of course, rituals like beginning Thanksgiving meals with five kernels of corn may become void of meaning, as holy communion or church attendance may also become empty rituals.

But Thanksgiving began for the purpose of thanking God for his provisions. I hope it does not become just another excuse to stuff our faces. From the Geneva Psalter comes a song the Pilgrims could have known and sung. "Praise God, from whom all blessings flow: praise him all creatures here below. Praise him above ye heavenly hosts. Praise Father, Son and Holy Ghost." This Thanksgiving, whether we have loved ones or a great feast or not, I pray we will have an attitude of thanksgiving toward "Father, Son and Holy Ghost."

Thanksgiving Day or turkey day?

Contrary to popular myth, the Pilgrims did not come to America for religious freedom. They did leave England because of religious persecution, but they fled first of all to Holland in 1608: By 1609, they had established themselves in the city of Leyden. They flourished as the lenient Dutch allowed them to worship freely as they saw fit.

But amid all their freedom, the Pilgrims had other concerns. They were afraid that the longer they stayed, the more their community would assimilate, with the loss of the strict emphasis on personal faith in Christ and piety. From our perspective now, we might question their wisdom, because the Dutch had their share of Christians as dedicated as the English ones. But the small Dutch nation was surrounded by the big bullies of England, France and Germany, so they had to adopt a national policy of toleration and acceptance of differences, or they would be smashed. So, strictness of doctrine or conduct was not as valued as it was among the Pilgrims. But we can be thankful for their concern to pass on the Christian faith undiluted. They crossed the Atlantic and endured severe conditions in 1620, in order to do all they could to preserve a strong Christian faith.

In the USA today, we all have freedom to worship or not as we please. But do we have the deep burden to pass on the faith and the willingness to sacrifice comfort or status in order to do that? We can be thankful truly for parents who sacrificed materially to support evangelism and missions and who lived out the faith in private as well as in public. How thankful we can be to know that others gave up selfish goals in order to do what they knew was best for us.

I was talking to a little girl and when the subject of her parents came up. She mentioned, "I do not have a father." I asked when he left, and she said it was a month ago, or maybe two, or maybe a year ago. She was not sure when he left, but she was definitely convinced that she did not have a father. I pray God will protect her from being scarred by the abandonment, and I hope her father will sacrifice pride or time or comfort of whatever is necessary to show the daughter that he cares for her.

Thanksgiving Day becomes just turkey day unless we have someone to thank. Deep in our hearts, we know that none of us deserves worship, but we give thanks to God, and to those who sacrificed so that we would be pointed to God by their words, attitudes and actions. And as the Pilgrims did on the first Thanksgiving Day, let us give thanks to the Creator for supplying all our needs. No doubt they thanked the Indians also for their help. But from the historical records we know that their foremost concern was to render thanks to the Triune God.

The Bible is much more positive than any worldly promise. God says in Psalm 84:11, “For the Lord God is a sun and shield; The Lord bestows favor and honor. No good thing does he withhold from those who walk uprightly.” That and many other precious promises for those who love and obey him, give us abundant cause for thanksgiving, even in the midst of difficulties we all face.

Practice hospitality.

"Practice hospitality," especially during holidays such as Thanksgiving and Christmas. It is a command for Christians, from Romans 12: So we have no choice if we want to walk with God, except among various methods. As a single person for many years, the holidays were the most difficult for me. Sometimes, I would invite myself over somewhere, but it is always unpleasant to do so. How much better it is when a group or a family takes the initiative and calls us over. Pray for God to guide us, then look around our neighborhoods and among our contacts and invite someone to Thanksgiving or Christmas dinner.

If we do not know of anyone, call the international house at your local university, or talk to a waiter with an accent, and invite them to come and to bring friends. That way they will not feel as isolated when they arrive. Offer transportation, for many students here from other countries do not have cars. By the way, if you can use your car later to take them to grocery stores, they can save much money. Often, they must shop at a local corner store that charges much higher prices.

By letting our thanksgiving to God overflow to others, we teach our children by example to curb greed and selfishness, and we build a bridge to other countries, because very often, foreign students stay in the USA for several years without once being invited into an American home. Can you believe that when we see ourselves as a hospitable people?

If we can afford to eat out, we can afford to bring someone over for at least a peanut butter sandwich, which most have never seen except in the movies. Also, please tip well, because Christians are known as cheap among the waiters and waitresses in tourist spots such as Sevier County by the Great Smoky Mountains. If you have a pastor, you might ask the person to stress to the congregation that they can quit being stingy with the hired help, and that will be a big boost towards hospitality, aside from inviting others over (Ok, emphasize the positive aspects also of being generous, do not mention repentance or the congregation may be offended).

We have food, clothes, shelter probably, and the ability to read this or we have someone to read it for us. We have a land of incredible opportunity—to which either we or our ancestors came (including Indians). We can worship freely by assembling together, or we can stay home if we wish. Churches often have Thanksgiving dinners and welcome outsiders, and that is positive. So, if we feel bashful to ask others to our house, that is one way to practice hospitality. Or we can do both. Ho Chi Ming was a student in Boston before he returned to lead Vietnam, and Jacque Chirac was a student in South Carolina before he became president of France. I often have wondered what a difference it would have made if they had been shown hospitality. Many are here who will go back to their countries and become leaders, but if they become ditch diggers, they still deserve to be shown compassion and care by us as American Christians (or American atheists, or otherwise, for that matter).

Jesus says to do unto others as we would have them do unto us. I have experienced so much kindness in different countries when I traveled alone. I cherish those memories of people taking me miles out of their way when I was hitchhiking, waking me up at a truck stop at about two in the morning because the driver heard I needed to go to London, etc. I ate meals in the homes of foreigners and am very thankful to those who showed care. I am not able to repay them many times, and I am obligated to pass hospitality on to others. And I enjoy and am so encouraged to do so. I do not always have a lot of money, so we can just put more water in the soup when others come! But it means a lot, especially when a person is alone in a foreign country. And if that sounds too difficult, look around for some Americans who would benefit from hospitality. I am sure we have a hundred million or so to choose from.

When internal restraints against evil behavior are removed by our acceptance of selfish and irresponsible philosophies, then only a dictatorship can insure individual safety and peace. I hope instead we opt for the Prince of Peace, Jesus Christ, who said in Matthew 11:29 "take my yoke upon you" ... Then when we know the lawgiver, we internalize the law, or in other words, the law is written upon our hearts by the Holy Spirit. When the law of God is written in our hearts, our Constitution will remain adequate to govern us, and we will avoid the extremes of a dictatorship on the one hand, and lawlessness on the other hand.

George Washington

The president of South Africa in 2001 noted that many think Africa is corrupt and inefficient. "They are right," he added. One cannot help but admire and respect such a humble and honest leader who was devoted to fighting such sins. What about the "old boys" network here and in every place? In every location, leaders emerge naturally and try to pass on jobs and benefits. The only difference is how these favors are passed on. Are they inherited by family and friends regardless of whether they are best for the jobs or not?

Or are the plums given to those of integrity and competence? Any government from the local to the international level benefits when leaders gather Godly people around them and delegate authority to them. As the Bible phrases it in Proverbs 13:34 Righteousness exalts a nation, but sin is a reproach to any people. All levels of government bring justice and a much better living environment when those in charge are honest, kind, and under the Lordship of God.

I know it is sometimes very difficult to tell which public figure is righteous and which. Is not. Some may claim to be trustworthy when the opposite is true, and the opponent may be more wonderful but humble. Sometimes a public forum will clearly show arrogance or humility, respect for others or contempt, competence or incompetence. It's sometimes asserted that plainer politicians like Abraham Lincoln can no longer get elected since handsome or beautiful candidates appeal to the masses more. If that is so, we harm ourselves very much.

When we celebrate the birth of our nation on July 4, I hope we respect and admire and choose more leaders like George Washington. Our third President Thomas Jefferson (who disagreed with him about many things) had this to say about him: "He was indeed, in every sense of the words, a wise, a good, and a great man." Yes, he owned slaves and was wrong for doing that, although John Adams did not, and was a good example in that area. It is always easier and much more pleasant to see the sins of others rather than our own sins!

While some revisionist historians sneered that Washington married his wife Martha for her money, he himself wrote to her... "There was never a moment in my life since I first knew you, in which it (my heart) did not cleave and cling to you with the warmest affection." By the way, if you want to understand our first president or anybody else in history, read some of their own writings instead of just reading the opinions about them!

He read the Bible daily, and different guests reported barging unintentionally into his room after nine o'clock at night and finding him alone. He was on his knees with an open Bible before him on a chair, reading aloud (as was the custom then). May God have mercy on us so that we do not prefer the witty to the wise, the arrogant to the good, the petty to the great. We are responsible to train ourselves in godliness so that we can recognize it and appreciate it in others who seek to be political or social or religious leaders.

True guilt and false guilt

"The righteous shall live by faith," Paul said in the book of Romans. But what if we think we are living by faith when we are not? What if our faith is in our feelings or logic or charm or education, and not in God? David prayed in the Psalms, "Declare me innocent from hidden faults." The prophet Jeremiah said, "The heart is deceitful above all things, and desperately sick; who can know it?" So, it is theoretically possibility to think all is well when it is not well.

Many have been blindsided by a demand for a divorce, for example, when they thought that all was well. But, as spouses should check with each other from time to time and sincerely ask how we can be a better spouse, so should we check in with God with some real prayer regularly. One song affirms, "It is well with my soul." But can we really know when all is well between us and God?

I struggle with that sometimes. I know I have salvation or "fire insurance," so I am not uneasy about that. But often it seems to me that if I were really, truly, walking with God as closely as possible, I would have more influence on others as I speak or write, to move others to either become followers of Jesus Christ or better disciples. At other times I wonder if I would be in difficulties or one sort or another if I were living as humbly before God as I should. I do not think such questions are unrealistic to ask, for it is entirely possible that our sins have caused problems for us or hindered our influence for Christ.

At other times, however, we experience what Paul did when he prayed for some hassle to be removed by God and got the answer, "My power is made perfect in weakness." His obstacle or "thorn in the flesh," was left intact, and it was never specified so that all of us can more easily relate to Paul. There was no need for Paul to have guilt in this case, for God revealed that the problem Paul had was for his own good, since he had to cling to God all the more in order to deal with it with grace and peace.

In his excellent book, *Guilt and Grace* (literally true and false guilt from the French), Dr. Paul Tournier encourages us to repent of true guilt and to refuse to accept false guilt. But how can we know the difference? Sometimes it is clear from the Bible that we are wrong by failing to do what it says or doing what it says not to do. At other times, we internalize personal or cultural or family expectations, and when we fail to meet them, we have false guilt. Goals for success can either be from God or from other sources. But if we are doing whatever the Bible says to do and as far as we know, avoiding what it says not to do, then any guilt we have is false.

The Scottish pastor Robert Murray M'Cheyne influenced many to pray as he did when he said, "Lord, make me as holy as a pardoned sinner can be." When we say that to God and mean it, we will be convicted often of impatience, unkindness, rudeness, selfishness, etc. If we pay people enough, they may be too greedy to point out these traits when we have them. But when at least we are honest with ourselves, we will be aware of them sooner or later.

Reading the Bible, by the way, cuts through the walls of self-deception we all like to build in order to think more highly of ourselves than we ought. That is why a proud heart makes it painful for us to pore over its pages. But when we pray for God to help us to understand and to apply it as we read the Gospels, Romans, Philippians, etc., we are cleansed by that humility and then there is the possibility that the Holy Spirit will guide us. When that happens, then we will live by the faith that patience, kindness, and other traits taught by the Bible are best for us.

And whether we have health or sickness, or wealth or poverty, or a job that has deep influence or not, we can have faith that we are being and doing what honors God. God does not call us to be anyone but ourselves with our gift mix of abilities and limitations, consciously dedicated to him. Just as the Holy Spirit convicts the Christian when we are out of his will, so he confirms and gives peace to us when we are in his will. May that happen to each of us, with both true and false guilt replaced with forgiveness and peace.

When the unmistakable consciousness of sin is gone, so is the unmistakable awareness of God.

"The church's consciousness of sin began to erode along with its awareness of God," said Dr. Richard Lovelace, in the book *Dynamics of Spiritual Life*, on page 87: The Bible teaches in Jeremiah 17:9 "The heart is deceitful above all things, and desperately sick; who can understand it?" So, there is unconscious motivation behind surface motives. "Sigmund Freud rediscovered this factor and recast it in an elaborate and profound secular mythology," notes Dr. Lovelace. Freud's colleague, Dr. Carl Jung, added that the unconscious affects our actions, and he claimed that the unconscious has both good and bad elements. He labeled the unconscious God. But if he is right, then no repentance is ever necessary, because we are with God whether right or wrong. Nor is praise ever deserved either if God is the author of both good and evil. Against these teachings, the Bible affirms that "God is light, and in him is no darkness at all." Furthermore, we not only commit sins, but we are sinners by nature. We have a bent for sinning, in other words, or we are naturally inclined to have attitudes and words and actions that rebel against God.

"Bidden or not, God is present." Jung had this carved over his front door (in Latin), and on his tombstone. He was indeed present, but as the judge and not as the demonic which he and his parents venerated. His last book finally admitted that his work had been influenced by this force, which had caused his clergy father to finally admit that he had turned his back on Christianity. His mother had reserved a bed where spirit couples were always welcome in their home, so she was devoid of the Holy Spirit also.

To become a Christian does not mean to have our natural bent for sinning taken away. As a matter of fact, the Christian becomes even more aware of our human opposition to things of God. At the same time the Christian has the Holy Spirit, who convicts us of not only individual sins but of our whole independence from God by nature. The Christian has a deeper awareness of his/her sin nature, while at the same time God is with us to confirm his great love for us, and his desire for us to live within his love.

But as the awareness of our sin has been undermined by our society in addition to our own selfishness, so has our unity with God. We still have sin in the general sense, and many specific varieties are clearly condemned in the Bible. But we have deceived ourselves into feeling that they really do not matter to God. We do not have adultery or fornication anymore, but affairs and hook ups. We do not steal but pilfer, and nobody dies anymore; instead, people just pass away. So even death, the last enemy, is trivialized.

As we try to hide from painful reality, so we become closed to joyful reality—the favor of God. We cannot have the peace and joy of fellowship with God until we reject whatever the Holy Spirit calls sin. "Do you renounce the devil, and all of his works and all of his ways?" So asks an ancient litany. But now we change it to something like, "Do you turn your back on anxiety and embrace your highest potential through a higher power?" Or we may say, "May the force be with you." That sounds good, but Jesus is God, and he says, "No one can come to me unless my Father draw him." People are drawn supernaturally to Jesus, or they do not come at all. That is a big deal. Few churches really meet with God so that the presence and power and awe of God enters the worship service. When that happens, the person is traumatized in a good way, by seeing our sins and how much we are opposed to a holy God, even the most holy of us. Then this jolt from above continues even after the service. "How about them Vols/Trojans/Gators?" Those thoughts are swept from our consciousness for a period of time when we see clearly the Holy God of the universe in the worship service. When we rationalize our sins, we may protect fake dignity and real pride, but the dignity of forsaking our sins and repenting and taking pride in the Lord of the universe is infinitely better.

Lord, send a revival, and let it begin in me.

When the Billy Graham organization was accused of having a $20 million "slush fund," it was put on page one of *The Charlotte Observer*. Further investigation revealed that the fund was for training evangelists at Wheaten College, to build a lay training center near Asheville, N.C. (which became "The Cove"), and to go to some student ministries. The correction was published in small paragraphs at the back of the paper. Some of Graham's family and friends fumed, and Billy had this to say about *The Charlotte Observer* reporters. "Bob Hodierne and Mary Bishop taught us some good lessons. We have learned some things from them (namely, to be more open and transparent)." Graham was more concerned for the honor of God than his own honor, and revival followed him wherever he went.

Do we have that kind of attitude when we think we are unfairly portrayed? Or do we want vengeance when God says, "Vengeance is mine, I will repay?" Do we stay gracious and forgiving, or do we pout and worry about our reputation and honor? We cannot follow Jesus well unless we are repentant about any of our crabby reactions to others. But how do we confront sin and still be gracious? I have not figured that out very well yet. And when I get my theology straight—as I normally am convinced that I have done, I must struggle to apply it well.

"Speak the truth in love," God commands us in the Bible. I am sure that sometimes when attacked I defend my honor instead of being concerned about the honor of God. And the fact that I have the courage to face people head on just adds to my pride in those cases. But if we have been forgiven, have salvation and friendship with Jesus Christ, we have the ability and therefore the responsibility to be Christlike. When was the last time we were accused of that trait? Perhaps we can recall a cartoon of an eagle with some turkeys, and the caption asked, "how can I fly when I am surrounded by turkeys?" But how can we be sure we are not one of the turkeys—especially if we blame them for keeping us from flying high?

If we are not reaching our full potential/flying like an eagle/being all that God has called us to be, it is only an excuse to blame anyone or any circumstance. That is because only we can keep ourselves from speaking the truth in love and living in that truth. Harsh criticism or tough circumstances can certainly pressure us to deviate from truth or to speak hatefully, but we can choose to be gracious and to trust that God always does what is best for those who love him (Romans 8:28), or we can choose not to trust that. When I love and obey God and trust Romans 8:28, I have peace and graciousness and encourage others Godward in at least in small ways, and when I do not, I am a hindrance to revival.

As a boy, I recall one preacher saying that he was going to "preach the truth if it harelips every one of you." Perhaps he should have had that attitude, but the way he said it made me think he would not grieve if we all developed harelips. I remember not sensing a lot of love as he spoke, and I am certain that the Holy Spirit was not with him in power. On the other hand, the Russian writer Solzhenitsyn wrote of a fellow prisoner who was very important in his salvation: a teacher. When asked what he would teach when he was released, the teacher said he would teach the truth. Solzhenitsyn replied that they would throw him back in jail the next day. The teacher lowered his head and gently answered, "Let them." Revival had come to his heart, and the fire of the Holy Spirit spread to engulf Solzhenitsyn also.

When we look around, we may be tempted to pray that others repent more, and no doubt that need is there. But if we are genuinely concerned about the salvation or growth in grace of others, our prayers for them will be effective only when we are righteous ourselves. That is because James 5:16 says the prayers of the righteous are effective, not the prayers of the unrighteous. As a boy growing up in east Tennessee, I often heard the song, "Lord, send a revival, and let it begin in me." When we have that attitude, we will not see ourselves as eagles and others as turkeys, but as people for whom Jesus Christ died.

Sincerity is not enough.

The Scottish philosopher David Hume was an atheist. Yet he sometimes would go and hear a preacher who was known to be a historic Christian. A friend asked why he went and remarked that he did not believe what he said, or did he? Hume responded that he did not believe what was preached- but the preacher did. "And it is refreshing," added Hume, "to hear someone who believes what he says." But do we listen because a person is sincere, or do we allow God the Holy Spirit to move us toward truth?

After I preached my first sermon in my first congregation, a woman who later became a good friend told me she asked a professor who attended what he thought. He replied, "Well, he was sincere." In other words, he did not believe what I said, although he liked the fact that I did. He later had a sex change operation, abandoned his wife and four children, and ran off with another man. I hope I have more positive influence through my writing, for my speaking days seem to be over.

I had my daughter tape a message to send out, but it was at Cades Cove in the National Park nearby, and people flushed the toilet near the mic so much it was drowned out. Another time, I had a person tape a sermon given at a church, and afterwards I was informed that the machine ate the tape. So, I must stick to the printed medium and hope and pray God works through this avenue. If you want to hear magnificent sermons, I suggest you go to www.sermonindex.net and listen to Rev. Jim Cymbala preach on prayer, or any of the many others collected over about a fifty-year period. The web host is a Canadian guy, Greg Gordon, who has done a great service by putting together some of the greatest preachers and their sermons, and personal stories of revival in various places.

True revival means that people get serious about serving God, return stolen property, and otherwise make restitution for any wrongs that were done. It means that concern for the things of God are awakened, and that we either begin for the first time, or that we live more fully, for his glory. It means that those who are truly converted to Christ begin to get more irritated at our own sins than the sins of others. I never see in the New Testament that Paul and Peter and other church leaders whined about how fourteen of the first fifteen emperors were homosexual, or that Caligula was a transvestite. I never read about Paul and others scared that Christians would lose their rights—they had no rights to lose. And yet the church grew by leaps and bounds. They had a hostile environment outside the churches, but inside the churches they had an environment conducive to the Word of God. We have the opposite now in many of our churches! The hostility to Godly preaching and living comes from inside the congregations so many times.

When Jim Cymbala began to pastor in Brooklyn, New York, about half of the eighteen to twenty left. He is a nice guy with a good sense of humor, unpretentious and humble. Several were not offended by any of that, but by his preaching from the Bible and trying to live it. If he had kissed their rears, he could have kept them, but then the church would not have grown to almost 10,000 with fourteen new churches planted in addition. During each of the services, about twenty are praying for the service that is going on. "My house shall be called a house of prayer," said Jesus. Preaching, singing, and doing good works is important, but when it is really a house of God, praying comes first and underlies all other activities. Otherwise, they are worthless in the eyes of God, even when praised by humans.

We may preach under God's guidance and have only a small group attend, and no atheist philosophers converted. But we are to be faithful to be all God calls us to be, and to do all he calls us to do, and to repent enough to recognize his voice and to obey him. If so, then our hands will be clean before God, and if not, then the blood of many will be on our hands.

1905 Lake Avenue adventures, Part 1

I glanced up from reading the newspaper and noticed a guy coming down the stairs with a gun in his hand. I asked as casually as possible, "Uh, what do you plan to do with that pistol?" He replied that he planned to shoot jackrabbits in the snow with it. This was while I was a student at UT in Knoxville, at 1905 Lake Avenue, just off campus. But nobody laughed at such a ridiculous statement.

I talked him into putting the pistol into a desk drawer overnight and assured him that it would be safe there. I also pointed out that he could then take it with him when he left the next morning. Fortunately, he took the advice and left without killing any of us. We had guns too, but he had the drop on us. We later found a needle upstairs he had disposed of after shooting up heroin.

He was just one of the many hitchhikers we befriended when I lived there. Not all students confront people high on drugs with drawn guns, but still I hope we pray for our loved ones when they go away to school. They face pressure to conform or to be lonely or perhaps poor, and need to have self-discipline once the parents are removed from their lives. It is tough to begin a new life away from home. Even the most dedicated Christian students need to find good relationships, and to have proper balance between study and leisure.

Groups such as Intervarsity, Campus Crusade for Christ and Navigators, as well as denominational organizations deserve our prayers too. In the heady atmosphere of a college or university, the student may be ashamed of parents who are less educated or who do not subscribe to the coolest magazine. But instead of giving up trying to influence them, I hope instead we give them relevant and practical prayers, and books also. Or perhaps we can recommend web sites that lift up Godly intelligence.

C.S. Lewis taught at Oxford and Cambridge in England and is at least as intelligent as any professor they will ever encounter or hear or read about. So even if they try to dismiss their Christian parents as morons relative to their cool professors (which may be a fact), C. S. Lewis will make the most hip professor seem like he or she is talking shallow drivel. He was a friend of J. R. Tolkien, C. K. Chesterton, and other profound thinkers, and also a deeply dedicated Christian. His book *Mere*

Christianity will appeal to any honest searcher for spiritual truth. Chuck Colson, the former hit man for President Nixon who was sent to prison, was surprised to finally read someone who presented Christianity with some sense, and so began to consider Christianity seriously. The book *God in the Dock* by Lewis is a series of essays that have timeless relevance. While I do not agree with everything he says (especially regarding women in the church), even then his reasoning is fair and respectful and formidable. The book *Know Why You Believe* by Paul Little also gives logical reasons for the Christian faith, as do many others. These and other authors let the Christian student know that Christianity has withstood assaults from thinkers in every culture and has survived intact. Ecclesiastes teaches us that there is nothing new under the sun, and the English journalist Malcolm Muggeridge added that there were only new people discovering old ideas in each generation. So, historic Christianity as well as the old heresies continue to be circulated. Present day thinkers such as Os Guiness, J. I. Packer, Tony Campolo, and others explain and defend historic Christianity very well. I would have benefitted very much by knowing about such people when I began university, and so will your children/grandchildren/friends.

1905 Lake Avenue adventures, Part 2

I was asleep upstairs in my room at 1905 Lake Avenue, when the door burst open. A guy who lived on the other side of the duplex stood there with a pistol in his hand and shouted, "Is Diane here?" I was glad to be able to answer, "No, she is not." One of his housemates had heard a cat meow while he was trying to study, grabbed his revolver, ran outside, and shot it dead. And back on our side of the duplex, one housemate was caught forging my name several times. Perhaps it was to fool the university into thinking he was still taking classes as a student, or for all I know, to try to withdraw my few funds from my bank account.

At first, only good and trustworthy friends shared the house, but then less responsible folks crept in. At one point, a housemate left during the summer, planning to return in the fall. To reserve a room, he agreed to pay rent throughout the summer. He did not, so I took his records, etc., to a pawn shop and sold them so I could pay the rent. He came back the very last day it was possible to redeem them.

Finally, only one guy and I were left. It was like pulling teeth to get him to pay any of his expenses. But I was cheered up when his dead grandmother left him some money, for I hoped he would then pay his share of the rent and utilities. Instead, he informed me that he planned to buy a motorcycle instead of paying his bills, for I would get a good job later!

I can only guess at what his lawyer father taught him, but I do know what my father, who was much poorer, taught me. When I related to him that I was considering joining the Presbyterian Church, he answered, "Pray about it and do what God wants you to do." Certainly, part of what God wants us all to do is to treat others as we want to be treated. It is safe to say that no one wants to be awakened by a jealous, crazy guy waving a gun, or to have a pet shot dead, or to have our name forged, or to have a thief mooch off us, especially when the thief has more money! But colorful experiences like these hopefully help us to recognize and appreciate people of integrity more by contrast. No matter how beautiful or charming a person is, if she/he is jealous, lying, or irresponsible, our relationship will be a foretaste of hell!

On the other hand, it means a lot to be with someone we trust will do what is right. No one does that at all times, neither you nor I. But when God is with us, we have a measure of supernatural peace when we do his will, and a measure of supernatural dread when we do not. But if there is no God who communicates his will to us, then it is just my opinion when I disagree with someone. Then neither you nor I have a right to condemn a housemate who chews tobacco and then drinks from my milk carton left in the refrigerator. Why does he not have that right, especially if he is a Nazi when Hitler was in power in Germany, or a communist when Stalin was in power in Russia, or a henchman of Pol Pot when he ruled Cambodia, etc.? It is because there is a God who clearly communicated his will to us, that we are to "whatever you wish that others would do to you, do also to them," to forgive, to be kind, not to return evil for evil, but to trust God when he said, "Vengeance is mine, I will repay."

Do not murder, whatever your religion or non-religion is.

The Muslim major who murdered unarmed and innocent victims at Fort Hood was wrong, because God exists and says, "Do not kill (murder)." I do not know what he was thinking, but whatever it was, it was evil. Christians, Muslims, Jews, atheists—people of all religions or of no religion—we all have enough evil and crazy people in our midst. Hopefully, we will not be like Fox News, which teaches that the Republicans can do no wrong, or like MSNBC, which teaches the Democrats can do no wrong. We Christians should condemn the crusades, etc., Jews should condemn kicking Palestinians out of their homes, etc., Muslims should condemn the conquest of Spain, etc. And when an individual does evil in the name of any religion, those in that group should be the first and the loudest to oppose it (or of no religion; think Hitler, Stalin, Pol Pot...).

Whatever Jesus meant when he said, "Love your enemies," surely we can agree he did not mean travel halfway across the world to kill them, to paraphrase Dr. Anthony Campolo, an evangelical Baptist minister and professor. He probably did not intend us to kill innocent women and children either, gently called "collateral damage" by our military. I am not a pacifist, although the Quakers, Mennonites and Amish may be right in this area. I am for self-defense, believing even the pacifist groups benefit from police protection.

But I understand how Muslims unite at least to some extent when a Muslim majority country is invaded (or with the case of Alexander the Great in Afghanistan, in pre-Muslim days). We have no legitimate business in Iraq or Afghanistan. As horrible as Husain was, at least Christians had freedom of worship there, unlike in Kuwait, which we defended when he attacked. So, whatever we were fighting for, it definitely was not freedom of religion.

We supported the Shah of Iran, a dictator, so instead of promoting democracy we helped unleash the forces of radical Islam there. Charley Wilson, a congressman from Texas, was moved by the plight of the Afghan refugees after the Soviet invasion. He finally got the congress to arm them, and now they are using arms we gave them to fight us. What kind of improvement is that for them? Do the terms "Vietnam" and "quagmire" ever come to mind? If we are Christians, do we honestly think

Christ is honored by these antics? Like Americans who would unite against an invader, so do other countries.

Well, the American workers at the military industrial complexes may be honored by fat paychecks, but they will probably eat more and die faster and have less health as a result. Criminals in power benefit in Afghanistan and Iraq. But they are "our criminals," someone has observed. But thinking Christianly, I am not convinced we should support criminals of any stripe whatsoever.

So, whether criminals call themselves Christian or Muslim or atheists, etc., I hope we do not support them. Instead, I hope we "do justice, and to love kindness, and to walk humbly with your God," as he requires us to do. May God help us to follow him with humility, so we can recognize justice and mercy when we see them and hold them in balance. None of us do that perfectly, but surely, we can all oppose murder, no matter what the pretext is.

Church growth thoughts

I have a doctorate in church growth and pastored relatively small churches, while some others did not even go to seminary and pastor relatively large churches. I could join some in mainline denominations that talk about smaller groups having more quality, but I am kept from doing that by Aesop's story of the fox who wanted some grapes. He jumped and jumped and failed to grab any of them. In disgust he walked away muttering that they were probably sour anyway (hence the expression "sour grapes").

More importantly, I have noticed congregations of all sizes that are dead spiritually and congregations of all sizes that are alive spiritually. When a person has charm and intelligence and good speaking ability, usually a church (or synagogue or mosque or business...) will grow. But as Christians, I hope and pray that we grow in grace or favor with God, as the Bible commands. Then we will be effective witnesses for Jesus, whatever the sizes of our congregations are. Ad we grow in grace we will be more kind, honest, faithful to our spouses, and hardworking people of integrity. Yet Gallup and all the other polls show just the opposite is happening in our country. Should we not be deeply concerned that whether we have ten or 10,000 in our congregation, we are converted and walking humbly with God? Yet that is rarely the emphasis in either mainline denominations, or independent growing churches either, for that matter. God and his call for repentance and holiness are not only dismissed by society in general, but much of church culture, also.

What can we do about this disrespect and trivialization of Christianity but search our own hearts to make sure we are not a part of it, and to repent when we are? Recently I have become increasingly convicted by the Holy Spirit of a sin of omission. It is something very difficult to do in my situation, and not really a part of my human nature to do. But that is an excellent way to know that God is with us and is moving us in a particular direction, since his ways and thoughts are so much higher than our ways or thoughts! Otherwise, we would always be just following our own feelings or logic and claiming God was guiding us. That happens frequently throughout history.

In the congregations of my childhood in east Tennessee, I recall with gratitude and awe how clearly and powerfully the Holy Spirit moved during sermons and other parts of the services. I was overjoyed at seminary to pore through the library and to see that was the norm throughout history among many kinds of churches in many countries. To be a part of that historic stream of Christianity we must humble ourselves, pray to remove all that is not from God in our lives, and to keep only that which is from God in our lives.

Jesus Christ has proved that he deserves our all, our abandonment to him to do with us what he wills. We have no reason to fear doing that, since he is perfect love and has all power and all knowledge. When we refuse to give him our all, we wound our families and others with relatively trivial pursuits and words and attitudes. How much better it is to be like the prophet Samuel, of whom the Bible said, "none of his words fell to the ground." Will we be remembered as such a person? I hope so.

In 1 Corinthians 2:4-5 Paul said "My speech and proclamation were not in plausible words of wisdom, but in demonstration of the Spirit and of power, so that your faith might rest not on the wisdom of men but in the power of God." Do we want our loved ones to have the fake kind of faith that depends on our charm or experience or learning, or the legitimate faith based on the power of God? I pray for the kind of speech and proclamation Paul spoke about, for myself and for you.

Some church leaders oppose Christianity.

I have worked with some who lived in opposition to clear and repeated teaching in the Bible, and yet were leaders in their churches. I wondered whether I should call their pastors and inform them or not. I decided against it for the following reasons. First of all, I am convinced that if the pastor were preaching in the power of the Holy Spirit, the pastor and other leaders would have enough spiritual discernment to know that something was dead up the creek (polluting the source of clean water, in other words). In that case I saw no reason to get specific with them unless harm was being caused to children. Also, if they were not humbling themselves before God enough to speak his words with his attitudes, they would only be amused or aggravated at me, or more than likely very glad to learn that other leaders in their church were also not caring what Jesus and the Holy Spirit taught or thought. Or, if they were genuinely concerned about holiness and righteousness, they might confront the offender before it was appropriate.

I recall that I was very irritated at a person in one of my congregations, and justifiably so in my mind. I planned to nail them to the wall during a sermon the next Sunday. But as I began to preach, I looked around and the person was not there! I was so convicted by the Holy Spirit for trying to do his job. His job is to convict the world of sin, according to John 16, and it is my job to say a good word about Jesus Christ when I have the chance. I am persuaded that as a minister or anyone else does that, encouragement in righteousness and conviction of sin will occur without getting up to slam someone for a particular sin.

Particular sins (lying stealing, getting revenge...) are not the main problem but outgrowths of the root of the problem—rebellion against the call of Jesus Christ to love and obey him as God/Savior and Lord. We can all avoid many sins and be an upstanding church member and still be in rebellion against Jesus Christ ruling our lives. Historically, those who most avoided the clearly destructive behaviors were the ones most resistant to the drawing of the Holy Spirit to repent and to become a sincere follower of Jesus Christ. But the closer we get to God, the more his otherness or holiness shows us our vast distance from him and the righteousness he demands.

Perhaps the pastors of fellow workers were not living in such deep rebellion against God as they were, but church leaders are especially responsible to pray for deeper and deeper layers of repentance in order to follow Jesus closely and to build up his people by encouraging holiness and discouraging whatever harms us. We are not to pretend to be beyond temptations that have overtaken my colleagues.

The British professor C.S. Lewis answered a question about gambling by noting that he was not especially proficient to discuss that field since that was one of the few sins he was not attracted to do. His was a very honest and profound reply (he was not in favor of gambling, by the way), and when we are as aware of our natural condition as he was, and add his courage, we can admit the same.

I am sure that we are not all tempted to do the same sins that my co-workers were doing, but we all are exempt from being drawn to only a few sins, and the rest we must guard against firmly or fall. Pride comes before a fall, the Bible teaches, and it is the most vicious and overriding sin that beckons each of us. Although God may call us to confront an individual about a certain sin at some point, he daily confronts us about our own sins of either transgression or omission (doing what he says not to do or failing to do what he asks us to do and be. May God have mercy on all of us!

The first great revival under the much abhorred Jonathan Edwards.

In 1735, the fire of the Holy Spirit fell in the town of Northampton, Massachusetts. The dry and introverted, yet brilliant and holy Jonathan Edwards, who later became president of Princeton, preached the gospel so that sinners quit giving excuses and were swept into the kingdom of God. He gave a report in his *A Faithful Narrative of the Surprising Work of God:* "And then it was, in the latter part of December, that the Spirit of God began extraordinarily to ... work amongst us ... And the work of conversion was carried on in a most astonishing manner and increased more and more; souls did, as it were, come by flocks to Jesus Christ ... This work of God, as it was carried on and the number of true saints multiplied, soon made a glorious alteration in the town, so that in the spring and summer following, Anno 1735, the town seemed to be full of the presence of God. It never was so full of love, nor so full of joy ... there were remarkable tokens of joy in families on the account of salvation's being brought unto them, parents rejoicing over their children as new born, and husbands over their wives, and wives over their husbands ... There were many instances of persons that came from abroad, on visit or on business ... (who) partook of that shower of divine blessing that God rained down here and went home rejoicing. Till at length the same work began to appear and prevail in several other towns in the country."

Across the pond, George Whitfield was converted and ordained on June 20, 1735: He was invited to address the nobility, where many repented and were saved while many others were outraged at the thought that they were sinners. Such snits always accompany the preaching of the gospel. Harriet Beecher Stowe complained that the sermons of Edwards on sin and suffering were "refined poetry of torture." And so they are for the proud and unrepentant, but for those who do not hold on to our sins they provide a doorway to heaven. Mark Twain had this to say about Jonathan Edwards: After staying up one night reading his treatise on the will, he reported that "Edwards's God shines red and hideous in the glow from the fires of hell, their only right and proper adornment. By God, I was ashamed to be in such company."

Well, Twain was probably our greatest American writer, but he rationalized his rejection of orthodox or historic Christianity, as one must when confronted with the claims of God to be holy and just as well as love. Edwards believed that Biblical preaching must point out the dangers of damnation, and while Biblical language about fire and torment is not perhaps literal, if not, then the reality is much worse. The Bible does state that the fear of God is the beginning of wisdom, not the love or any other trait. Other traits are there and wonderful, but we cannot approach him until we have an awe of how holy he is and by comparison how unholy or impure we are, even the most upright of us. That rubs our pride the wrong way, if we intend to keep our pride, but it paves the way for repentance, and then we will begin to see the beauty of God.

Baby busters (1965-1983) are the first generation in American history where a majority reject Christ.

The Bible teaches, and Christians affirm, that God was born and laid in a manger in Bethlehem over 2,000 years ago. Jesus added human flesh while he remained eternally God the Son, the second person of the Trinity. When I pastored in Toronto, I was in the Italian area and saw shops frequently with the signs "Carne." The word meant meat, so the incarnation was when God became meat or flesh and dwelled among us. Those of us who are Christian often have little appreciation of how far-fetched that sounds to others.

"Silent night, holy night ... round yon virgin mother and child, holy infant so tender and mild ..." was screeched harshly in mockery on a TV show I saw recently. The British stars then laughed as a branch was thrown in front of one of them skate boarding, causing a nasty fall. Estimates of British churchgoing ranges from one to seven percent, and contempt for anything that claims to be Christian is common. We are rapidly moving in that direction. Baby busters (those born between 1965 and 1983) are "the first generation in American history in which a majority of those who are seeking a religious faith to embrace are starting their spiritual journey with a faith group other than Christianity," says the researcher George Barna (www.barna.org).

Few Busters see Christianity as unique, or believe in the possibility of truth, or that the Bible is anything special (get some teens around you to be honest with you and this will become clear). Perhaps Christianity was just a way to make a living for their minister father or mother, or just a way to make business contacts for their churchgoing parents. Busters are discouraged that so few in the churches have the kind of supernatural encounter the Bible talks about as normal, or that the hymns teach about. Until people are gripped with the reality of God unmistakably, Christianity will naturally be seen as a religion that is fading away, as the Europeans and their descendants that have cradled that religion for the last 1,500 years are doing demographically.

When the virgin birth of Jesus (Matthew 1:20, 23, 25, Luke 1:26 to 35), the resurrection, and other miracles recorded in the Bible are considered in the churches as the teachings of either deliberate liars or sincere deluded folks, why would anyone expect (or want) this teaching to be passed on to our children/grandchildren? Given a choice of legends, I personally would prefer the Norse mythology, with cool Thor and no restrictions on my natural inclinations!

But as Peter stated, he and the other disciples did not follow cleverly invented fables. Jesus was eternal God who had the right and the power to be born in the unconventional way that Matthew and Luke describe. He chose to be born as a helpless baby in a manger because he determined that his influence over people would be supernatural- and not on account of his wealth or beauty or political power. When we rely on wealth or buildings or programs or anything else except the supernatural power of God to reach people, we become a stumbling block for those who would contact God. May God help us to sing with reverence the great Christmas carols "Silent Night," "Away in a Manger," and others that encourage us to adore Jesus Christ, and teach, "where meek souls will receive him still, the dear Christ enters in."

Does speaking and singing of God in a show time event promote or hinder revival?

Is God honored when he is mentioned and sung about in show time events? Maybe if I were a better entertainer, I would answer a resounding "Yes." Maybe it is sour grapes to even wonder about this issue, and Scottish genetic dourness inclines me to doubt that patriotism, University of Tennessee football, and corny jokes about sex, go together with singing and speaking of God. Perhaps those who mix those ingredients together are closer to God than I am, and I am sure they sometimes have more to show for their efforts. And I recall Paul telling us in Philippians 1:18 that he was thankful for those who preach the gospel, even though they do it under false pretenses. In addition, I am convinced that when God uses us, it is often in spite of ourselves instead of because of us. So, I am sure a word for Jesus can do much good, no matter what the motivation or circumstance. David Brainard preached to Indians in the 1700's through drunken interpreters and they were converted. After all, we benefit by putting faith in the words Jesus spoke, and not in the person who speaks about Jesus.

So, does it matter then when the good news of Jesus Christ is put on the same low level as the rest of the entertainment show whether outside or inside of a church service? I am persuaded that it matters a great deal. God can work any way he pleases, but he demands that his people walk humbly with him; that we worship him in spirit and in truth. Jim Cymbala began to pastor a church in Brooklyn, New York City, with about twenty people. Soon, about half of them left, for they were offended by the historic Christianity he preached (and lived). Together they built a church of several thousands. I attended a Tuesday night prayer meeting there once, when about two thousand gathered together. No one strutted or pranced about, nor was there high-tech wizardry. But the Holy Spirit was there in power. That is or should be the highest goal. There are no bad side effects of such meetings among those who humble themselves, so that God is approached with his blessing.

The Nazis had prisoners play classical music while their fellow inmates were murdered. So that entertainment did not inspire any Godliness at all! But great hymns and the reading of the Bible often does not inspire Godliness in people either. Why not? Jesus said that some read the Bible and think that they have life but will not come to him in order to have life. So, we can come to Jesus in a wild pagan festival or miss him completely in a historic Christian church service. The outcome depends on whether we are drawn by the Holy Spirit to him, and then accept that offer of friendship with God or not.

"Where two or three are gathered in my name, there am I among them," said Jesus. So, he shows up where people get together in his name/for his glory and honor. He does not arrive when we go to a place for our glory or entertainment. So, the reason we turn up at an event partly determines whether Jesus turns up or not. Do we gather to pick up women or men or business, to show off our clothes or speaking or singing abilities? Or do we gather for the purpose of worshiping Jesus in Spirit and in truth?

God may be present in relatively staid or wild settings. God does not order the method, only that we arrive with the sincere intention of coming into his presence with repentance and obedience. Instead of showing off, we will then see our need for deeper and deeper layers of repentance. The closer we get to God, the more we will see our lack of holiness or purity, and how we either need to be converted or to be more holy. Then we cease to focus on the sins of our spouse or parents or children, and pray, "God be merciful to me a sinner." If strutting and prancing about and calling attention to ourselves brings about such repentance, then I am in favor of it. But whatever hinders us from coming into the presence of God, I am against. Certainly, I was convicted of sin when I did such antics, and when I spoke without having a word from the Lord. If you want to fake having God with you and speaking his words, then you can influence some emotional and silly folks, no doubt. But whether we influence many or few, I hope we live in awe of God, remembering that he is holy. He is not a pal or a buffoon. I personally am afraid to talk about God and equate him with a country or a football team or other relatively trivial pursuits. God is above all cultures, and he will not share his glory with another person or event. To approach him, I am convinced that we must have reverence and awe.

Chinese Christians pray that American Christians have persecution.

The American missionary was about to leave China when his hosts, internal Chinese missionaries, said that they would pray for him. He turned around and asked them what they would pray. They were a bit reluctant to answer but admitted that they pray that we American Christians will be persecuted, because our churches are so weak. That is the opposite of what many American Christians pray, and God cannot answer prayer that is contradictory!

Are they right to pray that? The Bible promises that "all who desire to live a godly life in Christ Jesus will be persecuted." Many Christians in this country whine that prayer is not allowed in public schools when their prayers in church never get any higher than the ceilings. Many wail about how Christian influence is being lost, as they dump spouse after spouse. The pastor of a large cathedral in California groomed his son to take over the church but dumped him. I suspect he mentioned the "r" word in a sermon (repentance), for the father never mentioned that in any sermon that I heard or read.

We have many preaching prosperity gospel, promising that if we serve God we will have a better life, and wealth, and to be rich is a sign that God is really with us. But it may be a sign that we are mafia, or that we ripped off our siblings after our parents died, or that we have started a Ponzi scheme. Just come to Jesus and he will improve your life, is a common message in the USA. Your social contacts will multiply and deepen, your financial situation will improve, your personality will brighten, and your family and friends will adore you more, or so many claim. And sometimes that does happen. But everyone needs peace with God and forgiveness of sins and eternal life, whether we have any other benefits or not. Paul noted that if we do not have the hope of Christ, we are of all people most miserable, for we are always at odds with whatever culture we are in when we really do live for Jesus Christ.

Jesus had no place to lay his head, the Bible states. His first disciples suffered torture and death because they took the gospel to those who did not agree. Who among us is proud and arrogant enough to pretend to deserve better than that? The answer is millions of American Christians. When we compare the prayers of Chinese Christian to those of spoiled and arrogant American Christians who have a sense of entitlement, if I were betting, I would put my money on the Chinese.

Dr. James Kennedy told the story of a Christian congregation in the Soviet Union that met to celebrate Easter. Suddenly two soldiers burst into the building, accused everyone there of being parasites of the Soviet state, and insulted them in other ways. They assured them they all deserved to die but said there might be those there who were not Christian, and they had one minute to leave. After a mad stampede to the door, the soldiers laid their guns down and said to the few who remained, "Brothers, let us worship God." I suspect that was a real worship service!

I sincerely hope that we American Christians do not need persecution before we call important what God calls important and call trivial or demonic what God calls trivial or demonic. Do we read the Bible enough to know the difference, and do we pray to understand and to apply it in our lives? According to the Bible, if we are not suffering persecution, we are not living Godly in Christ Jesus!

Church going

"On a sleepy city sidewalk, wishing Lord, that I was stoned, for there's nothing like a Sunday makes a body feel alone. And there's nothing short of dying half as lonely as the sound, of a sleepy city sidewalk with Sunday morning coming down." When Kris Kristofferson wrote and sang the song "Sunday Morning Coming Down," it bothered me a lot, because I was far from God. Later I rededicated my life to Jesus Christ and started going to church again. After all, Hebrews 10:25 does teach us not to neglect to meet together for the purpose of encouraging one another in the Christian faith.

I did know the truth of the statement of John Calvin when he said, "Whenever we see the word of God purely preached and heard, there a church of God exists, even if it swarms with many faults." Critics of the church often mention the presence of hypocrites and use that as an excuse not to go. The father of one roommate mentioned the presence of hypocrites as a reason not to go. I replied that I would rather go to church with hypocrites than to go to hell with them. I like to think that I am more patient and diplomatic now. If I could relive that conversation, I hope I would explain how even hypocrisy is a testament that there is a higher standard which we agree we should try to achieve. And even the most sincere of us have blind spots and limitations that may not be apparent to anyone but our enemies until about a hundred years after we die!

How could they have claimed to be dedicated Christians and so materialistic, future generations may ask? If everyone did as we do, would the world be a better place or not? Would closing all the churches advance justice and mercy and honesty and forgiveness, or not? Probably not. Even churches we think have the most faults hopefully read the Bible and encourage others to love and obey Jesus Christ. At least some evil is restrained when we deliberately put ourselves under the preaching and teaching of the Bible regularly.

Then the Holy Spirit has a chance to convict us of sin and to encourage us in righteousness. The logic of scripture then causes us to at least consider accepting the reasoning of God when it conflicts with our own limited perspectives. Even when the sermon is not preached in the power of the Holy Spirit because of sin in the life of the speaker or a lack of prayer in the pews, the Bible is read, and people benefit from hearing truth. Hymns record the valiant faith of people who overcame huge obstacles to live for God, and virtues of honesty, forgiveness, kindness and justice are promoted (and hopefully repentance and holiness).

If we think the churches are full of hypocrites, even Jesus said to do what the Pharisees said, not what they did in their pretensions. And besides, if we really think churches need help and reform, why not throw ourselves into that struggle? The English professor C.S. Lewis became a Christian and very reluctantly began to go to church, for he considered the Anglican hymns "fifth-rate poems set to sixth-rate music." But he went anyway and noticed that they were being sung with "devotion and benefit by an old saint in elastic-side boots in the opposite pew, and then you realize that you aren't fit to clean those boots."

No Christian trusts the Bible very much.

If we Christians really believed Romans 8:28- that all things work together for good to them that love God- our relationships would be radically different. We would never be impatient/crabby with anyone, selfish or rude, or afraid of competition/loneliness/illness or poverty. So, what excuses do we use to tell ourselves not to trust that verse? If we accept so called "higher criticism" that relegates the Bible to fairy tale status, that could explain our belief that the verse is useless, but when that is the case why not quit pretending church is important and stay home on Sundays?

But if we are historic Christians who have therefore encountered the living God, then we can and should live by his teachings. It is an invalid reason on my part, but sometimes I do not put much faith in Romans 8:28 when I look at my circumstances and wonder if I really do love God enough for the verse to apply to me. But I (and all others) am responsible to love God with all my heart, soul, mind and strength. So, if I am not doing that, I am sinning against God. Therefore, I am not to wonder about how strong my faith is but to repent of any and all sin, and then to trust that I am where I am by God's appointment: geographically, physically, financially, and otherwise!

Sometimes I do have that attitude, but I am certain that for much of my life I do not. I was single and wanted to be married, sick and wanted to be well, I wanted to evangelize more and worried because I could do so little. Nothing is wrong with wanting any of these things to happen, but how do we balance peace in the present with desire for something more?

Frankly, I do not think that I do a very good job with the balance. I do ask God to forgive my worry, and for him to guide me, and to help me to trust him more. I do this very often and ask that I might pray that prayer more sincerely if possible. I notice that sometimes I am sorely tempted to complain or to be rude and have given in to such impulses not a few times. At other times I do recall that verse and I have peace and kindness instead of turmoil. I can by the help of God control what happens inside of me, as we all can, although we are rarely if ever, able to control whatever is outside of us.

Which of us has not experienced or seen a person being very irritable and rude interrupted by a telephone call, and answering the ring with a calm, polite, and even sweet voice? So, we know that we can turn hatefulness on and off when we choose to do so! We are responsible to be patient and kind and unselfish every minute of every day. Of course, that is impossible without depending on the Holy Spirit within the believer or building our lives on God's promises daily. I have no doubt that many of the readers, and hopefully all, do this better than I do.

I have learned over the years that I was not called to preach because I was closer to God than others, or that I heard the voice of God more clearly, or that I was locked into holiness. It was for the opposite reasons if anything. And when I think of Romans 8:28, one of my favorite verses, I am ashamed to have trusted it so few times in my life. But it does cheer me some to realize the great grace and mercy of God; that he remains faithful even when we do not. This means that even our past unbelief and fears are also bound up in that verse when we keep loving Jesus Christ. So, King David (who loved the Triune God before he was revealed as such) was promised by God that he would be king, and yet when he was chased by Saul, he was afraid he would be murdered. But David became king anyway! Even his weakness and the sin of unbelief in the promises of God, worked together for his good in his future to make him a wiser and more compassionate and more Godly person. May God in his mercy bind the strands of our lives together likewise.

Her boyfriend Charley

As I waited for my wife to finish work, the little girl on the bench beside me began to talk about her boyfriend Charley. I asked, "Well, is he good to you?" She answered, "Yes he is." I added that if she ever gets another boyfriend, I hope he will be good to her also.

Females are almost always more nurturing than males, while males typically encourage more independence in children. Both influences are very important. Unlike the little girl about six years old, females often pick guys who are mean and irresponsible. Why? That happens when the desire to nurture pushes out God's teaching for justice and truth. And males are to add mercy to our natural inclination to push kids out of the nest. We all need balance from God in order to encourage ourselves and others in what is best. Thomas Edison said, "No one knows more than one millionth of one percent about anything." That sounds about right.

If so, then it is the height of arrogance when we do not humbly ask God for guidance as we interact with our spouses and friends and everyone else. Every parent and every child is different, so what worked with us may not work with our children. But God is perfect love and knows each of us perfectly. Yet we depend on our own intelligence so often for guidance when God says, "Trust in the Lord with all your heart, and do not lean on your own understanding. In all your ways acknowledge him, and he will make straight your paths." This is a great promise for those who love and obey God.

I pray the little girl and Charley does that, and I and my family, and you and your family. It is so unnatural to do that, since the Bible says, "The heart is desperately wicked, who can know it?" In other words, we are all inclined to sin continually, and we know so little about our intentions and motives, as we observe ourselves as nurturing or supporting responsibility in others. May God help us to spend more time in the Bible which is at least a billion times better than the next best book, praying to understand and apply it in our daily lives. Perhaps God will then allow us to teach others, or if not, then our holy lives will then be powerful influences on others anyway. I know some of the people who had great impact on me never knew it. Who will be there with a holy life, when someday the little girl and Charley will reach the age of accountability or reason?

Evidence for the resurrection

The Koran (Sura/chapter 100 in English, 65 in Arabic) teaches that Jesus Christ did not really die on the cross, but only a likeness of him was there. This was written about 600 years after the crucifixion took place, much like someone now contradicting accounts of the arrival of Columbus to the new world in 1492 without new evidence. But at the time it happened, all the authorities, both Jewish and Roman as well as Christian, agreed that Jesus was in fact murdered on a cross.

In addition, he was seen there by many who were neither authorities nor Christians. Also, the great Jewish historian Josephus, known for his accuracy and honesty, taught that Jesus was crucified. Then too the famous Roman historian Tacitus affirmed that Jesus was crucified. Neither were friends of Christianity, and therefore had no motive whatsoever to lie to fit the Christian narrative. No, they did not just believe the eyewitness of the Christians either. The Christians had no status in that society. Therefore, Josephus believed the eyewitness accounts of the Jewish high priests, and Tacitus trusted the eyewitness stories of Pilate and the other Roman soldiers.

I never considered that the resurrection of Jesus could not be true, for I heard it from my parents, who were honest about everything else, and devout Christians. They really did get it right; and it was only much later that I examined the evidence for the resurrection myself. But for those both in churches and in other religions who never heard the Bible preached in the power of the Holy Spirit, it is normal for doubts to arise about the resurrection. But it is big deal, for Saint Paul said that our Christian faith is in vain if the resurrection did not really happen in history (1 Corinthians 15:14-17).

At the time Jesus was crucified, no one denied that it really happened. But Jewish authorities did try to deny the resurrection. They paid sixteen Roman guards who were guarding the tomb to say that someone had stolen the body of Jesus. But that could not be true. In the first place, sixteen professional and well-armed soldiers protected the tomb. The disciples were not well armed and would be no match for Roman soldiers. More importantly, they had no motive to steal the body. They did not understand his many promises that he would rise from the dead until after he had done so.

So, they did not look forward to his resurrection at all. Instead, they were totally devastated by the death of Jesus on the cross. In Luke 24:21, "But we had hoped that he was the one to redeem Israel," said two of his from the road to Emmaus, when Jesus joined them incognito after the resurrection. They had hoped he was the one who was promised in the Old Testament to save Israel, but when he died on the cross, that crushed all hopes in him that they had.

Even if the disciples had outmanned and outgunned (so to speak) the Roman guards, they had absolutely no incentive to fight, then to grab a dead body, then to spend the rest of their lives preaching that Jesus rose from the dead. As someone pointed out, some die for what they mistakenly believe is the truth, but no one dies for what they know is a lie.

Besides that, liars they were not. They gave the world the highest ethical and moral standards and lived them themselves. They taught us to trust that God will take care of us when we love and obey him without lying or manipulating to get ahead or exaggerating to help our situation. We lose peace with God when we do any of that if we ever had peace in the first place.

Besides, the tomb was empty when the disciples arrived on Sunday morning after Jesus was killed on the tree. No, they did not go to the wrong grave, as some assert. If they had done that, it was easy to ask and to find the site that belonged to Joseph of Arimathea. No, Jesus did not swoon and revive when he hit the cold stone either, then roll back a big rock, fight off Roman guards, and then convince his followers to lie that he had risen from the dead. Also, if he did all that unethical manipulation, no one records that he died and was buried again.

So, it takes much more faith to believe the swoon theory than what actually happened. Furthermore, Jesus was murdered on the cross. He was speared by a soldier so that blood and water came out. Blood and water separate in a body only after death. So, a dead corpse was carried inside the tomb.

In addition to all that evidence, the sepulcher was empty. How can we be sure of that? We know definitely the body of Jesus was not there because of the reactions of the Jews and Romans. When the disciples preached that Jesus was risen from the dead, all the Jewish or Roman authorities had to do to kill Christianity was to produce the body. If the guards were still there when Peter and John and Mary and the others proclaimed that Jesus was alive, they would show the corpse to one and all. They did not, only because they could not. So, the disciples had no motive at all steal the body, and neither did the Romans or Jews. The Romans wanted peace and the Jewish leaders wanted no competition for their respect and status. Besides, if either group had stolen the body, they would have produced it and killed the movement at once.

By the way, Mary was the first one who talked with Jesus after the resurrection. No one who made up a lie would record that a woman was the first to see Jesus. Women had no respect in that society. It would be the same if we wanted to start a new movement that was supernatural and had the town drunk to first announce it today.

Furthermore, over 500 in addition to the disciples saw Jesus after he rose from the dead. Some claim they hallucinated. But only a few hallucinate with such a psychological profile to make them do so. And this is only when they expect something to occur. A grandpa may die and someone may claim to see him afterwards, for example. Or as recently occurred, a celebrity died, and her daughter says she feels her from time to time. But none of these folks had the least hope that Jesus was resurrected from the dead, or that he would eat with them and talk with them afterwards, as did happen. As the angel said in Luke 24:6, “He is not here, but has risen."

It is easy to see the sins of others!

A black man told of visiting Mount Vernon, the home of George Washington. At one point the guide spoke of "the quarters," and his little girl asked her father what that meant. When he answered, "the slave quarters," she asked how anybody who owned slaves could be considered great. All the others on the tour were white, and they got really quiet.

George Washington was a great man who was a product of his time. Society was built on slavery, and as a rich farmer he benefited from that institution. And yet, there were Quakers in his society who debated the issue and then abandoned slavery. As he read his Bible, he came across the verse, "So whatever you wish that others would do to you, do also to them." He freed his slaves before he died, showing that he felt at least some true guilt.

One hundred years from now, I do not doubt that Christians can look back at us and often ask themselves how we could call ourselves Christians and have lived our lifestyles? It is easy to see the sins of others, now and in the past (especially when we are not attracted to those particular sins), and to congratulate ourselves because we are not like them. But are we really better than our ancestors?

How about the "needs" we have that would have been considered gaudy luxuries only a few years ago? How much of what we own is for the glory of God instead of for our own glory? How much of our travel or business or free time is spent on what honors God best?

Romans 12:2 "Do not be conformed to this world." If George Washington retired to his room at nine nightly to read his Bible, was deeply regarded as a man of integrity, and still owned slaves, what hope do the rest of us have to discern, "what is the will of God, what is good and acceptable and perfect?"

We can be free of conscious sin, and still have habits and attitudes underneath our consciousness that have yet to come to the surface. Sanctification is gradual—if it comes at all. No one becomes a Christian and then gets perfect in this life. As we read the Bible and plead for God to help us understand and apply it, God answers that prayer. But like all people, we are tempted to see in the Bible how others ought to repent before we do.

It is the work of the Holy Spirit to convict each of us of sin. As Oswald Chambers so insightfully states, "Conviction of sin is one of the rarest things that ever strikes a man (woman)." We are to pray for the gift of tears, as the Puritans prayed, and that we do not quench or grieve the Holy Spirit, but that we became all God wants us to be. This kind of prayer will not be answered overnight. But Jesus will begin to peel away layer after layer of selfishness and greed and whatever else prevents us from being like David, who was called in Acts 13:22 a man after God's own heart.

But-did David not commit adultery with Bathsheba and then have her husband murdered? And did he not have several wives? And was he not a lousy father? Yes, and all this was contrary to the will of God. David and George Washington and other great men are not to be our example in the ungodly things they did. We are responsible to follow Jesus Christ and not to gloat when we see someone choosing sins different than the ones we choose.

Public prayer in the name of Jesus?

When we pray aloud at a public gathering, should we use the name of Jesus? Or should we use the generic name God? I was invited to pray before a school commencement in Toronto, and the principal who had invited me informed me just as I was about to rise to speak that one of the faculty was offended when the name of Jesus was mentioned.

At a Rotary club meeting in Tennessee, I remember that guests who were invited to speak began with a phrase glorifying Allah (who excludes God the eternal Son Jesus Christ and God the Holy Spirit). I was not offended, nor was anyone else as far as I know, because I respect their right to say a good word about what is important to them. Although Allah is the Arabic word for God used before Islam began, now it is meant to exclude the Trinity.

In the not too distant past, the word *God* invoked in the USA and Europe caused the vast majority to automatically think also of Jesus and the Holy Spirit as part of the Trinity. Such is no longer the case as non-Christian forms of spirituality multiply.

Perhaps more important than whether the name of Jesus is mentioned in a particular prayer or not is the intention of the one who prays. Once I said a prayer before a meal, and I was asked by someone why I did not pray in the name of Jesus. I replied that I always pray in the name of Jesus (even when I do not end my prayers, "in the name of Jesus, amen." In other words I always pray in the name of the Trinity and for His sake. My prayers are always consciously for the glory of God the Father, God the Son Jesus Christ, and God the Holy Spirit.

Mentioning only the name of God may open the door for evangelism later in an atmosphere of respect, where the claims of Jesus can be presented more fully. There is a time to be discreet, to be diplomatic, to be slow to speak and quick to listen. At the same time we are to ask ourselves blunt questions about our motivation. If we do not mention the name of Jesus, it is very important that it not be because we are ashamed of him. This is because Jesus said if we are ashamed of him, he will be ashamed of us when he returns. That is a big deal since Jesus of the Bible is coming back as the judge of all the world.

So if we do not mention his name because we fear embarrassment or controversy, that is another issue entirely. Very few of us can ever be accused of speaking too much about Jesus Christ. In fact, our human nature tends to make us guilty of the opposite, to be silent when we should say a good word about Jesus Christ. One of the tasks of the Holy Spirit, according to John Chapter 16, is to glorify Jesus Christ. When we pray for his guidance, we who are Christian will have supernatural peace about when to speak the name of Jesus in public or in private, and when to follow him quietly.

Are we passing on faith or national culture?

Do you ever wonder why millions of immigrants continue to come to the USA when we are the third most populated country after China and India? Even the so-called native Americans came here from other lands, and unless our ancestors were criminals or missionaries, they almost certainly came here for economic reasons. If the Scots or the Germans had a great life in their own countries, they would have little incentive to leave, unless the Lord or the government prodded them out.

Every American should travel to a poor country and then it will be understood why several of the billions on earth want to come here. Why are some countries rich and others are poor? There are exceptions, but normally when a couple stays together with respect, works hard, doesn't waste money on expensive booze or drugs and doesn't steal or lie, a peaceful and relatively prosperous life results.

The same is true on a national scale. Yes, we have some evil folks in the USA, and waste and incompetence in all levels of government, etc. But we need to appreciate that it takes about four times longer to start a business in Europe than in the USA (one good reason not to rush to convert dollars to euros) and sixteen to 40 times longer in the Philippines and other developing countries. When a crooked government invents layers of bureaucracy to give jobs to their lackeys, the standard of life lowers dramatically for all but the most evil criminals.

Virtue brings a good, fair government and a society where people want to come to, instead of one they want to leave. Or as the Bible puts it much better, righteousness exalts a nation, but sin is a reproach to any people. Our nation will become like the nations our ancestors left if we cheat on our taxes, reward dishonesty, make bribery a way of life, glorify gambling, prostitution, attack historic Christianity, etc.

What are we doing personally to exalt/lift up/promote the best for our nation? Nothing, unless we are right with God and walking humbly with him. To do that means to be concerned for his glory, to be broken, repenting, and walking in the light. Does our family and others who interact with us, find us encouraging what is good and discouraging what is evil, first of all in ourselves? Do they see us not only talking about what is good but actually doing fair and honest and kind deeds? Can they trust us to treat them as well in private as we do when others are watching?

The USA is on top of the world presently. No one would question that we are far above all others economically, militarily, and culturally (well, the French would dispute the cultural point). But are we passing on the Christian faith as well as we pass on American culture? Statistically we are not, with very few exceptions.

After traveling more than I ever wanted to travel, I am glad to see that most Americans do not care what Europeans or Africans or Asians or South Americans think about us. But I am deeply grieved that so few care about what the Triune God thinks of us. As individuals and as a nation, we have been given much. God says in his word, "Everyone to whom much is given, of him much will be required." Do we have a clear idea of what God requires of us personally in order to be righteous in his sight? As one song so practically proposes, "Come let us pray until the power of the Lord comes down." When we do that, the Holy Spirit will cut through our rationalizations and will guide us to be righteous in specific ways that glorify Jesus Christ.

Do not fear the waning of Christianity.

Church goers increasingly see themselves as individuals firstly (I will follow the Bible only when it doesn't oppose my desires), Americans secondly (ethical or not), and Christians thirdly (when Jesus agrees with my logic and feelings). As a result, moral anarchy reigns in the USA Today, with increased lying, co-habitation, stealing, etc. My brother began to drive a truck again after an absence of about twenty years, and he remarked that unlike then, almost all the drivers are mad at something all the time now.

Personal holiness has been overthrown in favor of pleasure for many. This is especially true when people saw one thing preached in public and the opposite lived out at home. So, should we despair? No, because throughout history Christianity has waxed and waned. But we need to make sure that our homes are places where Christianity is practiced sincerely and wholeheartedly, and where we repent and ask forgiveness from God and each other.

It is not primarily the responsibility of the preacher or youth director or schoolteacher to raise Godly children, but of the parents. Sometimes others in the community can offset parents who get their ideas on relationships from the trashy magazines sold at the counters of Walmart and other grocery stores. But we are commanded by God to think about what is noble, good, and not to dream and scheme of how we can use others financially or socially or otherwise.

When Corrie Ten Boom was working as a watchmaker with her father, a rich customer once came into their shop, picked out a very expensive watch, pulled out a fat wad of bills and paid for it. Corrie said she was paying attention from the other room and was so thankful to God, since they had some large overdue bills (as was common). The customer talked of how he had taken his old watch to another watchmaker who could not repair it. Her father asked to see it, made a small adjustment, and then returned the money for the very expensive watch. He then spoke highly of the other watchmaker and encouraged the customer to return there for his business. When the customer answered that he had been back three times and still the watch had not been repaired, her father said to bring it to him, and he would repair it, for the young watchmaker would be as good as his father.

After the customer had left, Corrie stormed into the shop and asked her father, "How could you?" He replied that he had preached the funeral of the watchmaker's father, and it was wrong to take his customer. He added that there is blessed money and cursed money, and we are to trust God for the blessed money.

The Ten Booms attended the cathedral church in Haarlem, where the Bible was not respected as the Word of God. Guess which institution had more influence on Corrie, the church or the family? Of course, we are to encourage Godly churches and other parts of society. But we are individually to live by choosing right and refusing wrong on a daily basis, and especially with those in our homes. It is easier to seem wonderful in public- even mafia types are usually on good behavior at weddings, baptisms, and funerals! But I hope we love God enough to be honest and kind and fair even when we seem to benefit by disobeying God. Then we must choose between our logic or feelings as normal Americans, or what the risen Jesus Christ would have us do!

Education choices

Public schools find themselves competing with Christian schools and home schooling. If the public is allowed to take vouchers or tax credits and transfer them to alternative educational systems, the public schools will lose even more students. What are the pros and cons of each?

Public schools have advantages because public funds provide for a greater variety of subjects with supporting technology. So public education is less expensive for the family. Children there are also exposed to a representative slice of the area, and committed Christian students are free to form their own groups for nurture or outreach. As far as I knew, I was the only Christian at my high school, but now Christian pupils are more open and less ashamed of their faith than I was. Also, their faith gets tried in a secular setting.

Disadvantages of the public system include the fact that texts continue to almost completely delete references to the vast Christian influence in this country. Patrick Henry, for example, said, "This country was not founded by religionists but by Christians." Violence and lack of caring teachers is sometimes a great problem in public schools, but thankfully there are many wonderful exceptions.

Christian schools would cherish this quote by C.S. Lewis. "Education without religion, as useful as it is, seems rather to make a man a more clever devil." At a Christian school, a great advantage is that students have more encouragement to relate biblical teachings of justice and mercy in their private and public lives (in theory at least). Disadvantages include greater expenses, leaving only poorer Christian students to fend for themselves in public schools. Some schools also major on minors and neglect the themes of Christianity that benefit all of society.

Home schooling means fewer expenses, and a stronger unity among the family is possible as peer influence declines. The family can pass on truths and experiences and listen more to understand the unique needs of each child. It is a drawback, however, that even an extremely gifted family is rarely a match for a collection of teachers, with the variety of experience and wisdom they offer to students. More has been done to improve home schooling resources, and cooperative efforts among home schooling parents bring more social and intellectual opportunities than ever before.

Still, I personally prefer to have Christian children tough enough and loving enough to go to public schools and have strong influence there. But each child has different needs and interests, and it is up to the parents to prayerfully discern what is the best kind of education at a particular time in the life of a child. At any rate, the parents are not only responsible to be the primary teachers, but to teach their children what is worth learning.

Honesty

Honesty is not a glamour virtue, but I think it is the very minimum trait for a Christian. No relationship can flourish unless both can be relied on to tell the truth. To know the other is committed to saying what they believe to be real, is necessary in order to trust the other person. On the other hand, when we know another person has a track record of shading the truth to make themselves appear more noble or when truth inconveniences them, no relationship can thrive in that situation.

The Bible teaches that we are to speak the truth, in love, and sometimes it is better to stay silent rather than to say hurtful things. But it is not helpful to be deceptive when another asks how we like a hairstyle or a clothing item. Make a generally vague statement if necessary, but later our word will be devalued when others know we compliment even when we do not mean it!

So, what should we do if we are caught between being hateful or saying what is untrue? I think the problem belongs to any person who insists on hearing wonderful compliments or nothing. I hope we do not feel sad at the loss of such a person who is desperate for the false. Try to otherwise encourage the person, if possible, but not at the expense of lying!

We rightly expect our government to be honest, and the government in the USA operates on the premises that Americans are also trustworthy. Many governments in the world assume the opposite of their citizens, and laws to collect taxes are very oppressive because the government considers the business community to be crooked and does not expect them to abide by the rules. Honest businessmen in such a situation are severely handicapped. Are we as a country headed in the same direction? Unfortunately, studies have indicated that honesty is practiced less and less in the USA.

But the less honest our colleagues are, the more we suffer when we are honest. This will encourage more dishonesty in those who are honest because of cultural norms, or because it seems to be the most pragmatic course to take. But in an environment where honesty is not valued, one must have reasons beyond the financial or social to stay honest. When God is real to us, and we know that we have fellowship with him, then his commands are the basis for our choices. Then we choose to be honest because we love God, and we want to reflect his image. When others do that, it is easier to be honest. But when others choose to disobey God by being dishonest, we are still motivated and enabled to do that when we are friends with God through faith in Jesus Christ. Then if we lose money by being honest (as I have done), we can say it is money we do not really need. That is because God promises to supply ALL our needs (not necessarily all our wants) when we love and obey him, as Philippians 4:19 teaches. Sometimes we can see clearly and quickly that honesty is the best policy for us. New contracts or new friends may appear to strengthen and encourage us. At other times, the opposite may occur. Especially then, we need supernatural help from God to have his peace, and to keep on doing what we know is honest.

Choose Godly leaders.

In 2001 the president of South Africa said that many think that Africa is corrupt and inefficient. "They are right," he added. One cannot help but to admire and respect such a humble leader, who was hopefully able to fight such sins effectively.

What about "the old boy" network that abounds in every place? In all locations leaders naturally emerge and try to pass on jobs and benefits. The only difference is how these favors are passed on. Are they given to family and friends regardless of whether they are best for the job or not? Or are the plums given to those of integrity and competence? Any government from the local to the international level thrives when leaders gather Godly folks around them and delegate authority to them. As the Bible phrases it in Proverbs 14:34 (KJ21), "Righteousness exalteth a nation, but sin is a reproach to any people." All levels of government bring justice and a much better living environment when those in charge are honest, kind, and under the Lordship of Jesus Christ.

I know that it is sometimes very difficult to tell which public figure is a good person and which is not. Some may claim to be trustworthy when the opposite is true, and the alternative choice may be wonderful but much more humble. Sometimes a public forum will clearly show arrogance or humility, respect for others or contempt, competence or incompetence. It is sometimes asserted that plain politicians such as Abraham Lincoln can no longer be elected since handsome candidates appeal more to the masses. If that is true, then we deserve only handsome criminals.

As we celebrate the birth of our nation each July 4th, I hope we respect and admire and choose more leaders like George Washington. If he did nothing else than step down after two terms, he deserves great honor! Although certainly not perfect (freeing his slaves only as he was dying, for example), Thomas Jefferson, who disagreed with him on different matters, had this to say about him: "He was in every sense of the words, a wise, a good, and a great man."

While some revisionist historians sneered that George Washington married his wife Martha for her money, he himself wrote to her ... "there was never a moment in my life since I first knew you, in which it (my heart) did not cleave and cling to you with the warmest affection." By the way, it is much better to read the writings of famous people directly than to take second hand and often very biased opinions.

Washington read the Bible daily, and different guests reported barging unintentionally into his room after nine o'clock and finding him alone, on his knees with an open Bible before him on a chair, reading aloud, as was the custom then. May God have mercy on us, so that we do not prefer the witty to the wise, the evil to the good, and the petty to the great. We are responsible to train ourselves in Godliness so that we can recognize it and appreciate it in those who seek to be political or social or religious leaders.

The love of money

Mae West, among others who share credit, professed, "I've been rich and I've been poor, and rich is better." Money does solve a few problems, we must admit. We can be cool in summer and warm in winter. We can also eat more ice cream when we have wealth.

But having more money often brings a gnawing obsession to just have more. According to Juliet Schor in the book, *The Overspent American*, twenty-seven percent of households making over $100,000 a year (1998 figures) say they, "cannot afford to buy everything they need." Does the term greed or selfishness occur to the reader about now?

As our income rises, often our expectations rise even faster. If we are not careful, what we considered to be luxuries a few years ago we now call needs. So, we sometimes succumb to the temptation to really "need" new cars, new boats, European vacations, etc.

But when we define ourselves by what we have, it is never enough to give contentment. The average size of the American house has doubled in the last fifty years. So, to feel superior to others now in the housing category, we must probably quadruple the size of our house. May I add that God may lead some to have huge houses for various reasons, so individual circumstances differ!

When the nobility ruled, aristocrats passed laws so that the newly rich businessmen could not wear the same sort of clothes they wore. So, the desire to get worth and value by comparison to others is a constant theme throughout history.

Jesus says in Luke 12:15, "... be on your guard against all covetousness: for a one's life does not consist in the abundance of his possessions." Followers of Jesus and all others have trouble really trusting this on a day by day basis. Being a "good provider" is a worthy goal, and I should have been a better one. Boaz cared for Ruth very well, and we all need to pray for balance between living for Jesus Christ and providing well. Undoubtably we should guard against the love of money and still support ourselves in some ethical endeavors. May God give us wisdom in these work areas.

The Triune God is above every culture.

Anthropologist Carolyn Fluehr-Lobban agonized over the fact that her discipline's prime directive-cultural relativism- left her with no rationale for opposing rape or racial genocide in other cultures. In other words, anthropology asserts that there is no such thing as God who has communicated absolutes of truth or right or wrong. So yes, much of so-called higher education is definitely demonic!

According to anthropology, in Europe and the USA where Christianity has had strong influence, it may be wrong to rape and commit racial genocide. So, we were right to condemn the Nazis or communists or the slaughter of other ethnic groups in the Balkans, for example. But when Africans or Asians slaughter other tribes or neighboring groups, we as white people have cultural imperialism when we condemn this. Also, in non-European culture when rape occurs, we are being self-righteous and bigoted to oppose it, according to the cultural relativism preachers.

This sort of demonic excuse making has permeated European and American culture more and more, as people have sought to eliminate Christianity because it condemns lifestyles we choose. How convenient to steal, lie, commit adultery, etc., and to be able to rationalize that there is no God, therefore whatever we choose to do is okay.

"They thought it was an honor to be sacrificed ... They had a different idea of life and death." These are the words of Mexican First Lady Patricia Valasco Zedillo, as she and her husband escorted President Clinton and Mrs. Clinton around Mayan ruins in the Yucatán peninsula. She described child sacrifices performed there, explaining that the Mayans believed, "the universe was nourished" by the child murders.

There is no basis to oppose such practices unless there is a God who has revealed himself to be opposed to such action (yes, I know the Old Testament has extremely bloody sections, but they were for that time and place and not to be repeated since Jesus Christ came). To be personally disgusted by what the Mayans did is no more significant than to dislike liver or onions unless our choices reflect a higher power than ourselves.

This is not to say that anyone can know truth exhaustively, but as Francis Shaeffer put it, it is possible to know true truth. We have no excuse to sing as Frank Sinatra did, "I did it my way." When a person rapes or murders and says, "I did it my way," we have no basis to praise or to blame, unless we can appeal to a higher power who has clearly communicated his mind and love and power to us.

Christians affirm that God the Father, God the Son Jesus Christ, and God the Holy Spirit exist eternally, and gave a clear and accurate account of his will in the Bible. Those who reject this need to closely examine their own presuppositions. Where do they get their ideas and beliefs? How valid are the sources and the founders of their belief systems? Are they people of intelligence and integrity who treat others as they want to be treated? Do they have one standard for themselves and a higher standard for others?

Even those who do not follow Jesus Christ as God like to think he is a good man. But Jesus was not a good man; he was, as C.S. Lewis pointed out, a liar or a deluded lunatic, unless he was truly God. Lewis explains this theory, elaborating on how Jesus made such outrageous claims about himself. John 14:6 teaches, "I am the way, and the truth and the life." Colossians 1:16 teaches through the Holy Spirit that all things have been created through him and for him. Colossians 2:10 reminds us that Jesus is the head of every ruler and authority. He is the only legitimate reason for choosing good over cultural relativism!

Are we thankful?

Each individual and each society has problems, but in the USA, we are so favored by God that our gratitude should be overflowing to him daily. Most of us have comfortable homes and cars, and records show that these were very rare only a few years ago among my relatives, and probably yours, also. I remember touring castles in Europe, and I was struck by the fact that even the most wealthy and powerful families lived in perpetually dank and dark moldy homes, while the bulk of society lived in wretched conditions indeed-throughout history!

The custom of the bride standing on the left of the groom during a wedding developed because of danger to her. Most are right-handed, and men wore swords until relatively recently. When someone tried to nab the bride, the groom would unsheathe his sword quickly, slash his enemy, and if the bride were standing on his right, he might cut her nose off. The best man was also wearing a sword for similar practical reasons. I have done hundreds of weddings and never saw the need for such a display of force, so most weddings are much more genteel now.

When I was attending high school in east Tennessee, we had no drug problem or school shootings, but no one claimed to be Christian either openly, including me. Over 90 percent attended church then, but like myself, none of my peers ever seemed interested about what God thought or wanted. Now several are openly serving God in word and attitude and action.

Violent crimes have decreased in New York City from well over 2,000 yearly to just over 200 now, and much of our culture is similar, despite well publicized exceptions to that trend. We live in a country so wonderful that over one million immigrants enter each year, over one million enter illegally, and several hundred million more would come if possible. Yes, we have problems, but our problems are preferable to the problems of the countries people leave to come here, the third most populous country in the world.

There is no question that European culture will decrease in influence here. We were populated by the overflow of Europe, but they have chosen not to replace themselves for many decades now (and some wanted to have children but could not). But the most important issue is whether historic Christianity will further weaken. A smaller percentage of each county in the USA goes to church each year, and growing evangelical and fundamentalist churches have higher divorce rates than the non-church-going public. Do the great blessings that we have from God cause us to neglect honesty, honoring each other, and treating others as we want to be treated?

In the 1800's the French writer Alex de Tocqueville toured our country. He was deeply impressed with our work ethic, our wealth, and our natural resources. But most of all he was struck by the fact that Christianity was not only talked about, but it was lived out in the lives of many people. He wrote that America was great because America was good, and when it ceased to be good it would cease to be great. May God help us to make it (and your country) great in his eyes!

Show hospitality to students.

Some of the foreign students have worked in the USA for two or three years and told us that they had never been in an American home before. Each summer thousands of students from different states and countries work in this country. Will we be hospitable to them as the Holy Spirit asks many of us to do?

They are not here by accident, but they are here by God's appointment. That is because as Acts 17:26 assures us, God has established the times when we live, and also the boundaries where we live. Ho Chi Min was a student in Boston before he returned to lead Vietnam. If the Christians there had shown him the love of Christ, it is very possible that the Vietnam war would not have happened.

Jacques Chirac was a student in South Carolina before he returned to be the president of France. It is highly unlikely that France would be so secular and so contemptuous of Christianity if Christians had shown him kindness. And even if the foreigners and students go back and become ditch diggers, we are still commanded to show hospitality (Romans 12). How can we do that?

If we have the money to eat in a restaurant or to amuse ourselves where a summer student is hired, then we certainly have the money to invite them over for a home cooked meal. Even a peanut butter sandwich would be better than nothing. It would be a distinctly different cultural experience for almost all of them. They need to be invited into our homes to see how we live- especially if we are broken from our selfish ambitions, repenting of our sins, and walking in the light of Jesus Christ.

If we are not practicing hospitality to our spouse or children, repent first, ask Jesus to forgive us, and then we will be able to have positive impact on anyone we do welcome into our home. I have been privileged to be a guest in homes in different countries, and I assure you that I was much more favorably impressed with Brazilians, Dutch, and others who cared enough to bring me into their sanctuaries, where I ate and talked with them leisurely.

Another way to offer hospitality is to remember that visitors often do not have cars, for no other country is as dependent on cars as the USA. Offers to take them grocery shopping or to see natural beauty would be much appreciated. If the visitor is not in your age bracket or does not share your interests very much, try to find a committed Christian who may be more compatible or who is going through similar life experiences as a student or single person, etc.

If you see international students and are uncomfortable making contact with them, call Intervarsity or another organization to encourage them. If the international students are from Latin America or Africa, they are much more likely to evangelize your church youth group than to be evangelized. And if the international students are not Christian, they will have many valuable things to teach us anyway if we are humble enough to think that we Americans can still learn a few pointers about life.

God is bringing the world to our doorsteps. Can they say that they have met the living God through us after they have visited- or only that they met smug materialistic Americans who had a form of Godliness, but no supernatural connection with God. Our charm, education, and experiences can encourage them only in the most shallow and trivial ways, at best. That is why we need to plead for God to give us his words and his attitudes, so we can practice hospitality among those close to us, as well as to the strangers he brings into our paths.

No rules?

A restaurant advertises, "No Rules." Does that mean I can eat without paying? Or perhaps it is okay to dance on tables and stomp on the plates of the other diners? A radio station gives out bumper stickers that proclaim it as "Wild." So, they are saying that they are not impressed by Christian teachings on truth and treating others as we want to be treated? If someone went berserk and looted the station or kicked the windows out, do you think the owner would smile and say, "That is ok, they were just being wild?"

Those throughout history who eloquently advocated doing as we please, when examined closely, were found to apply those ideas only to themselves. "Free love," for example, meant that the guru had no restraints, but the followers had to obey the rules. "Power to the people" meant power to those shouting that slogan, usually not power to those with less education or money.

We are all attracted to the idea that we as individuals can do whatever we wish, while others need to be forgiving, fair, honest, and hard working. In other words, we all tend to magnify our rights and minimize our responsibilities. That is one reason the Bible is so offensive to all of us. C.S. Lewis said that before he became a Christian, he was outraged that the Bible taught God demanded our total obedience and wholehearted worship. But after he began to follow Jesus Christ, he discovered that God really deserved such devotion. His rules for behavior bring us the most fulfilling and interesting lives possible and deliver individuals and nations alike from disaster.

When we Christians rid ourselves of false guilt and cultural baggage not taught in the Bible, we become countercultural in a seemingly wild sense. But that kind of wildness will not bring on stabbings or unfaithfulness or evil insults either!

A strong streak of anti-authoritarianism has permeated the baby boomers, those born between 1946 and 1966: Some of that is good, for we should question authority. But we should not question from a selfish desire for our own comfort, but to know if an authority is right and holy before God. If so, we should support it, however much our rights are stifled or restricted.

Even a restaurant or radio station cannot survive if truly committed to no rules, or to wildness. Nor can we thrive as individuals or families or as a nation without behavioral boundaries. Then to what rules or standards of truth should we defer? We could live for money, or pleasure, and treat as trash or ignore anyone who does not help us to achieve those goals.

If we advocate no rules or wildness, it is illogical to object when others are true to their preferences of anarchy, even if we get clobbered in the process! But no nation can exist without laws to govern behavior, neither can we as individuals. When the laws of God are written in our hearts by supernatural conversion to Jesus Christ, then we are sure that God is real, and that his laws free us instead of constrain us. They free us to act justly and to love mercy and to walk humbly with the risen Jesus Christ.

Belief impacts behavior.

If you think it is not important to live by the Bible, try going to a dentist who also believes the Bible is full of fairy tales! Then you will be charged for extra work without being consulted, advised to have work that is not only unnecessary but causes more damages, so he will then make more profit. Or you may be among those who are treated for cancer when you are really healthy. The same is true for plumbers or craftsmen or mechanics, etc. When we see the Bible as a book of suggestions instead of the Word of God that it is, we often ignore, "So whatever you wish that others would do to you, do also to them." When the Holy Spirit is not within us to let us know when we sin, people need to count their spoons after we visit them, as the English writer Dr. Samuel Johnson observed.

Beliefs have direct impact on our behavior. We may be able to rip off some folks and get a fancier house, but we will then be a greedy and untrustworthy individual. Our children will then have contempt for us, but they will learn our ways, however, and will normally mimic us, becoming unscrupulous and then marrying such a person and continuing our traditions.

Try instead telephoning a church that teaches truth exists and that you can know it, and have them recommend professionals and craftsmen and tradesmen that you can trust will work with competence and integrity.

Surveys by Barna research show that the younger the persons are in the USA, the farther they are (as a group, not every individual is in this category) from believing that it is always wrong to lie, cheat, and otherwise sin. As folks who must sometimes get specialized care for ourselves, our pets, cars, or houses, that trend affects all of us negatively. Mockery of the Bible spawns unethical dentists, doctors, and others who will use ungodly practices to take advantage of us. We reap what we sow, whether we encourage our children to take Godly or ungodly traits into their workplaces.

I was honored to meet Dr. Broady, a physician who had a practice in Sevierville, Tennessee, before he died. During the Chinese civil war, he bravely protected his hospital there from soldiers, and later returned to work in the USA. When he delivered his first baby, not only did they refuse to pay him, but his gas was siphoned out of his car. From that beginning he slowly recovered financially and had a fulfilling and productive life. Perhaps he would have made more money if he had encouraged his patients to get needless services. But he left a much better legacy than greed! He was respected while he lived, and his memory is honored now. I might add that the prayers of the righteous keep on benefitting the recipients of their prayers, even after the righteous person dies.

Proverbs 10:7 says, "The memory of the righteous is a blessing, but the name of the wicked will rot." First of all, the recollection of the greedy wicked will be a stench in the nostrils of God-then among their family-and among all they mistreated. How much better it is to be like Dr. Broadly, and others who do their work as unto the Lord. God sees all, he is just, and he will repay us-even for the gas that is siphoned out of our car.

Hospitality

Romans 12:13: "... seek to show hospitality." I have received so much welcome kindness, I would have to be a real cad not to care about this subject deeply. While hitchhiking in Switzerland, for example, a guy and his nephew picked me up and took me to Geneva, where I stayed with them for two weeks. They took me camping with them in the Jura Mountains of France. Also, when my clothes got drenched, the next morning the grandmother had them washed and dried on an outside clothesline! In addition, they invited me to go to church with them, but at the time I was so far from God that I had no interest whatsoever.

I was treated with similar kindness in different states and countries. I have been honored to be associated with A Christian Ministry in the National Parks for several years, specifically with the support committee in the Great Smoky Mts with American students each summer.

My wife is Russian and very hospitable, so we continue contacts with several Russian students who arrive each summer, and many stay. Do not just comment on their accent when you hear a student, invite them to your church or to go hiking or to some other events. Very few ever see the inside of an American home, but most would be interested to do that. If you prefer non-Russians, you have a choice of many nationalities among the students.

Several in nursing homes get no visitors. Clear it with the staff first and bring a dog or cat there. I remember one man was so sick he could not sit up or speak. But from the time I brought my little dog to the time I left, he laughed with joy. I love dogs, and my reaction in such a situation would be similar. Especially if you live near such a facility, it would be good for the residents, you, and your peaceful pet.

Some near us may be house bound and need transportation or groceries or just a visit on occasion. Pray for guidance, or we could waste time and money enabling one to take drugs or to do other harmful pursuits. It is not hospitable but very destructive to encourage lazy or vicious behavior. It is much easier to see when others do that than to see when we do it ourselves! But love not only encourages in what is right and holy, but also discourages others in what is sinful and harmful to them.

Christians have received hospitality from God, who opened our hearts to see him at least partially as he is. I just saw a guy on a sidewalk with the message, "God is dope." No, God is a high with no bad side effects. His presence encourages and enables the Christian to show hospitality. Even if we are not called to do hospitality regularly, all of us are occasionally called by God to provide lodging or food or some other act of hospitality.

All of us veer out of the will of God.

Fenelon, who was an archbishop in Paris, France, said that a baby sees an apple and a diamond and regards them equally, and we should do the same. He wrote this in a letter to a small group of Christians in the royal court of King Louis XIV, arguably the most immoral royal court in the history of the world.

When we pass through the Christmas season, that is arguably the most greedy time of the year. On Thanksgiving Day, many employees must work that day or night so that selfish employers can serve greedy and silly materialists. Thank God for the few businesses who buck the trend to trash Thanksgiving Day. God bless them.

In the interest of full disclosure, I admit (to paraphrase C.S. Lewis), that consumerism/materialism is one of the few sins not attractive to me. Therefore, I can rail against those who "shop til you drop" without fear of being lumped in with them. But we who are not swayed by the sins of greed for material opulence ought not to look down our noses at those who are. We can be certain that we have other sins, besetting and appealing sins, that these hordes of shopping addicts do not have.

They may be open sins, and by the way, men usually have these more often, and therefore feel less welcome in church than woman whose sins are more acceptable to the general public. But all of us veer consciously and radically out of the will of God, since the Bible teaches us, "The heart is desperately wicked." If we are not tempted to show off materially, we are prone to be greedy for sexual pleasure, or status, or comfort, or safety, or for something else we crave more than to worship Jesus Christ as the name above all names. It is not wrong to have money or pleasure or praise, etc., unless we get those gifts by disobeying the clear teachings of the Bible.

Fenelon said, "Sometimes we find the most surprising faults in otherwise good people ... I ask you more than ever not to spare me if I need correction. Even if you mention a fault which isn't really there, there will be no harm done. If I find that your correction wounds me, then my irritability simply shows that you have touched a sore spot in my life."

I hope we have his attitude about material things this year. But even if we do not need to repent of materialism, we need to repent of hedonism or laziness or some other traits that hinder us from humbly walking with the risen Jesus Christ.

Don't give God excuses.

I was walking past the courthouse in Rogersville, Tennessee, when I noticed the preacher. He was giving a sermon at the top of his lungs to passersby and to a group of older men who were always there swapping knives. I thought to myself, "I am glad I do not have to do that. I am Presbyterian."

About two weeks later, I was visiting my parents again, and the Holy Spirit was still convicting me of my pride and arrogance. I drove out of the little town, and I was miserable. I knew it was the Lord's doing for the deep burden was not anything I had concocted. So, I said to God, "All right. I will go back to that courthouse, and I will preach, or read the Bible, or cry, or do anything you want me to do."

As soon as I said that to God, the burden lifted. He did not want me to do any of that, but he certainly wanted me to be willing to serve him any way he chose.

If we are from a mainline church, we are prone to look down our noses at anything that smacks of emotionalism. This is because we value reason and doing things decently and in order. On the other hand, if we are from a more exuberant tradition, we tend to be condescending towards those who are less demonstrative.

Let's face it, folks. There is some craziness in each denomination. As long as Jesus Christ is worshipped as Savior and Lord, I hope we wish them well instead of snickering at their more extreme actions. Just choose the craziness you tolerate best and join them!

The disciples were upset at one point because they saw another group that cast out demons in the name of Jesus, and he said to leave them alone. There are few enough Christians, and when we see another group more emotional or more analytical, let us pray for them and wish them well instead of feeling superior.

Professor C.S. Lewis had high regard for Billy Graham, who reached people for Jesus Christ he could not reach. And of course, Billy Graham had the utmost appreciation for Lewis and his outreach toward intellectuals. There is room for all kind of Christians as long as we have integrity and put Jesus first in our lives. Probably every Christian group has some who got that description.

Some may prefer wilder congregations for the excitement and adventure, while others may go to a more studious meeting to ponder and pray. When people love and obey Jesus Christ, he rewards them. When they do not, he will get them. So, we do not have to worry about it either way. We just need to be willing to get more starchy, or less starchy as the Holy Spirit leads.

Are we failing to be open to all God wants because we are afraid we will embarrass ourselves and others? I hope we get more concerned about whether we are an embarrassment to God or not.

I hope we get more concerned about his reputation than our own. I like the answer teens at the Brownsville Church of God in Florida gave when their peers would ask them if they went to that church where they flop like fish out of water. They answer, "Yes, why don't you come and flop with us? Are you thinking, "I am glad I do not have to do that—I am Presbyterian, or Baptist, or Orthodox, or whatever?

Robbers

I just joined a new fraternity—those who are the survivor of a home invasion and robbery. How do we think Christianly about such matters? I am more convinced than ever that Jesus calls all to repentance and salvation and holiness. None of my books on those topics were stolen, by the way. I am tempted to pray that the thieves will be shot dead during their next robbery, to keep additional people from experiencing the same injustice. Very rarely does one rob once and then quit, so the same persons will repeat the crime until they are either converted to follow Jesus Christ, or encounter a less supernatural force.

I think of the many who knowingly buy stolen property in this and other areas, and who therefore encourage more crime. Satan thanks you; I do not. I think of how drugs should probably be decriminalized, so the prices would drop dramatically, and no one would steal to support such an evil and stupid habit. I think of how one third of the Chinese were hooked on opium when the communists took over, and Mao promised that drug users would be shot. After about 10,000 were shot dead, the rest went cold turkey sober.

I do not suggest we take that approach, although if your house were broken into, the idea would have some charm to it. If your child is an addict, I suggest that you read the Bible and ask God to show you where you have gone wrong. If you pray this sincerely and still have peace with God, great. If not, then you as well as your son has the blood of the victims on your hands, and the blood of your own child is on your hands, unless you have lived a Godly, holy life before him.

It is tiresome to see parents act as if their child is an angel when in fact the person is a thug. If a society such as the mafia wants to rob, that is bad enough. But if such excuses appear in churches, then such places are under the domain of darkness instead of the light of Jesus Christ. If the intruders are from the south of the USA, it is almost certain that they went to a church somewhere. What did they hear there? Did they hear a good word about Jesus Christ? Or did they hear how wonderful we all are and how we just need to be nice?

No doubt thieves do think they are wonderful and deserve to steal what belongs to others. But that is a wicked sense of entitlement that is to be opposed by the churches instead of being encouraged at all! What do we encourage when we meet together? Do we encourage repentance and humble and deep reliance on Jesus Christ, or do we encourage others to follow their bliss, as Joseph Campbell taught? Bliss for some is to invade homes and to otherwise harm others.

Jesus rules in unexpected places.

It was Christmas Eve during World War 1: The German and allied armies faced each other in long trenches across the killing fields. Suddenly the English-speaking army began the beloved carol, "Silent Night."

The Germans listened and recognized the tune (the song is German). They then sang in their language, "Stille Nacht, Heilige Nacht! Alles schlaeft, einsam wacht ...." Allied troops began to run towards the Germans from their muddy trenches. The German officers tried to beat their men back, but to no avail. The Germans also rushed across the frigid no man's land to greet their enemies in a joyful, peaceful reunion. It was a gift from the Prince of peace.

People unite across all kinds of boundaries when they worship Jesus Christ. Soon after I rededicated my life to Jesus Christ, I was awestruck to see a TV special where others sang hymns I knew and loved in different languages. Later, I was able to observe that personally in different countries, and never without being deeply moved that the Triune God is universal, and for all people.

When we truly love Jesus Christ, there is a powerful supernatural bond through the Holy Spirit between us and others who worship him as God. A white motorist illustrated this by telling how tears streamed down his face as he listened to black pastor Tony Evans preaching of how this country needs to get back on the right path. He was stopped at a traffic light when a black woman pulled alongside of him, noticed his tears, and asked if he was listening to Evans. He answered yes, and they both agreed he was great. At the next light, they were both stopped again, and the woman rolled down her window a second time and spoke: "Although I am a Christian, I've been prejudiced all my life, not now. You've changed my heart."

After the Civil War in the USA, there was a reunion of soldiers from both sides. A Confederate told of how he was sent to kill a Union sentry. He had him in his sights when the Yankee began to sing, "Jesus, Lover of my Soul, let me to thy bosom fly ... other refuge have I none, hangs my helpless soul on thee, Leave O leave me not alone, still support and comfort me. All my trust on thee is stayed, all my help from thee I bring, cover my defenseless head, with the shadow of thy wings."

"I lowered my gun and could not kill him," the Southerner said. The Union man asked if it happened at a certain place at a certain time. When the Confederate said yes, the Union man said that he was the man. He said he was very scared and sang that song to keep his courage up, unaware that it saved his life until he heard that from his old enemy many years later.

Let us pray that the leaders of nations and races and factions as well as ordinary folks will listen to Jesus the prince of peace. As much as we love and obey him, we have peace within, and peace on earth. John 16:4 says, "But I have said these things to you, that when their hour comes you may remember that I told them to you."

God gives joy, not selfishness or greed.

Greed and selfishness run amok in our society. If you do not believe me, go to a mall sometime. Yes, I agree we all need shoes and clothes and food. But does anyone need 40 pairs of shoes, clothes we never wear, or other types of greed? I overheard several say that they do not need a particular item, but they want it. So, they buy it. Really, they hope to impress with the status multiple items bring to other materialistic folks.

I think it is Madonna who sings that she is a material girl. Well, she has buckets of money, but a string of divorces makes me seriously doubt that money has made her happy, because it makes no one else happy. The comedian Jim Carrey said he wished that everyone could be rich and famous for a month, because then everyone could see that money does not make a person happy.

But being holy as the Bible defines holiness does make a person content, whatever our money situation is. That is because we then get our worth and value from walking humbly with the risen Jesus Christ. He is with those who have been supernaturally delivered from the kingdom of darkness into his kingdom of light.

When we live by his teachings instead of allowing ourselves to be warped by the materialism of our culture, then we live relatively simply and do not envy what others possess. To do that, perhaps we must turn off the millions of ads that promote greed and selfishness and status. I felt deprived as a boy because my father did not allow us to have a television set, so I could not join the conversations riding the bus, and I assume we missed some good shows. But I am also sure we were much more content with what we had.

Robert Murray M'Cheyne noted that who we are on our knees before God is who we are, no more and no less. It is how God sees us, and we should see ourselves as he does. Yet all of us are tempted to be on our knees begging for approval from others! We tend to highly value the money or pleasure or status our fellow humans can provide. I agree that these are far superior to anything that a church that has a form of Godliness but denying the power of God can offer.

And even we who have experienced the unmistakable power of God in our lives are also deeply drawn to what the world system offers. We need to hide the Word of God in our hearts and pray much in order to walk humbly with him, and to repent much. There is a civil war raging within each Christian, for we keep our human nature after adding the nature of God through supernatural conversion. And even if we are not tempted to selfishness and greed, we will have other sins to fight. So, we never have a right to look down on those who have to struggle to be holy in areas that are easy for us!

The worst people in the world

Christians are the worst people in the world. No, I do not say that because of any pastoral problems I had. I say that because all of us sin, including Christians. But we have the law of God written in our hearts. We have the Holy Spirit, whom Jesus sends to each person who worshipped him as God and Lord.

John 16:13 says that he (the Spirit of Truth) will guide you into all truth. In other words, the Christian has God with us to guide us, directions from God, and the power to overcome sin. 1 John 4:4 says, "... he who is in you is greater than he who is in the world."

So, Christians have the ability to please God, yet we chose daily not to do that. We normally can avoid the grosser sins of murder, theft, etc. But even the most devout and sincere Christians must struggle daily against all kinds of more refined sins.

We are not always patient or kind, slow to be angry, or quick to forgive, for example. Yet we have been forgiven. Therefore, Christians are more able and responsible to forgive than those who are not forgiven by God.

Non-Christians are tempted to do whatever the Bible calls sin also, of course. But we Christians have the great and precious promise of Romans 8:28:..all things work together for good to them that love God. So, we are without excuse when we are impatient or unkind or want revenge. Psalm 84:11 says, "No good thing does he withhold from those who walk uprightly." So, when a promotion or health or a spouse is withheld, we have no excuse to fret.

Christians are commanded several times in the Bible not to worry. It is logical to worry when we are not certain that the Triune God loves us. But when we have been supernaturally converted to follow Jesus Christ as God and Lord, worry is a great sin and a great waste of time. Yet I and all Christians often refuse to trust God's great and precious promised to us. For these reasons we are the worst people in the world. God have mercy on us.

God gives favor; or not.

Exodus 11:3: "And the Lord gave the people favor in the sight of the Egyptians." And God also gives disfavor in the sight of some! The prophet Samuel was a very Godly man, yet he had no favor in the sight of his sons, nor did God have favor in their sight, because they chose to be wicked.

While I was in seminary, after much prayer I decided to run for the position of chaplain of the student body. The other student running called me up, and we had a prayer together. After we had a public presentation of our views, there was election, and he won. I was shocked because I was convinced (still am) that God wanted me to run. I was confident that therefore God wanted me to win, but he did not!

A. W. Tozer has brought deep and Godly encouragement to many (including myself) by his writings, and yet I found out only recently that his marriage was in terrible shape. I know nothing at all about his wife or her spiritual condition. I am sure that her husband was walking humbly with God, if not all the time, at least much of the time. Perhaps she was also, and their misunderstanding and struggles brought them closer to God. Or perhaps he or she or both were in person impatient, unkind, rude, etc., many times with each other.

Certainly, we should seek peace and pursue it, especially in our family, and forgive all wrongs whether real or imagined. As Mother Treasa said, "If you want to save the world, go home and love your family." I suspect he did that, and hopefully she did too. But it is entirely possible that they both were dedicated Christians and still had unfilled desires.

I naively assumed that since I went to a very Godly seminary I would have very deep and satisfying relationships there. That did happen to some extent, but not nearly as much as I had hoped. Whose fault was that? Although we are all sinners, I am convinced it was the fault of no one. I can look back and see a few things I should have done differently, but I do not think perfection in me would have changed where I pastored or who I married or any other important decision.

When we have strained relationships, especially among spouses, children or parents, I hope that we pray to be more irritated at our own sins than the sins of others. May God help us to see our own sins clearly and not to make excuses, but to sincerely repent of all sins.

In response to the question asking whether she had ever considered divorce or not, Ruth Graham answered no, but she had considered murder several times. Were she and Billy far from God when she had those thoughts? Was only one at fault, or neither? I hope such disappointing times drew them both closer to God, and I suspect that happened. Whether we have favor or disfavor in the eyes of others, I hope we pray to have favor in God's sight. Then we may or may not have favor in the eyes of our spouse or children or parents, etc.

Rev. Duncan Campbell and revival

Rev. Duncan Campbell (YouTube, www.sermonindex.net) spoke of the possibility of churches filled with people, and having many activities, without God being there at all. It is possible for a charming person to muscle up some fervor and excitement in a church, while at the same time working consciously for the other side. Or perhaps the presenter of the gospel is living a good life in sincerity, even as Saint Paul did before his conversion. Paul said that he was blameless as concerning the law, so he was a good ethical and moral man- he just opposed God himself.

Is Jesus Christ of the Bible honored? That is the most important question to ask about our own life, and any group we endorse. We know by checking our heart what motivates us, at least on a conscious level. We cannot see the hearts of others, but their attitudes and actions and words are good clues about their hearts. But God sees deeper still and calls all of us to deeper and deeper layers of repentance.

When God the Holy Spirit comes, then the community becomes God conscious. Talk about a sports team or other relatively trivial pursuit may still be present, but when God is really in our midst, we become concerned about how to best honor him in our daily lives. This becomes a common trait when God really visits a place with revival.

Hector McKinnon was concerned about the spiritual condition of the young in the settlement of Barvas on the Isle of Lewis in Scotland around 1950: He began to pray for revival and drew close to God himself with holiness and sincerity. He was told by God that Rev. Duncan Campbell would come at a certain time to commence a revival there.

At that very day, Rev. Campbell was sitting at a conference in Northern Ireland, when God the Holy Spirit spoke to him and told him that he was to leave for the isle of Barvas immediately. He mentioned this to his colleague, who said that he could not since he was to address the assembly that night. But he left and arrived on Barvas, where he knew no one. He asked a lad to take him to the nearest minister, and when told that there were none on the island, he asked to be directed to the nearest elder. He was led to Mr. McKinnon, who told him that he was expected and that a meeting was already set up that night. About 80 heard him preach, but it was an ordinary meeting, and Rev. Campbell said he feared that he had missed the guidance of God. But he reckoned that Mr.

McKinnon was closer to God than he was, for he assured his visitor that God was, "hovering." Soon many were drawn by the Holy Spirit to be converted, and revival spread throughout that small Scottish island.

Just previous to that event, Rev. Campbell had been approached by his sixteen-year-old Shena. She had told him that she was deeply concerned for him and had prayed much for him. Then she asked him how long it had been since he had led a soul to Christ. He had to admit it had been seventeen years. Furthermore, he was convicted of being against God consciously during that time, even as he had pastored and had been a speaker at many conferences on revival.

Shena further encouraged him, "Whatever it costs, go through with God." He took her advice and prayed to seek a renewal of brokenness before the Lord. That happened, and the power of God flowed through him again when he preached. He announced this breakthrough of deeper layers of repentance to his congregation, and five elders promptly left the church, saying that they did not want a fool as a minister. It is too bad that they considered repentance to be foolish!

He preached with renewed power, and hundreds became converted through his preaching. Perhaps we will get just as close to God and will see no results at all. Isaiah and Jeremiah were told by God to preach and not to worry whether anyone would believe or not, for they would not! Either way, we need to open ourselves up to be used by God, and to pray a prayer such as that prayed by the father of Rev. Campbell (who heard it from Rev. Robert Murray M'Cheyne), "Lord, make me as holy as a saved sinner can be."

Hold all things lightly.

I think most children are ashamed of their parents at some point, and when the parents are alcoholics or drug addicts or violent towards each other the shame is continual. When I was in the second grade, age seven, I remember being ashamed of our old car as Dad took me back and forth to school. He could have had a much better one, but now I know he supported the church and others who were less fortunate. Now I am ashamed that I valued status then more than acting justly, loving mercy, and walking humbly with God, as my parents did.

Recently I was with someone who kept noting how wonderful a certain house was, and she was sincere. I almost cried because it was very similar to houses I grew up in, which were much less impressive than my present house. And other houses are far more impressive than mine. But Christians, of all people, ought not to measure our worth and value by how fancy our house or car is. It was harmful and wrong to do so as a seven-year-old, and how much more so to measure ourselves by ungodly standards as a teen or older adult?

If we see even a few television ads, we will be prompted by very intelligent and crafty people to be more selfish and greedy. I am not against having good homes or cars or clothes, etc. But do we ever let God draw a line and hear him say, "This is enough for you?" Sometimes God wants us to live modestly because he knows that lifestyle will bring us more peace and calmness than luxury will bring. Sometimes God knows that more means more to tear up and to maintain, and less time to study the Bible and to pray how to apply it in specific situations. I do not pretend that I always have a good balance in these matters, but I do pray for that.

One may be called of God to pray many hours a day, or to be more active as a leader of commerce. God has blessed us all with abilities and limitations. But when our highest goal is to honor Jesus Christ, we get our purpose and meaning of life from that. Hopefully, my children are ashamed of me only when I do not walk humbly with Jesus Christ. As Corrie Ten Boom said, we are to hold all things lightly. Then when we lose house or health, etc., that is okay.

Godly leaders are vital to Christianity.

How did Harvard get so far from historic Christianity? It is our first university, founded in 1636: It is beyond dispute that it was begun by very Godly Christians for the purpose of training Christian ministers. For example, Rev. Thomas Shepard (along with Rev. John Harvard), was a founder.

Rev. Shepard was expelled from his English pulpit in 1630 and joined the Puritans who came to New England. He wrote treatises which included, "The Sincere Convert," and "The Sound Believer." He preached that true conversion requires a total change of heart, mind, and affections. He preached from the parable of the five wise and the five foolish virgins (Matthew 25), reasoning that we should expect, "a number of hypocrites mingling themselves with the purest of churches." The foolish virgins represented those who were satisfied with the temporary," blaze of outward profession" (the lamps taken with them)." The wise virgins stand for those who have the inward witness of the Holy Spirit (represented by the oil)."

For many years Harvard stayed true to the Christian faith, but by the mid-1700s it veered towards Unitarianism, the view that God is one and that faith in Jesus Christ is not important. Or as the humorist Garrison Keillor puts it, Unitarians do not worship, "what's his name."

What happened to Harvard has also occurred in many colleges and churches. Why? It is because the ruling group (trustees, elders, deacons) began to admit members on the basis of their wealth or personalities or because they had other admired skills. These are not bad in and of themselves. But to keep an institution Christian, new leaders must be supernaturally converted to Jesus Christ and must live holy lives. Then they will elect similar presidents, pastors, etc.

Once a group is committed to a non-Christian world view, it is extremely rare to return to Godliness. In other words, in the spiritual as well as the natural world, it is easier to have a baby than to raise the dead. So, Yale and Princeton were started after Harvard, in part to offset the apostasy that took over Harvard, and to promote historic Christianity. But as new universities and new churches form, they also go downhill unless they continue to elect leaders who are Godly.

Rev. Robert Murray M'Cheyne said that what a congregation needs most in a minister is holiness. I agree. Otherwise, skills will be used to advance the kingdom of darkness. 1 Timothy 5:22 teaches us to ordain no one quickly, until we know that they are truly and sincerely converted and walking with God. See how they treat family and friends, their fellow workers and neighbors. These can testify as to their character, and not just their reputation at large.

I have known very Godly, and very ungodly leaders who showed their fangs only in private. Do not be like the congregation that hired a mass murderer to oversee them. He was caught only after he began taunting police officers from a church computer. That is an extreme example, but it is inevitable that a group moves further away from Christian orthodoxy, unless we continue to choose governing members who act justly, love mercy, and who walk humbly with the risen Jesus Christ.

Straighten out pagans?

One of my wife's coworkers was surprised that I am friends with a person who has a lifestyle that is not Christian at all. She stated that it was strange since I am a conservative. But I am not a conservative, nor am I a liberal. I am a historic Christian, and within American culture sometimes that is considered conservative/reactionary, and sometimes liberal/radical. I am not placed on this earth to get people to change their lifestyles, but to point them to Jesus Christ. Then the Holy Spirit will change their ways when they need to be changed.

If I talk them into improving morally or changing some behavior, so what? They would then be no better off than the upright conservative types who are not drawn supernaturally to follow Jesus Christ as God and Lord. Then we would just have more Pharisees who were strict conservatives but unconverted, are arrogant and feeling superior to the liars and prostitutes and thieves, etc.

I encourage those close to me to be ethical, of course. But I tried and certainly hoped to point them to, "the Lamb of God, who takes away the sins of the world." We who are Christians are not called to make pagans straighten up, or those of other religions either. We have laws based on biblical teachings, for the most part, to encourage honesty and to punish dishonesty, and to otherwise support the good and to oppose what the Bible calls bad. These general principles are usually also upheld by others of different religions or those of no religion. Voltaire, the famous French atheist, preferred that his wife be Christian for she was more likely to be faithful to him, and he preferred his staff to be Christian for at least he knew that they would then be encouraged to be honest and hardworking and otherwise trustworthy.

But as tempting as it sometimes is, I very rarely try to straighten anyone out. If the Holy Spirit does not convict a person of sin, I have found that I only irritate the person who then becomes more emotionally wedded to whatever sin I oppose. So, I generally get along with pagans better than I do among Christians. That is because when I preach, I encourage Godliness and I preach against what the Bible calls sin. Those Christians who want to get closer to God welcome such remarks, while those who want to keep doing the opposite of whatever the New Testament teaches, probably get offended.

Why bother? Well, personally I could not care less what others do as long as they do no harm to me. But God has taught certain attitudes and behaviors are good and helpful while others are evil and unhelpful. Even when I cannot understand why, or even when such teachings contradict my own personal preferences, I am bound to preach the Word of God, not my feelings or my logic. But I am confident that on occasion I have substituted my own opinions in sermons and conversations alike. One preacher on the radio (Steve Brown), claims to be wrong about half the time. I think he is joking about the percentage, but the fact that he concedes to be wrong any time about anything, even in theory, is refreshing.

I do not doubt that sometimes I need to be more direct and confrontational with people, but since I tend to be that way, I consciously try to avoid that. We can all rationalize being quiet when we should speak out against wrong and speaking out when we should be quiet. May God help us have balance that honors him best. Either way, I am convinced that the first priority is to point others to Jesus Christ, who takes away the sins of the world, and not to rant to them about how terrible their sins are.

Rebellion is as the sin of witchcraft.

If a witch moved next door, many of us would be horrified. But the Bible teaches that rebellion is as the sin of witchcraft (1 Samuel 15:23). Are we as horrified of or own sins? No, and it is only because of our great wickedness that we consider witchcraft to be much worse than our sins of worry, complaining, impatience, rudeness, selfishness, lack of hospitality, etc.

Unless the Holy Spirit moves us deeply when we read the Bible he inspired, we become immune to what He teaches, seeing only where our spouse or children or neighbors need to repent and to walk humbly with God. Just because we do not murder or steal, we are tempted to feel that the Bible is not calling us to holiness, but to smugness and self-righteousness! But it is not doing that at all. Jesus said that the prostitutes and others who do what society considers outrageous will enter heaven before many in evangelical churches (my paraphrase).

It is a serious matter to deny in practice what we profess in theory. We have sniggered long enough at theological liberals who do not believe the supernatural elements of the Bible, because when we do the opposite of what the Bible clearly teaches and then pretend to be walking with the risen Jesus Christ, we are either void of the Holy Spirit (Jude 1:19) or we are deliberately rebelling against God the Holy Spirit. God is not mocked-we will reap what we sow. My parents were wonderful and Godly people, loving to me and my brother, and good to everyone. I am very thankful for them and sincerely doubt that I am as good a Christian as they were. I am concerned not to pass on to my children anything but pure Godliness, and I am sobered by the realization that my parents were great, and still not perfect. So, we all need to pray for layer after layer of repentance in order to hand down a holy legacy.

God calls us to be perfect. Is that our goal, or is it to compare ourselves favorably to our spouse or neighbor and then to congratulate ourselves that at least we are not as crabby or selfish or unkind as he or she is? Perhaps we are not, but our standard is not to be our spouse or King Saul, but Jesus Christ.

King Saul ruled Israel for forty years and was a good king by pagan comparison. But he grew more and more full of himself instead of more dependent on God. He not only did the opposite of what God told him through Samuel the prophet, but he lied and claimed that he did obey God. When he was confronted by Samuel, he finally admitted his sin, but then made excuses for it. That is when Samuel states that to obey God is better than to offer sacrifice of any kind, and that rebellion against the clear teaching of God is as bad as the sin of witchcraft/divination.

Are we any different from Saul? The Bible clearly says do not worry, so do we worry and then explain how intelligent it is to worry and how we have the right to do that, or to do anything else clearly called sin by the Holy Spirit who inspired the Bible? Jesus says, "Why do you call me 'Lord, Lord' and do not do what I tell you?" Even the most holy of Christians will be rebellious in some situations. May God convict us speedily and deeply of such sin, so that we do minimal damage before we again decide to begin to act justly and to love mercy and to walk humbly with God.

God did not blame the plight of the ancient Israelites on their pagan neighbors, but on their own sins. Today, we Christians like to think we are cornered by secularists and humanists, and in the recent past the communists and the fascists, but in fact it is our own rebellion against God that has sown the seeds of our own opposition. It is our own refusal to humble ourselves before God and to repent daily of our sins that weaken the influence of God in our families and in our society as a whole. May God help us to see not only murder and theft as terrible, but also worry and complaining and impatience and unkindness and other sins to be as wicked in his eyes as witchcraft/divination.

Amsterdam was good preparation for pastoring.

Working in Amsterdam, the drug, prostitution, and child pornography capital of Europe, was good preparation for pastoring churches when I rededicated my life to Jesus Christ. At one congregation, for example, an elder abandoned his wife and four children to have a sex change operation and ran off with another man. A church youth group met regularly on the steps of another church to smoke marijuana, and the Sunday school superintendent lived with a man unmarried. In my years of pastoring, I discovered only one thing that shocked me. That was when I would discover that a parishioner had a burden for the salvation of his or her children. Such folks lived Godly lives for they knew that God promises to answer only the prayers of the righteous (James 5:16). It may have been a church leader or not, but it was pleasing to God when a person would request prayer for a precious son or daughter to be converted or to be a more dedicated Christian. Especially when a pastor is well known to support evangelism, as I did, it is relatively easy to share such concerns.

As parents, we are to check ourselves occasionally to see if there is anything in us that is preventing those we love from developing in the faith. Maybe we need to ask forgiveness, to listen more, or to be more generous, or to quit doing something. It is not only the clear evil that we do that harms us and others, but also the trivial pursuits that crowd out the good and the righteous. Does what we say or do or think bring us closer to God? A better person? Smarter? If not, why do we waste our time?

We may need to look at what is going on in the culture, and when we do I hope we spend much of our time wondering and discussing what God is doing. He is moving and doing great things, and dedicated Christians are multiplying over the rest of the world. Barna research shows that overall (thank God for exceptions) the American churches are losing members and not keeping pace with the population growth, year by year. It is our responsibility to put into leadership dedicated Christians instead of child molesters, servants instead of bullies, and people who stand for what is right and against what is wrong. Even in the denominations that are run from the top down, local congregations may have much to say about those who are supported for leadership.

It is not enough to be sweet and polite in the Lord's work with people. It is necessary to want to please Jesus Christ above ourselves and above others, along with at least a few abilities in teaching, and so forth. Are Godly traits so difficult to discern? If so, please excuse yourself from committees that elevate those who will either advance or harm the cause of Jesus Christ.

Weddings

Weddings can be an early taste of bliss or disaster. The first wedding I conducted was set for ten in the morning. Friends came over from a nearby hospital during their morning break, but there was no bride. They returned during their lunch break, but the bride was yet to appear. Finally, after one in the afternoon, she appeared, and the wedding took place.

Yes, they had both received counseling. Yes, I had called to check on her, and she said her dress kept falling apart. Two hours after my call, she appeared. No, she did not have over a mile to the church, nor were there blizzards or other complications.

I was a bit annoyed, but I had several good conversations. The groom had the most difficult part. I joked that if he could get past this problem, the rest of the marriage would be easy.

The next wedding held out more hope. Although neither the bride nor the groom spoke any English basically, the sister of the bride did. Also, she assured me what a dedicated Christian her sister was, and how they were meant for each other. When they did not seem interested in going over the standard questions, I hoped it was because of the language barrier, so I did not grill them thoroughly, because I trusted her sister. One week later, the bride ran off with another man.

Lateness at weddings was so frequent that I contemplated requiring a $100 deposit, to be returned if the couple was no more than thirty minutes late. One time I warned the couple that if they were over 30 minutes late, I would leave. They were indeed over thirty minutes tardy, so I went home. Once there I reflected on how I had not made alternative plans. I also considered what a wonderful and deeply dedicated Christian the mother of the bride was. I thought they had learned their lesson, so I returned to the church. They showed up about twenty minutes later.

Between occurrences like the above, and squabbles over who sits where and who wears what and who speaks to whom, it should shock no one that some ministers prefer funerals to weddings. But over the years, weddings have become somewhat safer for ministers. An Anglican friend told me that when ministers were in the habit of asking, "If anyone has an objection, speak now or forever hold your peace," one man loudly said that he had an objection. "Well, come up here and tell me what it is," my friend instructed. He deemed it an unworthy objection, and the wedding continued.

Many weddings I did were deeply moving in positive ways, but the marriage is much more important than the wedding. According to the book *Fighting For Your Marriage*, how a couple works out differences is a much better indication of the success of the marriage than how they met, how long they knew each other, or how much they loved each other when they married. If the couple obeys 1 Corinthians 13 (love is patient, kind, unselfish ...), they will have a foretaste of heaven. Otherwise, they will have a foretaste of hell, even if the wedding goes off without a hitch.

Where "hypocrites tremble and sinners get terrified."

Do we want a church where "hypocrites tremble and sinners get terrified?" Rev. Zac Poonen, a pastor In Bangalore, India, asks this question. Or do we want a church where Ananias and Sapphira die of old age, after being church leaders for many years? Acts 5 records that the two were both struck dead in the Jerusalem church service, after pretending to be more holy than they really were. When they presented their money and were asked if that was a full amount, they answered yes but lied.

Hebrews says, "God is a consuming fire." If he is not in church services in the power of the Holy Spirit through brokenness and repentance, then such folks as Ananias and Sapphira become emboldened and eventually take over.

A mantra of, "God is love," is not enough. God is true and positive love, which means He is against all sin that harms us. If I say that I love my children but allow them to play with scorpions, that may be sentimental nonsense, but it is definitely not love.

If we are not convicted of our sins when we go to church, we can never enter the peace and joy God promises for those who love and obey him. Few Christians have an idea of the depth of love God has for us, and how much He hates the sin that destroys us. God is holy, and I hope we much prefer our families and friends be holy than happy, for without holiness, any happiness we have is shallow at best, and deceptively very harmful at worst.

A church where hypocrites are comfortable and where sinners who continue in whatever the Bible calls sin, are praised, will be just a social center at best. Soon even then, sins will pile up to make the place miserable for all. To speak of honor among any who value what the Bible does not value, is not wise. Would Ananias and Sapphira be welcomed as leaders in our church? Do we have the discernment, and do we care enough to value holiness, first of all in ourselves and next in those we place above us in leadership?

If you think so, so did the congregation that elected the Green River murderer as leader of their congregation. He had murdered about forty women in the northwest of the USA and had not been found. But he began to taunt the police and they traced his insults to a computer in the church where he was the president. He had not repented of his sins at all and felt at home there since "love" was stressed, and repentance and holiness were ignored so much that was comfortable there. He fit well in that congregation because he was among others who grieved and quenched the Holy Spirit. We can be certain that was the case, or they would never have elected such a criminal in the first place. May God help us to humble ourselves before the living God, so that we welcome trembling when we are hypocrites, and welcome the terror of the Lord when we are choosing to drift away from him and his holy ways.

Trust that the Holy Spirit can break through.

My mom looked at me sadly and said, "I am sorry you ever went to university." Her objection was not really to higher education, but because I showed absolutely no interest in living for Jesus Christ. She assumed that education had seduced me but in fact it was my own heart that had drifted away from Christianity. I said nothing because I had no interest in participating in such a discussion. Nor did I feel guilt of any sort at the time.

I was wrong. The Holy Spirit who came to dwell within me at age nine was dormant for many years. Only after ten car wrecks did I begin to think about God and what he wanted me to be and to do. I returned to follow Jesus Christ around age twenty-five, and I am sure the Godly prayers of my parents made a difference. James 5:26 promises that the prayer of a righteous man availeth much, or is powerful and effective. I thank God for parents who kept being faithful when I was not!

I have pondered often and much about a black spiritual (also sung by the rock group, The Rolling Stones) that I love dearly, called, "You got to Move." It goes like this. "He stayed in the fish, he stayed for days. He didn't eat, but he sure pray. And when the Lord got ready, Old Jonah moved.

You got to move. You got to move. You got to move. You got to move. When the Lord gets ready, you got to move.

You may be high. You may be low. You may be rich. Or you may be poor. But when the Lord gets ready, you got to move."

If we have children or grandchildren, we can be certain that they will not always follow the Lord or care what pleases Him. It is very painful at such times, because if we are loving and obeying Jesus Christ, great barriers will come between us. When that happens, pray that we repent and walk humbly with the risen Jesus Christ. Then He will give us the attitudes and words He wants us to have with them, and everyone else. We cannot manipulate the will of another person, nor should we try. Maybe the Holy Spirit will not draw them back until they have had certain experiences in order to better evangelize later. Conviction of sin is the supernatural work of the Holy Spirit, as John 16 assures us. Even though we may have no concern whatsoever about what others think, as I was for many years, He can still break through to us. As the black spiritual puts it so well, “When the Lord gets ready, you got to move.”

Impressions of New York City

I noticed that when someone walks toward you smiling in New York City, it means one of three things. Either the person is about to ask you for money, or about to kill you, or they are from the South. Yesterday a guy got on the subway approaching me, smiling. He was from Birmingham, Alabama. His stepson had an operation here to give part of his liver to his sister. The operation was successful.

So, there are many wonderful things about New York City, including great hospitals. The Alabama guy was on his way to an Italian festival in Lower Manhattan. Over 300 languages are spoken, so you have a good chance to fit in, no matter how strange others see you to be. Almost every weekend there is a parade of some sort, and thousands just ran the New York City marathon.

There are some very Godly churches here, such as Messiah's Reformed Fellowship (where we go), Calvery Baptist, Redeemer Presbyterian, and Brooklyn Tabernacle. My wife is Russian, so for orthodox Easter we went to Saint Nicholas Cathedral, on the Upper East Side. I noticed a guy standing near me (almost all stand for the whole service) who looked like a hit man for the Russian mafia. Near the end of the service, I glanced in his direction and saw tears flowing down his face like a river. I am 100 percent certain that he was not trying to impress me.

The living God/the Triune God, is at work in this city. There is very little cultural Christianity, as was the case in the South when I was growing up. Most who were not supernaturally converted to follow Jesus Christ as God and Lord abandoned church as soon as they left home. It happened here about a generation earlier. Huge church buildings on almost every block are mostly empty, and new sections such as Hudson Yards have no church buildings planned, as far as I can see. The same is true in Montreal and Toronto (where I pastored) and in Europe where churches are dying and being replaced by mosques.

We can blame the atheists who attacked Christianity to achieve paradise, and instead cleared a site for Islam. Or we can blame unconverted ministers, whom Saint Paul and Gilbert Tennant, who began Princeton, warned us about. But I blame the conservatives, who for the most part, knew the truth, but substituted a den of thieves for a house of prayer. With rare exceptions, eloquence and entertainment were preferred to preaching in the power of the Holy Spirit. New York City, the South, Paris, São Paulo, Delhi, Lagos, etc., do not need a renewal of churchianity, but supernaturally converted ministers and laity, who live holy lives.

The decline of Europe and the West

In 1950, one third of the world was Caucasian, by 1985 it was down to fifteen percent, and by 2020 the estimates are six to ten percent. Europeans and European descendants developed modern technology first, and not only conquered smallpox and more but invented contraception. My father was one of eleven children, raised on a tenant farm in east Tennessee, USA. He had two sons, and neither of us have biological children. Many of my friends have no biological children either, and that is duplicated among Europeans everywhere.

So, the future will definitely include fewer Europeans. So what? It means religiously, culturally, politically, psychologically, and probably financially, Europeans and their descendants will decrease in influence. Just recently, for example, the United Methodist Church voted to keep biblical standards regarding homosexuality. Although a majority of whites voted to bless and to encourage homosexual marriage and ordination, delegates from Africa and South America prevailed by sheer numbers.

For several decades now, churches in the West have been dying, for the most part. For example, by 2019, 500 churches in London were closed, while 423 mosques were opened. Meanwhile, revivals and supernatural conversions to Christ have marked China, Pakistan, Africa, and South America, etc. God bless them. May they not repeat our sins.

European materialism and hedonism has sown the seeds of our demise. If God wants to wipe out all the blonds and redheads and blue or green eyes, there will be less diversity, but in that case, I say, blessed be the name of the Lord. It is not the will of God that a type of hair or skin color be glorified, but that Jesus Christ who is God the eternal Son, be glorified.

We in the West have had very Godly and brilliant theologians (Calvin, Wesley, Spurgeon, etc.). In the future we can expect Europe to be more of a wasteland, barring a major revival. Let us not be too proud to accept Godly preaching from any culture. I saw recently that a seminary in the South from a historically biblical denomination wants to hire new faculty and said only minorities can apply. But people sin very much against God when they reject the Lord's anointed in favor of a particular color or background. Yes, Europeans and European descendants have elevated and revered many unconverted or backsliders to lead them. May God help the rest of the world to do better.

Predestination or not?

Why do two people go to the same church, hear the same sermons and hymns, and are sometimes even twins, and one becomes Christian while the other does not? Why does the same sermon or song (for example," ... for thee all the follies of sin I resign...) bring tears of sincere repentance to one, while another giggles or daydreams or plots evil?

Christians have historically emphasized the personal responsibility of the individual, or the sovereignty of God. But the Bible teaches both—that we are completely responsible for actions, and that God reigns. That seems contradictory to our finite minds because we can understand only what little of the mind of God that he chooses to reveal to us.

On the one hand, we are all clearly responsible to repent of our sins, to give our lives to Jesus Christ, and then to follow his teachings. On the other hand, God has all power, he opens and no one can shut, and he takes the initiative about how much and how to influence us. When we go to the extreme of human responsibility, we try to manipulate conversions by using emotion or mass psychology. We may think that if we just work hard enough, sing sixteen verses of "Just as I am," and plead enough, the resistance of the will can be broken.

Conversely, Presbyterians and others sometimes took the view that since God is sovereign, he will bring folks to him without our prayers, or personal testimonies or appeals for conversions. This genteel "wait and see" approach kills missions and ensures that very few children of such persons will become followers of Jesus Christ at all. Church growth statistics bear out this observation.

As contradictory as it seems to our limited minds, God wants us to trust that he has all power, does what he wants to do, and he wants to work through Christians to make disciples (Matthew 28:..go and make disciples). God chooses to work through the prayers of righteous people, and Godly examples and conversations to turn others to himself. We are commanded to be holy, to pray, and to work for the salvation of those lost without Christ.

Just before I went to seminary, I asked Dr. Ferguson (a very Godly Scot who was pastor of Cedar Springs and First Presbyterian Church, Knoxville, Tennessee) how we can reconcile God's sovereignty and our responsibility. He graciously discussed the matter and gave an illustration. It was like looking from the outside at a house, he continued, and seeing above the door verse 22:17 of Revelation, "Whosoever will, let him drink of the water of life freely." Then once you enter the house you see inside the verse that says your name was written in the Lamb's book of life before the foundation of the world. I am not totally satisfied with this, but I cannot fetch a better illustration.

Some understand this as predestination while others see it as teaching merely the foreknowledge of God. But it is clear from the Bible that Christians are to present to all the offer of salvation, be holy, and pray that God the Father draw individuals to his Son Jesus Christ. That is certainly our responsibility, and no one can know how strongly God initiates supernatural drawing in one person or another, or why. But we can rest assured that God will live up to his promises to be loving and just- whether he fits our theology or not!

Did man invent God?

Are you aware that many feel that God is just the result of our ideas? According to this theory, one group of ignorant people developed one idea in one place, another gullible bunch concocted a system of beliefs in another locale, and that is how the notion of God came about. Not a few in the churches hold such a view. But the many legends of good conquering evil, the need for forgiveness, and peace with a higher power, came from real historical events.

The truth was perverted when the German philosopher Schopenhauer taught that our true identity is in our identity and unity with all life. But our true identity is to have union with the risen Jesus, through whom and for whom all was created. Although Jesus Christ takes away our sins when we ask him to forgive us, and then give our lives to him, that is considered to be a legend by many. Dashing through fires of burning bales of hay is another way of cleansing us of our sins in one part of the world, carrying a huge rock around a pile of prayer stones three times counterclockwise is believed to free a person of guilt in another setting.

Pilgrimages, amulets worn, words chanted over and over, can all be sincere attempts to be friends with God. I remember in the past some carried a rabbit's foot or put a horseshoe above a door to try to bring them good luck—the favor of whatever power was higher than they were. The fact that there are so many varied attempts to placate a higher power convinces some that all thoughts of a higher power are bogus. Others say that no one can be certain of divine truth.

I appreciate more and more Francis Shaeffer, who noted that it is possible to know true truth, without knowing it exhaustively. Bombastic nonsense proclaiming to know how others should conduct every detail in their daily lives, or exactly how the world will end, has understandably caused many to doubt that it is possible to really know anything for certain. Yet we are to examine truth claims, to throw out those that are suspect, and to accept whatever has historical basis. Spiritual reality can spring from this. Jesus Christ lived, and died on the cross, as his enemies as well as friends taught. He rose again from the dead, because nothing less than an empty tomb would have kept the Romans and the Jews from laughing the claims of the resurrection away from potential converts.

They would gladly have shown that the followers of Jesus were a group of ignorant rabble who grabbed at psychological straws to bolster their weak and feeble emotional needs, except for the fact that Jesus rose from the dead.

Fortunately, among many in the churches who see Christianity as merely a social club where the supernatural is spoken of with their fingers crossed behind their backs, there are also many who have been transformed to follow Jesus Christ as God and Lord. As a matter of fact, people of integrity from all denominations have met this historic person and live for him.

Shame

"I haven't been ashamed since I was twelve years old," said a character in a Batman series movie. I understand. I could also say that about myself for several years. But it is nothing to brag about or to emulate.

To be without shame at least sometimes is the situation described in the Bible in 1 Timothy 4:2 ... having their conscience seared with a hot iron. And an Old Testament passage talks of those who do not know how to blush, describing people like the "Gotham" character. Is he a role model for our children? It is a very dangerous position to be in when we parade and celebrate our sins instead of confessing and turning from whatever the Bible calls sin. When sin is considered cool, and when what the Holy Spirit inspired Bible teaches is called uncool, we have embraced demons.

True guilt is to be embraced and valued highly, for it opens the door to repentance and salvation and holiness, through Jesus Christ. On the other hand, we should refuse to be ashamed because we don't fit into some cultural mold or expectations from someone else. Having a new car or trendy clothes may or may not be okay for us, because it depends on the path God has called us to pursue.

Nor should we accept condemnation from anyone because we are different. I remember a beauty contest winner declared that she won because she had a heritage of mixed race. That is as bad as an Asian winning such a competition and bragging it was because she had no European or African blood.

Whatever our heritage is, it is nothing to be ashamed of, nor our gift mix nor our limitations either. But I hope that I and each of us will be quickly and deeply ashamed when we do not act justly and love mercy and walk humbly with the living God. No one in the history of the world has done that naturally, so we need supernatural help in order to even want to do that! Our culture mocks shame regarding sin, more and more. But hopefully we will value the praise of God more than the praise of men and women and are ashamed only when we do not live for him.

God has no beginning.

Johnny Cash's voice beckons escorts to take him to Heavan in the song "Angel Band." Where did songwriter Ralph Stanley get such a notion? Well, those who follow Jesus Christ had near death experiences similar to that throughout history. Several spoke of angels drawing near them at such a time, especially before the advent of pain killing drugs.

Pastors see a fair amount of death and dying, and those I talked with much prefer funerals to weddings, especially when the weddings are elaborate. This is because weddings are often trivialized by discussions of how fast to trot down the aisle or who holds what flowers and so forth. Funerals, however, normally bring our far more respectful and civil behavior from folks. Everyone realizes it is easier to get a divorce than to raise the dead! Also, the contemplation of death tends to make us ponder if we are ready or not, and even the most hardened against the gospel wonder if the claims of Jesus might just be true. Those of us who accept the Bible as the word of God see life as linear and not cyclical- that history has a beginning and an end, and that we will not be recycled as either a higher or lower incarnation.

A man just told me that his parents only went to church for show, "like peacocks." He added that the gospel of Thomas and other writings were unfairly left out of the. Bible. I replied that ultimately one must rely on faith that God either inspired the Bible and those who compiled it, or he did not. Although Orthodox and Roman Catholics accept some books as belonging to the Old Testament (*Wisdom 1 and 2, Maccabees)* that Protestants reject, all agree on the New Testament books from Matthew through Revelation. The early church leaders were inspired by God and had no reason to include books such as Thomas that contradicted the canon.

These books teach that death for followers of Jesus Christ is not the end, but the beginning of a new and a much better life—one far superior than anyone can imagine.

"... we would rather be away from the body and at home with the Lord," wrote the apostle Paul about such individuals. It is not death that. Christians fear, but the process of dying or of leaving loved ones behind in various kinds of suffering and grief.

Our culture is for the most part very rich and seems to be heaven on earth. Unless we get a wasting sickness or emotional distress, few spend any time thinking of angel bands carting them off to glory. But although the average person has much more comfort than a king a few short years ago, at the same time God has put eternity in our hearts, says the writer of Ecclesiastes. Whatever else this means, we know that God has no beginning or end, that he invented time and is outside of time. And according to the Bible, we have no end either. For the past 1,000 years this has been the consensus of Europe because of the spread of Christianity. Our missionaries overcame the views of death offered by Druids, Vikings, Roman and Greek systems of belief. For quite a while historic Christian views of death have been challenged not only by other beliefs in Europe and among European descendants, but also in seminaries and in pulpits.

What can we do but pray to speak the truth and to speak it in love? In hospitals and in hospices and other institutions begun by Christians, it is increasingly problematic to say a good word about Jesus Christ as God. Even the most gentle and respectful conversation about Jesus Christ is often frowned upon. At times this could be because of insensitive and obnoxious witness by Christians, while on other occasions it is because of opposition to the claims Jesus Christ made about himself. Yet Jesus overcame death in history, and for his followers, death means, "My triumph has begun."

God is inclusive of all being?

Inclusive of all being? One prominent theologian writes that the highest stage of faith is to be "inclusive of all being." This is a phrase that is seldom quoted, but the idea is often accepted today. All this may sound progressive and positive, until we consider that "all being" includes love/hatred, honesty/dishonesty, kindness/cruelty, humility/arrogance, and other contradictions. To believe that we should accept what the Holy Spirit inspired Bible calls evil, is to show affinity with the Swiss psychoanalyst Carl Jung. He taught that our subconscious includes good and bad, and this is really God. So God, according to Jung, is both good and bad. In other words, God is considered to be inclusive of all being.

On the other hand, the Bible says in 1 John 1:5 that "God is light, and in him is no darkness at all." Other verses affirm that God is wholly and completely good and perfect. Aside from contradicting the Bible, there are other problems inherent in the view that the highest form of faith is to be "inclusive of all being."

If whatever exists is God, there is no valid basis for praising or blaming anyone for anything. With that theory, love and hatred, honesty and dishonesty, impatience and unkindness and rudeness and refusing to forgive are all different aspects of God. Our choices are merely cultural or temperamental, and equally pleasing to God, according to this teaching. Then those who do what the Bible calls righteous are never to be appreciated or praised, because if they wanted to murder or lie or steal, such choices would be equally valid. How bizarre it is that those who teach that God approves of everything usually want others to be kind and fair. That is plain selfish and unrealistic, because as Dostoyevsky understood, if there is no God of the Bible then anything is permissible.

If you were alone in a dark alley and saw five burly men coming toward you, would you prefer they thought God was "inclusive of all being," or would you prefer they had just come from a Bible study where they learned that God said to be holy and to exclude evil in their lives? The highest form of faith is not to be "inclusive of all being," as wonderful as that may sound at first. The highest form of faith is to love and to obey Jesus Christ, whom the Bible calls the name above all names. Then when others meet us in a dark alley, they will not need to worry!

God loves the "outcast."

He was a tall skinny guy from Greene County, Tennessee. At first, he was scary for us children to see, because he drooled constantly and slurred all his words. He also limped when he walked. But my father has a habit of making friends with Godly people, so only a few minutes after hearing him talk, I had a deep respect and admiration for him.

He was called by God to preach the gospel, and he was a wonderful man. I do not think he ever pastored, but I do know he was invited to preach at several churches. He would keep his appointments by hitchhiking to the services and would arrive on time.

Years after my father died, I would see the man selling pencils on the streets of Rogersville or Greeneville. I would go up to him, buy a few, and tell him I was Ray Marshall's boy. He would give a hoarse laugh—full of love for my father and joy for their fellowship in the faith.

Corrie Ten Boom (she and her Dutch family hid Jews from the Nazis and were imprisoned for their kindness) worked with mentally delayed children before World War 2. When the Nazis found out what she did, they mocked her for wasting her time. She answered that perhaps they were more loved by God than so called "normal" people.

It seems that outcasts bear a heavy burden in any society, but we are all outcasts at one time or another. We are too young, or too old and full of sickness and loneliness, too rich or too poor, or too something else to fit in with those around us at a particular time or place. I remember seeing a photograph of a billionaire in Texas named Marshall (a distant relative, I am convinced), who seemed to be drooling as much as the friend of my father did. He was about ninety-three, and had just married Anna Smith, a beautiful woman of about twenty-three. He died shortly afterwards, and the ex-wife and his children are having a big squabble over the inheritance (no, I am not in the running).

The billionaire was an outcast to his family at the end, or they would have settled everything peacefully beforehand. So I guess the biggest question is, "Who considers us an outcast?" Perhaps some whose opinion we value will see us as an outcast intellectually, physically, spiritually, emotionally, or financially. Perhaps there is nothing at all we can do about that.

But it is important that we are not among those of whom Jesus will say, "Depart from me, ye that work iniquity, I never knew you." He calls us to have friendship with him, the best friendship anyone can possibly have. My father's friend went to the Lord for refuge, and he showed less bitterness or self-pity than most so called "normal" folks. He was definitely not an outcast in God's eyes. That is all that matters, not only in the long run, but also in the short run.

God and evil both exist.

Cormac McCarthy is a writer who grew up in Knoxville, Tennessee. He is an atheist as far as I know but has a somewhat Christian view of evil. In his novel *All the Pretty Horses* a Mexican prisoner says, "Americans have ideas that are not so practical. They think that there are good and bad things. They are very superstitious, you know. It is the superstition of a godless people....evil is a true thing in Mexico. It goes about on its own legs. Maybe someday it will come to visit you."

In his film "No Country for Old Men," McCarthy shows evil as a living person, bringing havoc to many. Yet to hordes of Americans, neither God nor evil seems real. That includes several churchgoers. Churches are usually where we hear eloquent sermons, see ritual or hysteria, or social community. But Jesus says, "My house shall be called a house of prayer." It is to be a place where we meet unmistakably with the living God, in other words, to know and then to do his will.

As we do that, we see the need to repent of the evil in our own hearts, and then to bring the light of Christ to others around us. When we do this, we are confronted not just by evil in a general sense, but by the evil one called Satan. For most of us, however, good and bad are merely our own personal preferences. Fewer and fewer Americans have the Christian world view that the Triune God exists and has given his teachings about what is righteous and what is sinful. Few accept that truth is real, even though we cannot know it exhaustively, as Francis Schaefer noted.

John Calvin taught, "It is the height of evil when the sinner is so completely void of shame that he is not only pleased with his own vices (vices as described by the Bible), and will not tolerate their condemnation, but also encourages them in others by his comment and approval." Yet I have in mind, as Cormac McCarthy does, something even more sinister than that. Recently a small boy was terrorized almost every night by seeing what he thought was a man standing at a particular spot in in his room. A minister came and prayed in the name of Jesus Christ, commanding all evil spirits to leave. They did, and the boy had only a slight occurrence once after that. Such things have happened throughout history, as Roman Catholics and Orthodox as well as Protestants (minus the holy water and vestments and crosses and other rituals) attest.

The Bible teaches that although God has all power, in his sovereignty he allowed the angel Lucifer to rebel, and to take one third of the angels with him against God. Lucifer became known as Satan, or the devil. And his followers are called evil spirits. It is curious to me that McCarthy has even the slightest acquaintance with them because, speaking personally, when I held hands with the devil for several years, I was blissfully unaware of Satan or his minions. It was only after I repented and began to walk with God again that I encountered demonic opposition from time to time. Until then I believed the Bible when it spoke of evil, but I had no personal conscious interaction while I was walking on the wild side.

But the good news is that Jesus has all power in heaven and in earth. When we are supernaturally drawn to become one of his followers, we become his friend and are under his protection. This does not mean we are then immune to troubles of various sorts. But it does mean that we can walk humbly and peacefully with him, with his words and attitudes and actions, throughout our life. No evil person or evil spirit or difficult circumstance can keep us from doing that.

So, is Jesus Christ really God?

Is Jesus Christ truly God? I am 100 percent convinced he is, yet many disagree. Even in the churches several doubt or flatly deny the deity of Jesus when they get open and honest. So here is some evidence for the historic Christian view.

After the resurrection, Thomas was told by the risen Jesus to stick his hand in his side and Thomas answered in John 20:28..."My Lord and my God." Lord is from the Greek word Kyrios, which is YHWH in Hebrew. God is Theos in Greek and Elohim in Hebrew. So, there is no question he was calling Jesus God. Did Jesus correct him, and say he was only a prophet? No. He said in verse 29, "Have you believed because you have seen me? Blessed are those who have not seen and yet have believed."

In John 10:30 Jesus says, "I and the Father are one." No one else can truthfully say that. He is one with God the Father in being and essence, not just in purpose or goals. So that excludes him from being only a mere prophet. As C.S. Lewis pointed out, the claims of Jesus in the Bible make him either a liar, a lunatic, or God. It is impossible to be just a good prophet and not God.

In John 10:31-33 the Jews who heard him say, "I and the Father are one," wanted to stone him because they understood he made himself to be God, and they thought he was being blasphemous, since they did not see him as God. Do you not think that they understood Aramaic, the language of Jesus, much better than someone who comes along hundreds of years later and claims Jesus was saying here that he was merely a prophet?

Others feel that Jesus is only speaking metaphorically about being God, since in verses 34-36 Jesus points out that the judges were called gods, so why did his listeners claim he was blaspheming when he said he was the Son of God? But Jesus was using a common rabbinical method of arguing from the lesser to the greater. Since the judges were called gods because they had the word of God, how much more should they honor Jesus, who is the Word who became flesh (John 1:14), and is now standing in front of them?

John 17:5 says, "And now, Father, glorify me in your own presence with the glory that I had with you before the world existed ... you loved me before the foundation of the world." So, the Trinity was together in heaven before Jesus added human flesh to walk among us.

John 1:1 says, "In the beginning was the Word (Jesus), and the Word was with God (the Father), and the Word (Jesus) was God (the eternal second person of the Trinity)." John 1:14 says, "And the Word became flesh and dwelt among us." That is what Christmas is about, at least for Christians. God the Son limited himself to a human body for about thirty-three years. He voluntarily and temporarily gave up much of his glory. So he said in that situation, "My Father is greater than I." Does that not prove that God the Father is greater? No, because Jesus was at that time still in his human body with our limitations of pain, fatigue, hunger, etc.

In Matthew 28, we see Jesus was given all power in heaven and in earth. He shall judge the living and the dead at his return, and there is no other name under heaven by which we must be saved. So may we give Jesus his due, and worship him in spirit and in truth.

Seasonal songs

Are we celebrating Christmas by singing songs such as "Silent Night," or "Grandma Got Run Over by a Reindeer?" Depending on our grandma, we might celebrate by singing both with glee (in that case, we probably need to forgive grandma). But whatever generation we count ourselves to be in, I hope we get encouraged to be broken, repenting, and walking in the light of Jesus Christ. It is not important whether we achieved our goals as long as we are broken from our own sins of omission and commission.

In other words, we can all honestly say that we have failed to do all the good we should have done. Perhaps we should have given more money or visited more sick relatives or sad folks, etc. Or we might have sinned by actively treating someone with scorn or mockery, or insults or other sorts of abuse. "Vengeance is mine, I will repay," says the Lord, is one of my least favorite Bible verses.

But if we worship a god who caters to our every whim and who exists for our comfort and pleasure, we need only to look in the mirror to identify the god we serve. Such a god is an imaginary friend. But we all need to worship the Triune God of the universe, with all power and perfect love.

The historic resurrection of Jesus Christ, with all its evidence, helps us to acknowledge the babe in the manger as incarnate deity. If you can get peace and joy and meaning by singing silly holiday songs, have at it. But our sins are forgiven, and we have peace with the God of the universe, and we have eternal life, when we internalize the words of such carols as "Let every heart prepare him room, and heaven and nature sing."

I appreciate nature probably as much as anyone and love to hike the Great Smoky Mountains around my house in Tennessee. God made billions of flowers that only he ever sees, and when I view some on hikes, I am grateful. It is a great gift to be friends with the creator, and to be able to direct thanks to him. The Bible teaches that everything was made through him/Jesus Christ, and for him. If we wanted to reach ants, the best way would be to become an ant, with ant consciousness. And so, Jesus Christ, God the eternal Son, added a human body with our awareness and limitations, in addition to remaining God. Christians have disagreed exactly how the God nature and the human nature co-exist in the person of Jesus Christ, but all historic Christians accept that God the Son became flesh, was born in a manger, and walked among us.

I pastored in the Italian area of Toronto, and in many stores, I began to notice signs that said "Carne." When I looked in, I could see big slabs of meat hanging there. The incarnation means that God became meat or flesh, to dwell among us. Jesus grew in stature and in wisdom and became fully aware that he existed eternally before he was born on earth. He walked here as one of us, 100 percent human and 100 percent God, for about thirty-three years. He was crucified, buried, rose from the dead, returned to heaven, and will come again as the judge of all the earth. So, I hope the seasonally silly songs do not divert us from worshiping Jesus as God, either for the first time, or more deeply.

Feuerbach

Did you ever wonder why the University of Tennessee has a Department of Religion and not a Department of Theology? Almost all secular universities have studies of religion instead of studies of God (theology), because of the premise that God is an invention of mankind. Feuerbach, the German philosopher, said, "You are what you eat." Whatever we take in from our culture, in other words, is how God is conceived by people. God is a warrior in a harsh culture. God is therefore a nurturer in a more tranquil culture. But either way, God is seen to be only an extension of the minds of individuals.

On the other hand, Christian universities and seminaries traditionally have departments of theology to signify that God is the proper subject of study. God exists above all cultures and reveals himself and his teachings in the Bible. Therefore, learning in a Christian setting is based on the premise that we are to learn from God who has communicated clearly to us.

Yet Feuerbach claimed that the resurrection is merely the culmination of the wishes of people to transcend death. It is similar to other deities in different cultures. In each culture, God reflects that culture. In Northern European culture, God has blue eyes and blond hair, in African culture God is black, in Asian culture he looks Asian, and so on. God has been warped by each culture and by each person in his own image, and each Christian needs to beware of that. Indeed, the Bible warns us repeatedly against these tendencies. But in opposition to Feuerbach, the Bible claims to be inspired by God and to stand above all cultures and all individual preferences, instead of being "the dream of humankind."

What is concerning to me is the number of those in the churches who reflect the worldview of Feuerbach. A friend was at a conference using a bathroom stall, and he was shocked when he overheard ministers discussing how they did not believe in the resurrection. In public they would use the historic Christian terms but would mean the opposite. Yet those in the pews would often never know the difference. They might have been conservative, but so few cared about preaching in the power of the Holy Spirit, they opened the gate to wolves in sheep's clothing.

I also think clues about where the hearts of church leaders truly are will become apparent when evangelism is discussed. When one accepts the clear and repeated Biblical teaching that we are in radical need of repentance and salvation, this flies in the face of every culture. It is also objectionable to every individual who reads Paul in Romans 7, when he says, "nothing good dwells in me." Therefore, we have incredible need of God, not just to improve, but to quicken us with receiving the Holy Spirit.

We need a new heart, in other words, a heart of flesh instead of a heart of stone. We need, according to the Bible, to be supernaturally converted through receiving Jesus Christ as Savior and Lord. One who preaches and who believes this, will not always follow Jesus consistently (speaking for myself). But such a person knows the fallacy of the statement "the consciousness of God is nothing but the consciousness of the species." That is a very logical comment for one who has not yet met the risen Jesus Christ. And it is ridiculous to get mad at those who are dead (spiritually). When the Triune God is a reality in our lives, we have burdens that such folks also come into fellowship with the living God.

Repentance and holiness

I have a doctorate in church growth and pastored relatively small churches, while some others did not even go to seminary and pastor relatively large churches. I could join some in mainline denominations that talk about smaller groups having more quality, but I am kept from doing that by a story in Aesop's Fables. He told of a fox who saw some grapes that looked great, so he jumped and jumped but failed to grab any of them. Finally in disgust he walked away, muttering that they were probably sour anyway (hence the expression "sour grapes)."

More importantly, I have noticed congregations of all sizes that are dead spiritually, and congregations of all sizes that are alive spiritually. When a person has charm and intelligence and a good speaking ability, usually a church (or synagogue or mosque or business...) will grow. But as Christians I hope and pray that we grow in grace, or favor with the Triune God as the Bible commands, whatever else happens.

Then we will be effective witnesses for Jesus, whatever the sizes of our congregations are. As we grow in grace, we will be more kind, honest, faithful to our spouse, and hardworking people of integrity. Yet Gallup and other polls show the opposite is happening. Should we not be deeply concerned that whether we have a congregation of ten or 10,000, we are supernaturally converted and walking humbly with God? Yet that is rarely the emphasis in either mainline denominations, or independent growing church either. So, God and his call for repentance and holiness is not only dismissed by society in general, but by much of church culture also.

What can we do about this disrespect and trivialization of Christianity, except to search our hearts to make sure we are not a part of it, and to repent when we are? Recently I have become more and more convicted by the Holy Spirit of a sin of omission. It is something very difficult to do in my situation, and not really a part of my human nature to do. But that is an excellent way to know that God is with us and moving us in a specific direction, since his ways and thoughts are so much higher than our ways or thoughts. Otherwise, we would always be just following our own feelings or logic and claiming that God was guiding us. That happens frequently throughout history!

In the congregations of my childhood in east Tennessee, I recall with gratitude and awe how clearly and powerfully the Holy Spirit moved during sermons and other parts of the services. I was overjoyed at seminary to pore through the library and to see that was the norm throughout history among many kinds of denominations in many countries.

To be a part of that historic legitimate stream of Christianity we must humble ourselves, pray to remove all that is not from God in our lives, and to keep only that which is from God in our lives. Jesus Christ has proved that he deserves our all, our abandonment to him to do with us what he wills. We have no reason to fear doing that, since he is perfect love and has all power and all knowledge.

When we refuse to give him our all, we wound our family and others with relatively trivial pursuits and words and attitudes. How much better it is to be like the prophet Samuel, of whom the Bible says, "none of his words fell to the ground." None were wasted, in other words. Will we be remembered as such a person? I hope so.

In 1 Corinthians 2:4-5 Paul said, "My speech and my message were not in plausible words of wisdom, but in demonstration of the Spirit and of power, so that your faith might rest not on the wisdom of men but in the power of God." Do we want our loved ones to have the fake kind of faith that depends on our charm or experience or learning, or the legitimate faith based on the supernatural power of God? I pray for the kind of speech and proclamation Paul spoke about, for myself and for you.

God loves us?

A professor at the University of North Carolina published a book that teaches the problem of suffering drove him from being a fundamentalist, evangelical Christian, to being an agnostic. It was not just his own pain that bothered him, but the anguish of others. He looked at the standard defenses of God for allowing such torture and rejected them. I understand how he could do that. If we say people suffer because they do wrong, we can always see innocents who have as many or worse difficulties. My mother was very Godly, yet her cancer was probably as terrible as the concentration camps of the Nazis, or at least it certainly seemed that way.

If we claim that suffering is redemptive, we can see many who get bitter when they are deprived of happiness, and who attack those who had nothing to do with their situations caused by mean parents/neighbors, etc. Also, natural disasters kill millions, presumably the righteous along with the unrighteous. Certainty dictators of nations as well as individual thugs, cause evil that their victims did nothing to deserve.

The problem of pain and resurfaces in every generation, for as Ecclesiastes declares, “There is nothing new under the sun.” The English publisher Malcolm Muggeridge observed that there is nothing new, only old things happening to new people! And the prophet Job noted that the little ones of the wicked dance about with few cares, while the righteous suffer. The fact is, no one has more than a smattering of insight as to why anyone has suffering or joy, or whether we deserve either. Another fact is that all of us are dying, and after we die, I do not think it will matter to us a great deal whether we were murdered, or a tree fell on us, or that we died. And although the professor said he went from being Christian to agnostic (not knowing whether God exists or not), because he was bothered by suffering (everyone who ever lived can say the same), does not make his analysis a true view of reality.

From the Augustinian/Calvinistic view of salvation, which I hold both by theology and experience, once one is Christian, the individual cannot remove himself out of that group even by suicide. Therefore, I am convinced that the professor was either never really Christian, and that he gave merely an emotional or intellectual assent to God, or that he really is a Christian who is deeply struggling with how God can be both loving and all powerful and still allow suffering. To many, God is either loving and weak, or all powerful and mean to allow people to have deep pain. If we are honest, all Christians have these thoughts from time to time, that if God were truly good, he would fit our logic and feelings in difficult situations.

But the Bible teaches that God is both all-powerful and perfect love. This teaching is offensive to everyone sooner or later. Certainly, it seemed hateful to me in my relatively minor sufferings. Especially at those times I look at the cross.

Christianity is not a set of myths of fairy tales but is rooted in history that really happened. Jesus was murdered on the cross. And bodily rose from the dead. He suffered for our sins, the completely innocent lamb of God, died for the completely guilty. When we are supernaturally drawn by God the Father to accept his offer of salvation, we begin to follow Jesus Christ as God and Lord. Then the Holy Spirit dwells within us, to encourage and comfort us when we honor Jesus Christ, and to convict us when we do not (mainly through the Bible and never in contradiction to the Bible.

When we suffer (as people of every religion and no religion do), we can draw near to the Triune God, or rebel by beginning to trust our own opinion of what should happen, and when. I have done that more than a few times. But the Holy Spirit stays with the Christian to give us peace when we keep on obeying and worshipping Jesus Christ, and then ask for forgiveness when we do not. Ultimately, and sometimes the only way we can be sure that God loves us in particular circumstances, is because God the eternal Son Jesus Christ, died on the cross for us.

Christians should be thankful.

A student in Minnesota plotted to kill others at his school and was discovered and stopped before he could carry out his plans. A local official said, "Some would call them lucky, but I am sure that God protected them." Immediately after showing that segment, a news anchor said, "They were lucky, certainly." So, both were sure of opposite views!

There are problems with both world views. The problem with the Christian view is why do the righteous suffer? We understand when lazy thieves or murderers "get what they deserve." But when we believe the many clear and repeated verses that teach God reigns, and then see innocent children and adults shot and gassed or lose land or jobs through no fault of their own, it is hard to trust that God is good and kind. And when we ourselves have suffered, we have all resented that situation.

Yet we are called by God to "be holy." We are not called to be happy. Happiness without holiness is shallow at best, and very harmful at worst. As all things work together for good when we love God, even the happy times work against us to make us immune to friendship with God when we do not know him.

God promised through the prophet Micaiah that King Ahab would die in a certain battle. Even though the king disguised himself, toward the end of the conflict a soldier shot his arrow into the air without aiming, and it killed King Ahab. Even though it probably seemed like chance to the soldier, it was prophesied, and then fulfilled by one who was not conscious of doing the will of God.

For one who believes in chance or luck, the problems are magnified. Why praise or blame anyone for anything if all is chance? And if only some things are chance, which are which and how do we tell the difference? Why work or study hard if chance determines whether you get a job or not? But if God has all power in heaven and in earth, as Jesus states he has in Matthew, why do we bother to study or work either? It is because the Holy Spirit who inspired the Bible commands us to study to show ourselves approved by God, and says those who do not work should not eat (I am sure the sick are excepted).

Within his sovereignty, God has given us free will, and the responsibility to act justly, to love mercy, and to walk humbly with him. The teen in Minnesota who wanted to murder his classmates refused to do that. He consciously and intentionally planned to massacre innocent people who were defenseless. I am convinced that the town official who said that God protected them is correct.

Now why did God not protect the children in the state of Connecticut or Colorado or the Jews in Nazi Germany. Neither I nor anyone else knows for sure. I reiterate that God gives us free will, and we can use it to do great good or great evil. In everything, in the midst of any circumstances, Christians are to give thanks for our salvation, and then for using any and all situations to mold using into his image. God opens doors and no one can shut them, he sets one up and brings another one down. Blessed be the name of the Lord anyway, who truly reigns.

Carry the fire with you.

When it was time to preach, the minister announced in a fearful voice that he did not have the message. What an honest and brave and humble soul! I saw him take his Bible, walk over to another minister, and ask him if he had the message. He nodded his head to indicate no, and it was passed to another preacher who said the same. The third time the Bible was offered, a minister nodded yes, and he preached with power as the fire of the Holy Spirit fell in that place.

What would you or your pastor do in that situation? Would we have said words anyway if we were not conscious of the Holy Spirit resting upon us in power before we dared to speak in the name of the Lord? Or would the awe of God inspire us to find another who was anointed for that time and place?

John Wesley would not ask his lay preachers how large the crowds were, or how much money was raised when he met with them. No, he would ask, "Who of you is really alive to God, so as to carry fire with him wherever he goes?" Is that our concern? It was the concern of Saint Paul. He said he was determined not to know anything except Jesus Christ crucified. In other words, Paul was not interested in impressing people with his knowledge or experiences or human wisdom, but only in having words from God. We are commanded in the Bible to speak the very words of God (1 Peter 4:11). How much more important it is to do that from the pulpit than in everyday conversations! I cringe when I consider how sometimes I was concerned to impress with my intelligence or education or experiences. No doubt a few ignorant and silly folks may be awed if we have enough charm (or perhaps millions). But I hope and pray that we are determined to carry fire with us wherever we go- the fire of the Holy Spirit.

How do we do that? First of all, we must be supernaturally converted, drawn by the Holy Spirit to say Jesus is Lord/the one we worship and obey. Next, if we hope to be a preacher or pastor, we must be called by God to preach. All Christians are called to be faithful witnesses for Jesus Christ, to tell what he has done for us, and to encourage all to love and to live for him. But some are specifically set apart to preach the gospel. This is not a choice we make, but a supernatural drawing to do so. Everyone throughout history who has been impressed consciously by

God in this direction can say with Saint Paul, "Woe to me if I do not preach the gospel." The burden of the Lord is laid on some individuals to publicly proclaim the story of Jesus Christ and what that means for the listeners.

After salvation and a distinct/clear call to preach, in order to preach with the anointing of the Holy Spirit, the preacher must be holy. I know of no better way to encourage holiness than to quote the three questions an African evangelist would ask of those he met. "Are you broken? Are you repenting? Are you walking in the light?"

Psalms tells us that a broken and contrite heart will not be despised by God. All other kinds of hearts are despised! To be broken is to have Godly sorrow for all our sins—not just sins that are condemned by most pagans, but also rudeness, ingratitude, complaining, impatience, and unkindness ... for these rebellions are in the same category as witchcraft (1 Samuel 15:23).

Repenting means not only to be sorry for our sins, but to turn from them. We will be totally sanctified only when we die, but we are responsible before God to have layer after layer of repentance as we invite Jesus to control every area of our lives. As we become more aware of more areas we need to surrender to him, we are to renounce our own sovereignty in those compartments of time, money, daydreams ...

To walk in the light of Jesus Christ is to pray constantly for guidance, and that he encourages those hopes and plans and thoughts that are from him, and that he discourages those hopes and plans and thoughts that are not from him. By constant brokenness and constant repentance, we will be able to discern the light of Jesus Christ from the gaudy brilliance of our culture and personal preferences.

Exciting church services?

"Exciting" is a popular way to advertise church services so that outsiders will be attracted. I suppose that is preferable to bragging how boring churches are. But whether people jump up and down or bungee jump off balconies, is more of a cultural choice than anything taught by the Holy Spirit through the Bible. In Sweden I noticed even a Pentecostal service was calm, while Presbyterian churches in Brazil have more animated worship than is typical in the USA. When God is in the midst unmistakably, that is much more important, and I have seen that to be true in high liturgical churches where incense is flipped, as well as in more informal churches where people shout and dance about. The Bible teaches that Christians have this treasure (the Holy Spirit) in earthen vessels, so that the glory will go to God and not to us.

When the glory goes to God, then worship has reached the peak of significance, no matter how formal or informal the style is. God tells us that he draws near to those who have humble and contrite/repentant hearts. Arguments and insults toward those who like more quiet or loud services, detract from what is loved by God. We can have proud and self-serving motives with any form of worship—it can easily be "a form of worship denying the power thereof." Or we can draw near to God with sincerity and deep love and obedience in almost any type of worship. When we do that, we never have boredom. That is because we know that God has all power and is perfect love, and that he causes all things to work together for our good, as Romans 8:28 teaches.

Therefore, I hope we go to church to worship, to listen and to obey the voice of God, and not to be entertained. If others have great or mediocre music, eloquent or stammering preaching, I hope we still are not impressed unless the speaker is supernaturally converted, called by God to preach, and living a holy life so that the words are from God and with his attitudes. Otherwise, our souls are bleak and barren, even if we value being entertained for a few minutes with a shallow display of vanity. In that condition we will crave more and more amusements (a means not, and muse means to think) instead of welcoming the Holy Spirit shining on us to guide us into truth and away from any and all sin that harms us and others.

Plain unadorned Congregational churches in New England or Lutheran churches in Sweden or very elaborate Orthodox churches give no hint of whether the people meet to glorify Jesus Christ or not. Neither the outward appearances nor the method of worship make the hearts of the people open to say yes and amen to the will of God. Furthermore, even being surrounded by Godly people does not guarantee that we ourselves are Godly, and as soon as possible we may choose not to attend either a wild or a tame congregation.

The boy Samuel was raised by very excited priests. But they were evil (1 Samuel 8:1-3). Amazingly, he did choose to follow God, even before he had learned to recognize the voice of God. When God did speak the first time to Samuel, he assumed it was the evil high priest Eli. To his great credit Eli did not claim it was he, but he recommended to Samuel that if God spoke again to answer "Speak, for your servant hears."

Whether we prefer relatively rowdy or low-key worship services because of our personality and cultural backgrounds, I hope we earnestly and humbly pray as Samuel did, that he was a servant, and wanted to hear from God. And unlike the high priest Eli, I hope we pray that for ourselves at least several times daily.

Sins in public ministry?

Ministers who preach against sins and are discovered to be practicing the same sins are often in the news. Every minister has been guilty of this, although we are not all guilty of the same sins. The evangelist Billy Graham had the practice of praying each morning that God would help him to do nothing that day that would destroy his life's work. His was an honest prayer, and a good example for us all.

It is only by the great mercy of God that many of us with strong constitutions are not in jail for murder, or did not desert a military post because of cowardice, or steal because of greed, or have sex outside of marriage because of lust, etc. One cannot read the Bible without seeing that these and other sins are clearly and repeatedly condemned. So, when we do them, I hope we sincerely repent, and then pray to be holy, and neither excuse such behavior in ourselves nor support it in others.

But since we have all sinned, as the Bible states, should that keep us from a public ministry? Probably at least for a while, if the sins were public that brought dishonor to the name of Jesus Christ. Then if the individual has remorse and a change of behavior, in some cases the person should be reinstated. But even then, the public will continue to be distracted by memories of the rebellion against God, long after the sin is abandoned. So, I am sure it is far better for everyone when we preach the truth and then live it!

If the sins were private, or just in the mind, these are offensive to God also, and no excuse for them is acceptable to God either. But when the person is contrite and genuinely sorry and repents earnestly and truly wants to honor Jesus, what better person can represent Jesus Christ? Only the naive and those who have yet to be exposed to various temptations can say that they have never had a wide range of selfish and destructive thoughts and attitudes. Such folks then have only a limited range of sinful inclinations.

Jonathan Edwards, the president of Princeton who led the first great revival in the USA, wrote many times of his vileness before God, although he led a holy life. We can be certain of that, or he would not have been the catalyst for revival. Perhaps he was plagued by desires for revenge against those who tried to destroy him, although God says, "vengeance is mine, and I will repay." Or maybe he had yearnings for more status or money or health, etc.

It really does not matter, for as Saint Paul had his "thorn in the flesh," we all have to fight against internal urges that will destroy us if we give in to them. So even the most Godly people (Edwards) must repent a lot, or we will be counted by God as being among the most ungodly. Only Jesus Christ, both 100 percent God and 100 percent human, is exempt from the need for repentance.

The president of the National Association Of Evangelicals was recently found to be involved in an affair and removed. Did the majority who elected him pray until they knew he was God's choice? Or did he have other traits they valued more highly? Not long ago a minister of a mega church was accused of affairs with four different guys, after preaching a prosperity gospel (give money to me and you will get rich). He was anointed, they said. I do not doubt that, but if so, it was another spirit and not the Holy Spirit. I have seen strutting and arrogance elsewhere in pulpits, as ignorant and gullible folks were caught up in emotion they mistook for the Holy Spirit. So that is a common occurrence.

"He must increase, but I must decrease," John the Baptist said about Jesus. That is a good indication about the motives of the minister, when we see that attitude in action. Then Jesus is lifted up whether we have money or love or status or not, and the first word of the gospel becomes prominent in our ministry. The first word of the gospel is "repent," by the way. It is loudly absent among those who try to fleece others and who otherwise try to use others selfishly. From such turn away, and turn towards those who act justly, who love mercy, and who walk humbly with the risen Jesus Christ. May God help us to be among those who do that.

Congregations need the presence of the Holy Spirit.

I appreciated my seminary education very much. I enjoyed the friendships, the professors, the courses, the field work, and the beauty of the campus and the surrounding Boston area. But for me the most rewarding experience was the library. There I read historical accounts in other countries and cultures, about what I had seen as a boy growing up in east Tennessee.

I had relatively poor and uneducated parents who went to churches where they felt welcome, among similar folks. But these churches had something that made the plain and unadorned walls and furnishings acquire glory- because the King of Glory would enter. As a result, there was never even once a time in my life when I was not sure that God was real. The preaching, the teaching, the singing, and the testimonies, were for the most part infused with the Holy Spirit, as people spoke under his influence. The supernatural was not a myth in my background, but it was an integral part of our lives. "Jesus was a part of our family," said Corrie Ten Boom, the Dutch woman whose family delivered Jews from the Nazis and were imprisoned for doing that. And so, Jesus was a part of our family, and of many other families in those churches.

When I was called by God to preach, and after ten car wrecks decided to listen, I knew that in my case that meant that I had to go to seminary. The only information I had was that they were also called "cemeteries," since those who attended and then pastored brought death to the church services, extinguishing any fire of the Holy Spirit or evidence of his work. I thought if I had to go to a school where they did not know the Holy Spirit from a hole in the ground, I might as well go to one with a good academic reputation and at least learn some church history. I was steered by a Godly Presbyterian minister to some at least as academically respected as any, with professors who depended on the Holy Spirit to guide them.

I wept when I read in the library of Gordon Conwell accounts of Christians in the past who also preached in the power of the Holy Spirit, with people coming to Christ and having often radically changed lives. I knew that in my childhood I had seen vibrant Christianity. I was profoundly encouraged to know that was the norm not only in the New Testament, but throughout history.

When the elders of the Scottish churches looked for a new pastor, it was common (according to Dr. William Fitch, Scottish pastor in Glasgow, Scotland, and Toronto, Canada), for them to ask, "Does he have the anointing?" When the potential minister has the anointing of the Holy Spirit- a witness between the preacher and the listener- it means several things. Firstly, it means that the preacher has passed from the power of Satan into the kingdom of God. Secondly, it means that the person has really been called by God to preach the gospel of Jesus Christ. Thirdly, it means that the person is walking humbly with God at that time (that is, sins are forgiven, and he is earnestly trying to please God in word and attitude). And it most certainly indicates that this is the minister approved by God for that time and place.

I grieve when I consider that many children will not grow up in churches where the powerful and unmistakable presence of God is there in the services. I want that for them, and I pray that we will humble ourselves so that we will bring the power and presence and love of God to those we contact. God can save anyway he wishes. But normally he wishes to touch people through others who bring the fire of the Holy Spirit with them!

Evan Roberts

Evan Roberts was the catalyst for the great revival that swept the little country of Wales during 1904-1905: Sometimes he would say that there was someone in the service hindering the move of the Holy Spirit. He would invite them to repent, or he would call their name out loud. His was no idle threat because he had done that before. As long as we are offended by the idea of that practice in our church services, we will never see revival. When we hold on to grudges or to any attitude or behavior that the Bible calls sin, we will grieve the Holy Spirit. Then our churches will be filled by those who would consider a person such as Evan Roberts to be rude or judgmental.

But the Bible says, "judgement begins at the house of God." When it really is the house of God, then holiness will cause us to separate from sin. Yes, love begins at the house of God also, but not the "love" that says if it feels good then do it. That attitude is weakness and not love and causes great harm.

Evan Roberts would pray that the Holy Spirit would "bend us." Then the Holy Spirit would move mightily, and thousands would be supernaturally converted to follow Jesus Christ. May the God of the universe visit us again with such power. Probably the methods would differ a bit compared to those of the Welsh in 1904: Roberts would speak for no more than five to seven minutes, and his words were anointed with power. Then great waves of singing would convey the power of the Holy Spirit to the listeners, also in Welsh language. Hearts would be penetrated with repentance and a desire to honor Jesus Christ.

I have seen revival, although not on that scale. Revival is when the people of God are revived, or caused to live again by the power of the Holy Spirit. We easily become choked by the worries of this world, and by fears, unless we keep on thinking Christianly about everything of importance. If we are not careful, our hearts become hardened to things of God and need to be melted again. When the fire of the Holy Spirit falls, then those who hinder the work of the Holy Spirit either repent, or we get so uncomfortable that we leave. This happened when Rev. Jim Cymbala began to pastor a small church in Brooklyn, New York City. As he preached the gospel and lived it, about ten of the twenty church members left. Then the church began to grow in Godly ways until it is what is today, with about 2,000 coming out Tuesday nights for prayer meetings. And yes, they do much social outreach also.

For several years I would go to church just to please my parents, during high school and when I visited them while in university. I am certain I was a hindrance then to the move of the Holy Spirit in those gatherings. The Bible says that even Jesus could do no mighty works when he was surrounded by unbelief (he only healed a few).

I am convinced that all of us at some times, and most of us at most times, do not want Jesus to do mighty works among us in our churches. We are often wedded to notions of what is best for us without wanting God's opinion. But it is then that we quench and grieve the Holy Spirit, even if we manage to avoid sins that even most pagans condemn. We can be honest, faithful to our spouse, kind, etc., and still hinder the Holy Spirit. That is because God calls each person to love and to obey him in holiness. He calls us to see on the one hand that our "hearts are desperately wicked," and on the other hand that God loves us anyway.

Revival in Wales

If your name is Davies, Edwards, Evans, Hughes, Jenkins, Jones, Lewis, Price, or Williams, then you are either Welsh or of Welsh descent. Your relatives in the little country of Wales were drawn by the Holy Spirit into a mighty revival in the year of our Lord, one thousand, nine hundred and four. A 26-year-old coal miner named Evan Roberts became the point man used by God to unleash this supernatural outpouring that produced more than 100,000 converts and transformed lives in that green part of Great Britain. He had prayed for revival for over eleven years and had worked as a Sunday School Superintendent at Moriah Calvinistic Methodist Church, and later as an evangelist.

Crime rates dropped when conversions to Jesus Christ took place. Drunks reformed, pubs lost customers, and honesty gained a much stronger foothold among the Welsh. People returned money they had stolen and forgave grudges as they either began or deepened their walk with the risen Jesus Christ.

I am always disappointed to see announcements of ministers who promise to come to a city and bring revival with great signs and wonders. In the first place, all we can promise is hysteria from gullible folks if we manipulate them cleverly. In the second place, even when a minister is walking closely enough with God not to brag about how God will work, we cannot promise that the listeners will be open to the Holy Spirit. There was none of braggart about Evan Roberts. Therefore, God the Holy Spirit had free reigns to work through him.

A party of young men who had left a pub heard singing in the Moriah Church in 1904 and fled over the fields to get away. But they "were compelled to return by a power that they could not explain which seemed to draw them into the chapel where they went forward and confessed their sins" (www.moriah.org.uk). Only the Triune God does that sort of thing!

A Mrs. Kees reported that her father would get drunk almost every day after work at the Kingsbridge Inn on his way home, and her mother would fetch him and drag him to their home. Once at a rugby game, he became so uneasy that he could no longer enjoy the event and was drawn by the Holy Spirit to a meeting at Moriah, where he was converted to follow Jesus Christ. "Our home life was completely changed," she related.

Can God do such miracles in the rich and smug USA? God has brought sweeping revivals different times throughout our history. We cannot manufacture or manipulate a moving of the Holy Spirit at all. But we can pray to be sincerely open to God. "Pray for the gift of tears," some of the early New England puritans advised. In other words, we can pray that God helps us to see how far from him we naturally are, and how much we need his forgiveness and guidance in our lives.

Evan Roberts preached that the hearers should confess all known sin, deal with and get rid of anything doubtful in their lives, be ready to obey the Holy Spirit instantly, and confess Jesus Christ publicly. He added that there could be no blessing from God on anyone who had unkind thoughts about anyone else. It does no good to confess our sins until we get a glimpse of how holy God is, and therefore how much he hates sin.

In fact, that is why God the eternal Son Jesus Christ came, to seek and to save those who are lost, and to die on the cross as a substitute for our sins. As far as anything doubtful in our lives, even when others approve of us, are we giving ourselves wholeheartedly to follow Jesus Christ? Do we start fifteen minutes late, get caught in traffic, and then tell those who patiently waited for us that we are late because we were caught in traffic? What about obeying the Holy Spirit instantly? Would we recognize his voice from our own selfish mental notes?

John 16 assures us that if it really is the Holy Spirit who is prompting us to start or stop or do something differently, then he always glorifies Jesus Christ—his claim to have all power in heaven and in earth and his call for all to follow him as Lord. If we have begun to do that consciously, have we grieved the Holy Spirit, or do we continue to cultivate an openness to him? Normally the Holy Spirit does not lead dramatically but gently, as we mentally assent to be and to do whatever honors Jesus Christ best. Also have we confessed Jesus Christ personally, to a parent or friend, if not in a church service? By this act we witness for him and for his presence in our life. We then encourage those who already follow Jesus, and we also point to him for those who have not yet become his friend.

Decades after the Welsh revival, the lives of many thousands were still being impacted. When that has happened to us, may we pray that Jesus will not be Lord just at the time of our salvation, but more and more each day.

Preach self-improvement?

"People want to do good because they are good—that's their nature." So said Stephen Covy in USA weekend. It is certainly our nature to want to hear that, so many oblige with countless sermons and books supporting this basic instinct. I like to hear that too, and I am at least as offended as anyone else when the Bible says I am a sinner, in radical need of repentance and salvation (all have sinned, there is none righteous, no not one...), and also that I desperately need to depend on God daily.

It is a great temptation for the church to ignore these major themes throughout the Bible, and thus to undercut evangelism. Why bother and irritate folks by pointing them to Jesus Christ as Savior from our sins if we are inherently wonderful, and therefore just need to knock off a few rough edges?

But such thinking tends to make pompous, condescending Pharisees instead of dependent followers of Jesus Christ, like the apostle Paul, for example. He had been a dedicated Christian many years before he stated in Romans 7 that there was no good thing in him. He had suffered for the gospel because he lived it out in the midst of much persecution. He asserted that his nature was not good, so we can trust him or Covey but not both of them! Paul admitted that he not only needed supernatural conversion, but a continual reliance on Jesus in order to overcome his inherently sinful nature.

Paul, under the influence of the Holy Spirit, never preached the need for self-improvement or a better self-image, but more and more conscious dependence on Jesus. The realization that we never get good ultimately by God's standards, is not depressing, but instead it makes us more approachable as we plead for God to fill our minds with his thoughts, our emotions with his attitudes, and that he guides our hopes and steps. The New England theologian Jonathan Edwards pointed out that we "have an aversion to him (God)," because of his holiness and purity. And his immutability irritates us even more, as we become aware of the fact that he will never lower his standards to ours. Edwards was not preaching this to pagans, but to Christian believers!

Far from being depressive insight, to accept our radical need for Jesus to be our Savior from sin and to be Lord of our life, brings us the most abundant life possible. A continual dependence on Jesus for help and guidance brings more of him and less of us to influence others. Far from obliterating our personalities, this frees us to be all that we can be.

God's words with his attitudes?

Second Timothy 3:5 speaks of those who are "having the appearance of godliness, but denying its power. Avoid such people." We live in a time when the power of God is very rare in the churches, whether city or rural, large or small. At my first seminary I began to attend a church nearby where several professors went. Truth was proclaimed, but one Sunday, I could not stand it anymore to keep quiet about what I was thinking. So, after the service, I stated to the pastor that he did not preach in the power of the Holy Spirit and quoted the above verse. He replied that it referred to those who led silly women astray.

So, he was convinced that as long as he did not do the open sins referred to in that passage, and was preaching truth, it was unimportant to preach under the guidance of the Holy Spirit. He was wrong.

We are to speak the very words of God, and with his attitudes, in every sermon and in every conversation. Truth that is not from God for a particular time and place is irrelevant, and thus trivialized in the minds of the hearers. Unless we are broken and contrite, and filled with the Holy Spirit, the words we speak have no power to convict the hearers of sin, leading to salvation and then holiness. But when we have what Scottish elders called "the anointing," then sinners are converted, and saints draw near to God to become more holy.

A pastor from Texas told of praying for more closeness to God, and that prayer was answered. He was to speak soon after that at a Christian conference, but said he watched something on TV that he should not have watched. He then lost that close fellowship with God, or anointing, and was much relieved when another pastor was led by God to preach in his place. He spoke on repentance, and at the end he asked all who wanted to get closer to God to come to the front for prayer.

The prodigal told himself that he would go up, and those who saw him would think that he just needed to read the Bible more or to pray more. Then the speaker said that he was not referring to those who just felt that they needed to read the Bible more or to pray more, but to those who had been truly wicked. The Texan went up anyway, now being completely convicted of his sin. Would he have been convicted of sin at any church you have attended?

Someone said that repentance is one of the rarest things to ever strike a person. But it is common when humble ministers with broken hearts preach. None of us always do that, but I hope we are always deeply disappointed when we do not. I was so encouraged to hear Corrie Ten Boom speak when she was in Knoxville, Tennessee. I recall her showing a flashlight that would not shine. But then she removed a cloth, and then it worked. She illustrated that our sins block the flow of the light of God also, and our relationship with God is broken until we remove them.

Does that seem simplistic? Does it seem more sophisticated to preach or to converse without the guidance of the Holy Spirit? If so, then our preaching will be "the appearance of godliness, but denying its power" From such we are to turn away.

The Anointing

"Does he have the anointing?" Scottish elders would ask this question of prospective ministers. In other words, they were asking if the person was Christian, and called by God to preach, and spoke under the influence of God or not.

But when spiritual discernment is low or nonexistent, other questions are on the minds of the pulpit committee. Sometimes they wonder if the minister is a great orator, or is he in good physical shape? But Saint Paul noted in 2 Corinthians 10:10 that others complained about him, "His bodily presence is weak, and his speech of no account." Paul is not at all against health or good speaking skills, but he teaches under the influence of the Holy Spirit that these traits are not important for a preacher.

Instead, the most important question is, "Does he have the anointing?" To give assent to the Apostle's Creed and the Niceness Creed is good, but the person can say they believe and yet not really internalize these summaries of the Christian faith. The creeds are for those who are already supernaturally converted to Jesus Christ, in order to build them up in the faith. They are not primarily meant to lead someone to Christian faith.

Preaching with the anointing does that. Otherwise, some are, as 2 Timothy 3:5 states, "Having the appearance of godliness, but denying its power" Do not encourage such folks, but encourage those like Paul, Calvin, Knox, Wesley, and Spurgeon, who preach the gospel in power. We can have orthodox and historic Christian words, in other words, but not speak them at the right time and place, with attitudes that are from God. To do that we must be born again, called by God to preach, and humbly walking with God as we prepare and deliver the sermons. Then we have the "anointing," or the clear presence of God accompanying our words as we preach. Our words become a very clear and powerful witness for, or against those who listen. Another factor is the congregation, because even Jesus could do no mighty works when he was surrounded by unbelief (he only healed a few in his humanness). We might be in the center of God's will when we preach, yet our words from God can hit demonic shields and bounce off, with no sense of the anointing.

"Does the potential pastor have a history of developing large congregations?" That is another common concern a pulpit committee may have. That may be important, but sometimes to preach and to live truth means that others are driven away, especially when they are called to give up some sin they value highly. It is almost certain that Paul had small congregations.

"Does the potential pastor have a wonderful family?" Again, this is not a bad question in and of itself. Yet Paul had no family at all, although he belonged to the Sanhedrin and only married people could serve. So, they either made an exception for Paul, or his wife had died earlier.

"Is the minister intelligent and highly educated?" These are common concerns of a pulpit committee. Again, these are not wrong to ask. Paul was at least as intelligent and as highly educated as anyone of his day. So, he certainly was not opposed to either: to glory in ignorance is no virtue at all.

But Paul had his priorities straight, and he encourages us to do the same. He proclaimed in 1 Corinthians 2:1-5 these words: "And I, when I came to you, brothers, did not come proclaiming to you the testimony of God with lofty speech or wisdom. For I decided to know nothing among you except Jesus Christ and him crucified. And I was with you in weakness, and in fear and much trembling. And my speech and my message were not in plausible words of wisdom, but in demonstration of the Spirit and of power, so that your faith might not rest in the wisdom of men, but in the power of God." May we preach like that or encourage those who do.

God's message?

When I asked if his pastor preached in the power of the Holy Spirit, he acted as if I had asked for his personality profile, or world view. So, he answered that he was a good man, with practical sermons. But how can anyone know if the pastor is a good man unless God is with him unmistakably? He may say good words and act wonderfully in public and be the opposite in private. I dated a woman at the University of Tennessee whose father was a pastor in Chattanooga, who beat her mother very much. I am sure he did not mention doing that from the pulpit.

Furthermore, the man who ignored my question implied that it is impractical to empathize the spiritual. No, it is impractical to stress the emotional or just our opinions without hearing from God before and as we speak. Preaching with the anointing of the Holy Spirit is very practical, for then God speaks to us clearly and deeply, to encourage us in doing what is right, and where we need to repent and change. That is what we need. And that is what we desire also, unless we are determined to live without conscious dependence on God.

But God has all knowledge and understanding of every person and every circumstance. Therefore, it is logical to want to hear words from him in church services especially, and not my opinion or your opinion. Those who are converted to follow Jesus Christ as God, and who are called by God to preach, and who repent much and then pray for his guidance, do preach under his direction.

I am very sad that such historic Christian preaching is so rarely heard or understood when it is written about. Our observations and melodious voices may impress the evil and the ignorant, but they will help only in very shallow and trivial ways. How incredibly important it is to have the very words of God, as 2 Peter 4:11 commands us to have. It is especially critical when we dare to speak in his name.

1 Corinthians 4:20 says, "For the kingdom of God does not consist in talk but in power." The words are important, but they are not God. They just point to God. But even good words will be inappropriate and will have little impact unless they are birthed by the Holy Spirit, and delivered by those who are broken, repenting, and walking in the light of Jesus Christ.

I heard Dr. Stephen Olford preach at Park Street Church in Boston, and he had the anointing. God was clearly with him. About 300 gave their lives to Christ that Sunday. One was a person I had been praying for and encouraging to follow Jesus. She started thinking and acting Christianly. After returning to Tennessee, I would hear him on the radio, and I would always quit switching stations then. I listened because I knew he listened to God. Therefore, the words were inspired for any and all who heard them, in person or on the radio or by any other medium. He preached with the anointing, so his words were a strong witness for or against all who heard them. May God forgive us for daring to converse or to preach without getting our words from him. And yes, I have needed and asked forgiveness for doing that. Have you also?

Loss of a spouse

Ezekiel 24:15-18 records that God told Ezekiel that his wife, the delight of his eyes, would die, but he should not mourn (at least in a conventional way). So she died in the evening, and the next day he did as God had commanded him. If I outlive my spouse, I hope and I pray that I continue to do whatever God commands me to do. It would be so easy to be bitter at God, and complaining. But the Lord gives and the Lord takes away, blessed be the name of the Lord.

I heard the sermon based on that verse that Rev. Dr. E. V. Hill preached at the funeral of his wife. He saw her as a partner in the ministry, and a great source of encouragement. Once he came home to a candlelight dinner, but when he tried to flip the lights on in the house, they would not come on. She explained that she did not have the money to pay the electric bill, and cried. She tried to shield him from the pain of their poverty at that time.

On another occasion, people threatened to kill him the next day. When he arose, his wife was not there. When he looked out the window the car was gone. In a few minutes she returned, and he asked her where she had been. She replied that everything was fine, that she had expected a bomb to be planted in the car but it was not.

The third story he told about her was when he invested money into a gas station. She had recommended that he not do that, but he thought he could make it work. He lost everything in the business venture. When he came home she said that she had done some figuring. Since he did not smoke or drink, she thought that it was about even, so she would forget about his huge mistake!

I hope my children attract such spouses to themselves, and are attracted to such people of principle. I would like to think that if they are godly, that will happen. But I am sure that is not a certain outcome for the saints. King David married the daughter of King Saul, and she mocked him when he danced in the streets for the purpose of honoring God. In the New Testament, after all that David went through, he was called a man after God's own heart.

Hosea, the Godly Old Testament prophet, was commanded by God to marry Gomer, a prostitute, and to take her back time after time when she was unfaithful. This was to show the people of Israel how God took them back repeatedly when they were unfaithful to him. I know some think that is not literal in meaning, but I am convinced it is. That is because the lesson is much more powerful if the passage is real instead of theoretical, and God uses the most powerful stories possible in the Bible to teach us his ways.

Whether we suffer the loss of a loved one through death or divorce or some other painful circumstance, I hope and pray that the next morning, as with Ezekiel, we will either begin, or continue to do whatever God calls us to do. That is not easy usually. But it is the only way to honor God in that situation. And it brings the most abundant life possible.

New England tombstones

Tombstones in New England tend to be more reflective than those in the rest of the United States. One says, "As you are now, so once was I. As I am now, so you will be. Therefore, get ready and follow me." A wag added, "To follow you I am not content, until I know which way you went."

A funeral brings closure, at least somewhat, and reminds us that death is a part of life. At such times I say words about the deceased, but I keep the focus on Jesus Christ and the fact that he conquered death. As a result of joining our lives to him by a conscious commitment as Savior and Lord, we also have the assurance of overcoming death.

In the play *Macbeth*, character Macbeth utters, "Life is a tale told by an idiot, full of sound and fury, signifying nothing." Shakespeare voiced the honest opinion of many when he said that. But the Bible teaches us that our choices about Jesus Christ have eternal significance for better or for worse, so they truly do matter. Therefore, life has much significance.

Death comes to all of us, and to prepare for it means that we can live fully now. Otherwise, we cringe when we pass a funeral home or the subject of death comes up. Through friendship with Jesus Christ, we can say as the Dutch Christian Corrie Ten Boom used to say, "The best is yet to come."

The Christian faith is never more meaningful than when I stand at the grave side and say the words Jesus spoke to Martha, "I am the resurrection and the life. He that believeth in me, though he were dead, yet shall he live: And whosoever liveth and believeth in me shall never die." John 11:25-26:

These precious promises continue to comfort his friends. This does not mean that Christians do not grieve when one we love has died—of course we suffer loss. But the promises of one who overcame death help, when we love and obey him as God and Lord.

As David said about his son who died, "I cannot bring him back, but I can go to him." I wish, I pray, that each reader will have not just some psychological hope of better things to come after death, but the assurance that God is real, and through Jesus Christ there is friendship that will overcome even the last enemy—death.

"The ugliest baby I have ever seen "

Just after I was born, one of my aunts said to my mom, "That is the ugliest baby I have ever seen." Mom did not like her a lot before that, and she liked her a lot less after that. I think my nose was mashed in, but to hear someone say that about your first born was especially difficult.

Ephesians 4:15 encourages us to speak the truth in love. Even when we know something to be accurate, it is not truth in the biblical sense unless we add love to it. Love means to seek the highest good of the other person without expecting a reward, as it is used in this verse.

Conservatives who are passionate about truth tend to splinter into several different churches as they really care about what is right in all aspects of life. Liberals who tend to stress love, are more tolerant of different views. Truth is very important, yet those who think that way need to ask themselves what is most important, and not to be arrogant about knowing more than it is possible to know about a situation.

Francis Schaefer affirmed truth but added that it is possible to know truth without knowing it exhaustively. In other words, different forms of baptism and church government and interpretations of prophecy are possible without calling those who differ lunatics or people who deliberately twist scripture. On the other hand, those who emphasize love need to guard against the popular modern notion that truth does not matter as long as we love each other. Love takes some bizarre turns unless it is anchored to biblical truth. In the name of love, probably as much or more evil has been done as in the name of truth. We know several who tell others that if they really love them, they will do the opposite of what the Bible teaches in all kinds of areas. The results are not loving when others have been used for selfish gains.

We are not to jettison truth because some claim to know it exhaustively, nor are we to throw love out because it has been twisted for selfish purposes. When we read the Bible for ourselves, we see that Jesus Christ is "full of grace and truth." If we claim to worship Jesus as God and Lord, then certainly we are to see him as our example. Otherwise, we will write him off as an obscure person, even when we rightly admit that he is historical.

I was mad. So, I set aside a section of the sermon to straighten out a particular individual. I have no recollection now who it was or what the issue was. But I noticed the person was not in the congregation that Sunday. It was then that the Holy Spirit convicted me deeply and painfully for trying to do his job, without his permission. Whether the individual needed to repent or not, definitely I was not called to confront him or her at that time and place.

Romans 12:19 says, "Vengeance is mine, I will repay." That is one of my least favorite Bible verses. But we are to focus on saying a good word about Jesus instead of mulling over how we can get revenge. As we speak of his glory and his character and his deity, if the Holy Spirit does not work in the hearts of people to honor him and to convict them of sin, no word or attitude from us will convince anyone to change.

I know when I am attacked, I tend to defend myself, and to make excuses for my behavior or attitudes. But as Christians we are to accept criticism gracefully – to "eat the fish and to throw away the bones." God help us to do that more.

When the gospel is preached in the power of the Holy Spirit, listeners are strongly encouraged in righteousness and discouraged in sin. Saint Paul named Alexander the coppersmith as a bad person and warned folks to avoid him, for example. In the great Welsh revival, Evan Roberts would sometimes call out an individual by name who was quenching the Holy Spirit.

I have seen this happen (I was the one justifiably called out), with the glory going to Jesus Christ, so such should be welcomed. But in all of Paul's writings this happened only a few times. The remainder of his writings promoted righteousness, and when sin was mentioned specifically (as in 1 Corinthians 6:9-11), Paul said, "And such were some of you. But you were washed, you were sanctified." Paul had no interest in calling attention to their sins they had forsaken. But only God knows if our listeners are still in their sins, or recently added some, or if they are holy and walking humbly with Jesus Christ as God and Lord.

But whether from behind a pulpit or in a conversation, we are all commanded by God in 1 Peter 4:11, "whoever speaks, as one who speaks oracles of God." When we do that, then our words and attitudes will be from God to encourage righteousness and to discourage sin. Otherwise, even if we speak truth, it will not be for that time and place or for the benefit of those who hear us.

Repentance

Jesus died on the cross for our sins—not for our dysfunctions, not for our mistakes, or because we might be sick at times. According to the Bible there are no dysfunctional families, but only sinners who may make excuses for our sins. But people who shoot up schools are often considered unbalanced or crazy, but not sinners. Then why do such folks never shoot up a police station instead of planning for months to murder unarmed children and adults? It is because they are sinners, who carefully choose their innocent victims, and who often wear body armor to protect themselves.

So why do we hear all these calls for counseling instead of calls for repentance? It is because much of the country doesn't value personal responsibility for our actions. So we call murderers sick only when we agree they are not responsible for their actions. Then they need therapy to understand themselves, we feel. But people already understand that they are wrong to murder children, for example. They just want to perpetuate the myth that we are not responsible for our actions.

We have become a country where no one commits adultery anymore. That is condemned in the Bible, so we just have affairs, because that sounds better. The Bible is against fornication also, or sex before marriage. But we refuse to use biblical terms, so we just call it premarital sex. When I did that, since I was Christian, the Holy Spirit stayed with me to convict and to make me miserable.

No one lies anymore either, so we fool ourselves with thinking we do not need to repent, because we just tell fibs. Neither do we steal to require repentance, but we use some other cliche to describe taking things that do not belong to us. We use any excuse to get around the clear and repeated teachings of the Bible. We do not even die anymore in this country—we just "pass," as if life is only a football game. Yet the Bible teaches that we die, and "after death the judgement."

Do we like to imagine that we are too sophisticated to use the words of the Bible that are labeled sin, and that we can therefore shy away from the repeated calls to repent before we die and face the judge of all the earth, the risen Jesus Christ? I understand that the word repentance sounds harsh when we want to keep on sinning (I have been in that situation myself), and when we want to be encouraged in that state. But repentance is the only word that opens the door to heaven. In 1 Corinthians 15:3, we learned that Christ died for our sins. We are not to repent of our sicknesses or mistakes—just our sins!

Parents influence children.

The singer Doc Watson tells the story of how he was very hungry, and after a quick prayer, he began to eat his meal. His wife interrupted to inform him that their granddaughter (I think her name was Katy) wanted to pray. She was a little girl who prayed for just about everyone she ever met before she finished. When she did end the prayer, Doc commented, "That was a long prayer, Katy." She waited about a moment and answered, "It was better than yours."

Children are to be trained in righteousness, even when they embarrass us by being consistent! I know much harm has been done by people who tried to force children to believe the same way they believe. On the other hand, much harm has been done by those who contend it is wrong to try to influence children by our beliefs. If we do not have beliefs we consider worthy of passing on, we should get new ones. If we do have beliefs we consider to be helpful, it is cruel and evil not to try to pass them on to those we are responsible for raising. The philosophy "Let children choose without our intervention" may sound noble, but whether we love Jesus Christ or not, consistently or not, we do pass on a set of beliefs and values to those around us. We do that more or less intentionally, more or less effectively, but we do have an impact on others we meet.

At the same time, I hope we remember that each child has worth and value. Each child deserves respect and considerate behavior from us, whether the child accepts or rejects our cherished beliefs. Children notice if we are more concerned with our social standing than their salvation. If we pressure them to accept our beliefs because we pastor or want to otherwise protect our status, they understandably will rebel.

Sometimes I wore a sweatshirt given to me by a friend that read, "God is dead." Nietzsche. Below that was the phrase, "Nietzsche is dead." God. I can only surmise what kind of father Nietzsche had. I know he was a German clergyman who did not believe in God. So, he did not pass Christian faith on to his son, who considered the religious to be weaklings and who built the foundation for Nazi theology. The Swedish film maker Ingmar Bergman made films full of despair and hypocritical pastors. His father was a Swedish pastor who didn't believe in God either. He then passed that faith on to Ingmar.

Carl Jung, the Swiss psychotherapist, also was the son of a pastor. The poor father finally gave up any pretentions of a Christian faith, and his mother kept a bed reserved for spirit couples. Carl inherited his affinity with the supernatural from his mother. So, Christianity was only "a form of godliness, denying the power thereof," to these influential thinkers of the twentieth century.

On the other hand, how wonderful it is when people have committed themselves supernaturally to the God of the Bible, and he is an unmistakable presence with them. The children around them then see them as approachable, and humble enough to admit when the prayers of children are more sincere than their own.

Children

Dr. James Dobson states, "a world without children is a world without newness, regeneration, color and vigor." I might add, it is also a world without wonder, innocence, and hope. Perhaps some of the nursing homes in your area can learn from the Mennonites in Toronto, who erected nursing homes with a section for young families. How terrible to be isolated from other generations and to be stuck in the narrow confines of our peers. This tends to encourage the natural tendency of each generation to think that it is both smarter and more Godly than the preceding and following generations. I pity baby boomers or any other group that segregates itself and has friends only in its own age span.

Brian Aldiss writes, "When childhood dies, its corpses are called adults and they enter society, one of the politer names of hell." That is a tad extreme, although the increasing viciousness shown to children makes the thought more and more appropriate. A man who raped and murdered an innocent seven-year-old girl named Megan was found guilty of his crime. This was the third such incident for him. If we must get sentimental and feel sorry for anyone, I hope we collect our warm sympathy for the victims. Probably the criminal had some difficulties in childhood, as millions did who do not murder and rape. But we all are responsible to treat others as we want to be treated, no matter what happened in our past.

Children are the most vulnerable members of our society. When the father leaves the mother for another woman, the children feel abandoned. They feel abandoned because they are abandoned. Even when it is not the fault of the father, when children are separated from him by divorce, the same abandonment occurs.

Many writers are credited with saying that there are no illegitimate children. There are only illegitimate parents. One man shot up a classroom in Ottawa, Canada, and explained that he was mad at his parents. Innocent students suffered for the evil of his parents (and his evil), and this is repeated regularly in many societies. When children are abused by neglect or active ungodly words, attitudes or actions, they must struggle throughout life to overcome rage, lack of trust, and desires for revenge.

Jesus says in Luke 9:48: "Whoever receives this child in my name receives me." He has some very threatening words for those who would harm children. Let us be very thankful and as supportive as possible for Godly institutions such as Church of God Home for Children and Wear's Valley Ranch in Sevier County, Tennessee, and throughout the world. Some institutions are not Godly, of course, so pray for discernment and wisdom in this area.

Even if we cannot be part of a major established undertaking, we can pray for those children we meet. Ask God to give us words and attitudes that will encourage them in his ways. Try to arrange programs and activities in our churches and among our friends for the children in our midst. If we have nieces or nephews let us do good to them as we have the opportunity. If we are single and do not have friends or relatives who have children, we can walk with God, and then he will honor our prayers on behalf of the children we encounter.

Top needs of men and women are different.

In his book *His Needs, Her Needs*, Dr. Willard S. Hartley Jr., asserts that research shows the top needs of women and men are radically different. Women list their priorities in order of importance and put affection (non-sexual touching) at number one. In cultures where touching of any sort is minimal (Northern European, for example) I suppose this is even more critical.

Number two is conversation. In conflicts, eighty-five percent of men withdraw because men are usually less verbal, even in pleasant circumstances. If you observe couples walking on a city sidewalk, you will notice that the woman is talking about eighty-five percent of the time.

Number three in importance for woman is romance. Instead of something practical like an iron for a birthday, it means to express love in ways that show unique appreciation. I do not think that I do that well at all.

Number four is honesty/openness or transparency. I am not sure women would say this if they knew how much guys are different, but seriously, it is impossible to have a good relationship without trustworthiness.

Number five is financial support/ security. Money covers a multitude of sins for many. This expressed need is or was especially high in the south of the USA where women were traditionally not as encouraged to be independent.

The five needs men said are most important were as follows. Sex is number one. Maybe this is one reason so few single guys go to church, although not that many single women go either. For women, sex was rated number thirteen, right behind gardening. Of course, individuals vary, but still, that is a rather large gap for most.

Men say the second most important need is recreational companionship. Something shared is twice as good when pleasant (hiking, movies...), and half as bad when unpleasant. I enjoyed my single life until I was 50, but I much prefer being married.

Number three in importance was attractiveness. Yes, I realize it sounds as shallow and unspiritual as romance sounds to men. Number four is domestic support. That sounds like a joke to say "support," since most guys tend not to see dust bunnies or dirty windows at all. Number five is admiration or respect. This is not to say women do not crave this also, but it was lower on their scale of needs. Historically, men tended to define themselves by accomplishments, no matter what their inner qualities were. I suppose the number five need of both reinforces the other.

None of these "needs" are condemned by the Bible, and each can be appropriate within certain contexts. Christians do not cease to be normal women or men. So although all individuals would not fit the molds above, I suspect the Christian population would not differ in general.

At the same time, we are taught in Matthew 6 to seek first the kingdom of God, and all these things (all our needs) will be added unto us. Therefore, for the Christian, the first priority for both women and men is to put God and his will first. His will may or may not include what we would put on our list of "needs." When his will conflicts with our will, we are tempted to sulk and pout, or to rationalize why our "needs" are more important than obeying Christ. Then we will see clearly whether we follow Jesus by faith, or just when he fits our idea of what we need. From time to time we have all followed our feelings or logic when the Bible told us to do or think the opposite.

Harvard and historic Christianity

How did Harvard get so far from historic Christianity? It is our first university in the USA, founded in 1636: It is beyond dispute that it was begun by very Godly Christians for the purpose of training Christian ministers. For example, Rev. Thomas Shepard (along with Rev. John Harvard), was an important founder.

He was expelled from his English pulpit in 1630 and joined the Puritans who came to New England. He wrote treatises which included "The Sincere Convert," and "The Sound Believer." He preached that true conversion requires a total change of heart, mind, and affections. He preached from the parable of the five wise and the five foolish virgins (Matthew 25), reasoning that we should expect "a number of hypocrites mingling themselves with the purest of churches." The foolish virgins represented those who were satisfied with the temporary "blaze of outward profession (the lamp taken with them)." The wise virgins stood for those who have the inward witness of the Holy Spirit (the oil).

For many years Harvard stayed true to the Christian faith, but by the mid-1700s it had veered toward Unitarianism. This is the view that God is one, but faith in Jesus as God is not important. Or as the humorist Garrison Keillor put it, Unitarians do not worship "what's his name." What happened at Harvard has also occurred at many universities and churches. Why? It is because the ruling group (trustees, elders, deacons) began to admit other leaders on the basis of their wealth or personalities or because they had other admired skills. These characteristics are not bad in and of themselves. But to keep an institution Christian, new leaders must be supernaturally converted to Jesus Christ and lead holy lives. Then they will choose historic Christian and devout presidents or pastors, etc.

Once a group is committed to a non-Christian world view, it is extremely rare to return to godliness. In other words, in the spiritual as well as in the natural world, it is easier to have a baby than to raise the dead. So, Yale and Princeton were started after Harvard, in large part to offset the apostasy that overran Harvard, and to promote historic Christianity. By historic Christianity I mean supernatural conversion to follow Jesus Christ as God and Lord, belief in the Trinity, and acceptance of the Bible as the word of God. As new universities and churches form, they also go downhill unless they continue to promote leaders who are Godly.

Rev. Robert Murray M'Cheyne said that what a congregation needs most in a minister is holiness. I agree. Otherwise, skills and personality will be used to advance the kingdom of darkness. 1 Timothy 5:22 teaches us to ordain no one quickly, or to lay hands on no one soon, until we know they are truly and sincerely converted, and walking humbly with God. First of all, see how they treat family and friends, their fellow workers, and neighbors. These can testify as to their character, and not just their public reputation.

I have been privileged to know very Godly leaders, and also very ungodly leaders who showed their fangs in private. Do not be like the congregation that hired a mass murderer to oversee them. He was caught only after he began taunting police from a church computer! That is an extreme example, but it is inevitable that a group moves away from Christian orthodoxy, unless we continue to choose governing body members who act justly, who love mercy, and who walk humbly with the risen Jesus Christ.

The preacher and the stripper

During one of my pastorates, I became friends with a neighboring pastor who related this story about one of his ministerial colleagues. The individual began to frequent a strip joint and fell in love with one of the strippers. Her husband was in prison but was due to be released around that time period. One day the minister arrived at the club, but when he searched for his significant other, he was told that she was gone. The management had seen the situation develop and had arranged for her to be moved to another part of the country for his safety. They would not tell him where she was working, and he never saw her again.

We may think that God delivered him from a severe beating or worse, which he richly deserved. At the same time, I hope we are reminded of the many times we ourselves have been protected from selfish and irresponsible decisions that we have all made. Much of what passes for good is lack of opportunity to do evil, as someone has profoundly observed. Or our personality or cowardice prevents us from doing more mischief at times.

As the reader reads, each of us can fill in the blanks and details of how the Lord has protected us from our crazy and sometimes sinful schemes. Sometimes while hiking in the Great Smoky Mountains with someone, I started to make a critical remark, stubbed my toe, and while regaining my balance the conversation shifted. I then would reflect on what I was about to say and would be supernaturally convinced that it was inappropriate for that occasion.

When we walk with the Lord Jesus, he does nudge us and normally keep us from the disaster that offhand unthinking comments would bring to us. On the other hand, if we quench and ignore the Holy Spirit who lives within each follower of Jesus, God will allow us to go farther and farther from his will. Or as the Bible so profoundly puts it, he turns us over to reprobate minds!

Many admit after years of marital hell that they had absolutely no peace from God when they married. They ignored signals and clear signs that the person was not right for them, and forged ahead anyway because of loneliness or lust or being too proud to call it off, etc. So, when we persist in what the Bible calls sin, God has no obligation to keep protecting us from its consequences. Unlike the minister who was sheltered by the underworld, God normally lets us face the music when we harden our hearts against his love.

"Everyone to whom much was given, of him much will be required," God tells us in the Bible. When God is with us, as he is through the Holy Spirit given to each believer, we are then more responsible to obey God that those who do not know him. We then must quench and grieve the Holy Spirit to lie or steal or commit fornication or adultery, or to do the other sins the Bible condemns. Christian excuses then look more pathetic to God than one who acts in accordance with a Godless culture who does not have the law of God written on the heart.

Even if we have not hoped to dump our wife for a stripper, we all need to repent daily for opposing the will of God. Our little bouts of pride, selfishness, rudeness, etc., escalate unless we go to God for help to follow him again. We do not do that by feeling superior to those who sin in ways we are not tempted to sin, but by humbly and sincerely searching the Bible for guidance. In it we are confronted by the Holy Spirit, whose job it is to convict us of sin as John 16 tells us, who reminds us of what Jesus taught us to do, and who always glorifies Jesus Christ as God.

When a person considers it selfishness to be concerned with inner holiness, you had better count your silverware after they visit you, remarked Samuel Johnson. This is because belief influences behavior- not perfectly, as the minister above illustrates, for we may have orthodox Christian beliefs and contradict them. Or the minister may have been unconverted and just pretending to be a follower of Jesus Christ. How much better it is to both be supernaturally converted, and then to act in a Godly way!

Canada and the USA

A retired newspaper editor told me this story when he learned I had worked in Toronto. Just after the Sun Sphere in Knoxville, Tennessee, was shattered by gunshots, he was in Toronto riding in a taxi. He had mentioned to the driver that he was from Knoxville, and he later remarked how beautiful a particular glass building was. The taxi driver said it was too bad we could not have nice glass buildings in Tennessee. Well, we are not all trigger-happy savages, but relative to Canadians, we are very violent. There are one-hundred times more murders in the USA than in Canada. Yes, we do have about ten times more people, but that is still a ratio of ten murders to every one in Canada. Why is this?

I have two theories to explain the difference. The first one is that our country was born in violence. The revolution that overthrew the yoke of Great Britain also encouraged a contempt for authority that continued as the colonists pushed west. Often the biggest bully became the law, whereas in Canada settlers continued to respect authority. I know many of the founding fathers were dedicated Christians (as was John Wesley who opposed the revolution), and perhaps they did the right thing. But the fact is that our nation was drenched in blood and Canada was not. Their history of the westward expansion is relatively boring- because it was considerably more peaceful.

Another huge factor of the fierceness in the USA is the introduction of slavery. Colonists in Jamestown, Virginia, were approached by a Spanish slaver who wanted to trade slaves for food, and the practice first took root in this country. Slavery brutalized master and slave alike. It was an evil institution, and throughout history it was practiced by people of the same race as well as toward other races. Some Christians recognized it as evil and opposed it, while others treated people as they did not want to be treated, thus completely contradicting the words of Jesus Christ. Abraham Lincoln spoke eloquently when he said, “As I would not be a slave, so I would not be a master.”

Canada has its own problems, but the legacy of revolution and slavery are not among them. They have achieved a free and prosperous and peaceful country without these traditions (they did have slavery but thanks to Wilberforce and others in the British parliament it was abolished long before it was in the USA).

"O, we are not that violent," I protested to a Canadian friend who was appalled at the viciousness level. Then he told me of driving down I-75 near Atlanta when he suddenly noticed a man in a car beside him pointing a gun in his direction. He said he assumed he had cut him off in traffic unintentionally. He sped up and finally lost him at an exit. I confess that I proceeded to relate some true stories much more violent just to shock him.

May God give us the gift to see ourselves not only as others see us, but as God himself sees us. I love my country at least as much as anyone else does, but God says in the book of Isaiah that all nations are as vanity before him. I hope we consciously put the Triune God first in our lives, above any national or ethnic pretensions.

Church attendance

When I heard Kris Kristofferson sing “Sunday Morning Coming Down,” it made me sad and uneasy because I was not attending church then. But I later rededicated my life to Jesus and came back. After all, Hebrews 10:25 does teach us not to neglect to meet together for the purpose of encouraging one another.

I did know the truth of the statement of John Calvin when he said, Whenever the word of God is preached and heard, there a church of God exists, even if it swarms with many faults.” Critics of the church often mention the presence of hypocrites and use that as an excuse not to go. The father of one roommate learned that I had begun to attend church again and mentioned that he did not go because of all the hypocrites there. I replied that I would rather go to church with them then to go to hell with them.

I like to think I am more diplomatic and patient now. If I could relive that conversation, I hope I would explain how even hypocrisy is a testament that there is a higher standard which we agree we should try to achieve. And even the most sincere of us have blind spots and limitations that may not be apparent to anyone until a hundred years after we die! How could they have claimed to be dedicated Christians and so materialistic or hedonistic, future generations may ask.

If everyone did as we do, would the world be better off or not? If we refuse to go to church, would the world be better off without churches? Probably not. Even the churches we think have the most faults read the Bible and encourage us to love and obey Jesus Christ. At least some evil is restrained when we deliberately put ourselves under the preaching and teaching of the Bible regularly (even when the priests or ministers do not). Then the Holy Spirit has a chance to convict us of sin and to cheer us in righteousness. The logic of scripture then causes us to at least consider accepting the reasoning of God when it conflicts with our own limited perspectives.

Even when the sermon is not preached in the power of the Holy Spirit because of sin in the life of the speaker or a lack of prayer in the pews, the Bible is read, and the Holy Spirit can build on that. Hymns record the valiant faith of people who overcame huge obstacles to live for God, and virtues of honesty, forgiveness, kindness and justice are promoted.

If we think the churches are full of Pharisees, even Jesus says do what the Pharisees say, not what they do in their pretentiousness. And besides, if we think churches need help and reform (as I think), why not bring ourselves into that struggle? The English professor C.S. Lewis became a Christian and very reluctantly began to go to church. He considered the hymns "fifth-rate poems set to sixth-rate music." But he went anyway and noticed that they were being sung with "devotion and benefit by an old saint in elastic-side boots in the opposite pew, and then you realize that you aren't fit to clean those boots."

Get supernatural peace about important decisions.

"Peace I leave with you; my peace I give to you. Not as the world gives do I give to you. Let not your heart be troubled, neither let them be afraid." John 14::27. Do we "pray through" until we have this supernatural peace Jesus promises to those who love and obey him? Or do we have troubled and fearful hearts about our important decisions?

If we do not have the supernatural peace Jesus talks about, it is a good idea to get it before we ruin our lives. When I pastored in Toronto, I almost married someone I had no business to even date. If you were still unmarried at age 40, you understand that I got tired (very) of being single, especially on weekends and holidays. I finally found someone who wanted to be with me, and who was appealing to me- at least on some levels. My friends were not impressed, but I slogged on anyway.

I did value peace with God, however, and the more I prayed about the matter the less peace I had from God, so I called it off. Those who knew me at all could have predicted disaster if we had married, so peace from God may seem an unnecessary shield of protection to need. But if you think so, look at how many marriage catastrophes we see in almost every church, not to mention in general society. Emotional and physical and intellectual and financial attraction is no match for selfishness! And we do get selfish unless we seek and value the peace that comes from unselfishly putting God first in our life. Then God will give us the best spouse for us, the best job for us, and the best place to live.

This may or may not be the best in the eyes of others. It may be best to live in a dump for our spiritual growth, to wait until we are 50 years old to marry (as in my case), or to have what others do not value in order to have the peace Jesus wants to give. We are all challenged daily to go our own way, or to find and to follow the will of God for our lives, which will then bring his peace.

We should "pray through" until we have peace or lack of peace from God about an important matter, especially about whom to marry, what job to do, or where to live. A choice of chocolate or strawberry ice cream may not affect us that much, but our choice of a mate will impact us in many ways every day we live!

Oswald Chambers says profoundly," The good is the enemy of the best." I would hate to go through life thinking that my wife was ok, or even good, but always wondering if I had missed God's best for me. Most have these misgivings about a spouse or a job or some other choice we made. How much better it is to seek the counsel of Godly friends, to read the Bible to see the mind of God, and to "pray through" until we have the assurance that God gives us his peace to proceed with a plan or hope that we have. God knows all things and is perfect love, while the most brilliant of us has very limited knowledge (Thomas Edison said nobody knows more than one millionth of one percent about anything), and a heart that the Bible describes as "desperately wicked." So it is both stupid and arrogantly evil for Christians not to humble ourselves enough to pray that God gives us his supernatural peace in the important decisions we must make.

The divinity of the Holy Spirit

I have been interacting lately with several who do not believe in the Trinity of God the Father, God the eternal Son Jesus Christ, and God the Holy Spirit. So after presenting evidence for the divinity of Jesus Christ, I want to do the same for God the Holy Spirit. The Holy Spirit (or Holy Ghost from the German, whereas spirit is from the Latin) is considered the "red-headed stepchild" of the Trinity, even by many Christians. Someone has profoundly noted that if he left the earth, many churches would not notice but would continue as normal. When we have talented people, it is possible to have sermons and singing and teaching and programs without any dependence on the Holy Spirit at all. But that is terrible, since "no man can say Jesus is the Lord, but by the Holy Ghost." In other words, Jesus is not really our Lord or ruler we worship, unless we consciously rely on the Holy Spirit to guide our words, thoughts, and actions.

The Holy Spirit is God, as Acts 5:3-4 clearly teaches. In that passage, Peter told Ananias that he lied to the Holy Spirit and not just to them as individuals, but to God himself. The Holy Spirit is not just a force, but a person who comforts the Christian. John 14:16 says, "And I (Jesus) will ask the Father, and he will give you another Helper, to be with you forever." No human could be with millions of people forever, so this refers to the third person of the Trinity.

In John 14::26 it is clear that the "Comforter" is "the Holy Spirit, whom the Father will send in my name, he will teach you all things and bring to your remembrance all that I have said to you." So the Holy Spirit teaches, as no mere wind or force can do. In the midst of conversations we can remember the words of Jesus that honor him best when we really do live for Jesus Christ.

John 16::14 says, "He (the Holy Spirit or Holy Ghost) will glorify me," reminding us, for example, that all things were made by Jesus and for Jesus. It is nothing to brag about if we have a spirit around us, unless that spirit is the Holy Spirit who always glorifies Jesus Christ. That is the only spirit I want around me.

Ephesians 4:30 says, "And do not grieve the Holy Spirit of God." So, the Holy Spirit can be saddened by our independent nature unless we consciously pay attention to his promptings and learn to recognize his desires above our own and those of others.

1 Thessalonians 5:19 says, "Do not quench the Spirit." Do not put out the fire of the Spirit by letting bullies determine how to organize church activities or lead them, in other words. Elevate holy people of prayer as leaders, otherwise the rich and high-status folks or poor and low-status individuals, will bring a church farther and farther from godliness.

But do not all people have the Holy Spirit? No, definitely not. Acts 5:32 mentions "the Holy Spirit, whom God has given to those who obey him." So, obedience to the Triune God is a precondition for the Holy Ghost. Also, Jude 1:19 teaches that some are devoid of the Spirit. The law of God is not written in their hearts, in other words. But through the Holy Spirit we have God with us, and his law within us also. Sadly, we can still choose to do evil, however. But when we are indwelt by the Holy Spirit, we have the power to be holy, and to walk humbly with God.

A clear break between good and evil is not for our children?

George Washington said, "let us with caution indulge the supposition that morality can be maintained without religion. Whatever may be conceded to the influence of refined education on minds ... reason and experience both forbid us to expect that national morality can prevail in exclusion of religious principles."

Hitler proved that Washington was right, for he won over the great German universities long before he influenced the masses. As we can testify (if we are honest) about ourselves, our neighbors, and spouses, education just makes a person more refined not better.

Our second president, John Adams, wrote, "We have no government armed with power capable of contending with human passions unbridled by morality and religion ... our constitution was made only for a moral and religious people. It is wholly inadequate of any other." Are we still a moral and religious people?

A George Barna study found that fifty-seven percent of evangelical youth do not believe in an absolute standard of truth. In other words, sometimes it is okay to do the opposite of what the Bible clearly teaches. Therefore, even when truth is preached and taught as being real and clear and unchanging, what the Bible calls sin is okay when the individual wants to make an exception.

In the not too distant past, most of those who did what the Bible calls wrong admitted they were wrong and did what they wanted to do anyway. But now the whole notion of truth is outdated for many, and several are outraged at the very teaching that anyone can know truth at all.

I hope instead we opt for the Prince of Peace, Jesus Christ, who said in Matthew 11:29, "take my yoke upon you." Then we internalize the law when we know the lawgiver. When the law of God is written in our hearts, our constitution will remain adequate to govern us, and we will avoid the extremes of a dictatorship on the one hand, and lawlessness on the other.

Shot full of holes

The Scots were sent on horses during a World War 1 battle to charge German machine guns, so of course they were slaughtered. On the next cavalry charge by Canadians, a horse stepped on the back of Duncan Campbell, who was lying on the ground shot full of holes. He groaned, so a Canadian noticed that he was still alive, and carried him to a makeshift hospital. As he was being transported, Duncan thought he was about to die. But instead of being bothered by that, he was so very sad that although he was converted, he had led no one to Jesus Christ yet.

At the hospital, a nurse sang a Christian hymn in Gaelic, and Duncan recited a psalm in that language. The Canadians requested him to speak about Jesus in English, for they wanted to understand, but he was unable to do so. His pain was so great that he could only speak his first language (as is the case for all who are in such a situation, so if you marry someone who speaks English as a second tongue, try to learn their language also, at least enough to encourage them in times of great distress).

But the power of God was so strong then that the Canadians were converted anyway, all seven of them. We, however, do not have to be shot full of holes before we have a great enduement of power from on high. According to J. Edwin Orr, who deeply influenced Billy Graham, "... Obedient Christians may claim by faith a victory over sin, enter upon a closer walk with God, fully committing their lives to God, and be filled with the Spirit for whatever service he may direct."

That is a very different message than merely enlisting people for Christ with no repentance/life change. But without repentance over our rebellion against God and then fully surrendering our lives to him, we will not have his hand upon our lives. We may have accomplished many great things, but it is most important that God be pleased with us.

Acts 13: records that the church at Antioch worshipped the Lord (Jesus) and fasted, and the Holy Spirit spoke to them. When was the last time that happened at your church? Hopefully, it was recently. At Antioch, the Spirit said in Acts 13:2, "Set apart for me Barnabus and Saul (Paul) for the work to which I have called them." The next verse states, "So, being sent out by the Holy Spirit, they went down to ..."

How encouraging it is to know that we have been sent out to a particular place or work by the Holy Spirit, and not by our love of money or adventure or praise or comfort. That is why I had other students at my seminary gather and pray with me about my choices of where to go. I got peace about direction, and sorely needed that assurance later! It is useless to have a short prayer for guidance and then assume God will bless our feelings and logic.

I hope we fast and pray to humble ourselves before the Lord, to give up all that is not from him, and to keep only what is pleasing to him. In other words, do we pray to be more open to the leading of the Holy Spirit and the filling of the Holy Spirit (without being shot full of holes as Duncan Campbell was)? Luke 11:13 If ye then being evil (relative to God) know how to give good gifts unto your children: how more shall your Heavenly Father give the Holy Spirit to them that ask him?

Unregenerate folks never pray such a prayer, but one for salvation and mercy and forgiveness. So, the prayer in Luke is not for the sake of the non-Christians, but for those of us who are, so that we will have the infilling of the Holy Spirit, or enduement of power for service. So, we are to ask, and it shall be given, seek and we will find, knock and the door will be opened for us. The Greek text clearly means to keep on asking and keep on seeking and keep on knocking for the power to make our lives count for Jesus Christ. As we do that, "the Christian will find out for himself what stands in the way of the filling of his vessel with the Holy Spirit," says Dr. Orr in his book *My All, His All.* What stands in the way for me, and for you now, of being fully surrendered to God and filled with the Holy Spirit for his service?

The Smith sisters

Peggy and Christine were sisters, eighty-four and eighty-two years old. Unkind folks might look at them and see a useless drain on society, and even the most uplifting would normally see them as no longer able to make any significant contribution to society. But from God's perspective, we know that they were the key to changing thousands of lives in Scotland. They walked with God, and so their prayers were powerful and effective, as is the case with all such individuals. James 5:16 says, "The prayer of a righteous person has great power as it is working."

Their prayers for revival of Christians and for the salvation of the unconverted led to a massive move of God on the isle of Lewis from 1949-1950. They had been burdened about the drift away from Christianity they had witnessed in their community, and the spiritual deadness of their churches. Several from their congregation were persuaded to also pray a few nights a week, in a barn near the home of the Smith sisters. They thus drew near to God, for as the Bible says, "Draw near to God, and he will draw near to you."

As they prayed, God showed them that Duncan Campbell was the person to preach, so he was invited. He was able to build upon the Godly foundation laid by the sisters and their congregation. So, God came down in power, with Christians becoming more Godly and many non-Christians converted. Could that happen wherever the reader is? No, it could not—unless Christians become more concerned about the glory of God than our own glory/comfort/status. Jesus is the same yesterday, today, and forever, the Bible assures us. So, the change is not in God but in us if he does not move among us in powerful ways.

How else can one really be drawn to God? C.S. Lewis and other intellectuals are confronted by the evidence and logic of the resurrection, and by the historic nature of Christianity. But even he had to be drawn supernaturally, in order to pass from the power of darkness into the kingdom of light.

I know that Paul said in Philippians 1:18 that he was thankful the gospel was preached even when it was done under false pretenses, because truth was presented. And even then, a few will put their faith in the words and not be distracted by a messenger who is not Godly. But it is an infinitely more powerful presentation of the gospel when the person who proclaims it, also lives it.

Billy Graham preached basically the same as any preacher who believes historic Christian truth. But he was not only called and gifted to evangelize, but he had personal holiness which made his words much more powerful. No one else is called by God or gifted to be Billy Graham, but no one else has our unique mixture of abilities and limitations either.

We may be in the center of the will of God, and still hit the wall in terms of seeing results of prayers answered for ourselves or our loved ones. But we are all to walk by faith and not by sight. Some missionaries see tremendous results while others may be just as Godly and see no or very few results. I think of a Swedish missionary to Africa whose wife died there, and whose little girl was given to missionary friends. He left a very bitter man, remarried, and forbade his Swedish family to even mention God. But the only little boy who was allowed to help them was supernaturally converted, led most of his village to Christ, and became a devout Christian leader in his country.

Meanwhile the daughter married and lived in Seattle, and one day received a magazine in Swedish with a picture of a tombstone and her mother's name on it. She got a professor to translate it, and was reunited with her father in Sweden, who finally again began to follow Jesus Christ as Lord. I have not quite experienced the bitterness the Swedish missionary did, nor have you probably. But we all get discouraged when our prayers are not answered, or when we suffer great loss as he did. No doubt the Smith sisters had their share of discouragement also. But they kept on praying for personal repentance and holiness and revival, until it came.

Be ourselves?

Parents normally love their children more than their children love them, and that is the way it should be. After all, we are commanded by God to grow in grace, or favor with him, and parents have more years than our children have in order to do that. Therefore, we parents are more responsible to act justly, to love mercy, and to walk humbly with God. We are to be examples, in other words, and to repent when we are not.

Perhaps the example of repentance is one of the greatest gifts we can bestow upon them, since all have sinned, and fall short of the glory of God. If we pretend otherwise, we will lose respect and love anyway. So, we parents are to show kindness and patience, etc., even if we think our children do not! If we do want to encourage them in godliness, we can be sure we will either fail to speak truth on occasions when we should, but fear losing their love, or we will speak truth sometimes more harshly than we should.

We have all heard that we should "be ourselves," and especially inside our homes. But the British professor C. S. Lewis points out that we will have total chaos in our homes if we heed that advice. Among our family above all people, it is important that we allow the Holy Spirit to guide us, and to curb our natural instincts to bully or to be rude or selfish. To advise that we are to just "be ourselves" shows that whoever said that does not know either people or the Bible well at all!

Even when we love our children with respect, we parents are still prone to be selfish, worried, and to give too much or too little advice. Assuming we pray to encourage our children in Godliness and to discourage them in what is harmful, we will from time to time still err on the side of harsh "justice" or weak "love." What can we do but pray that the Holy Spirit convict us of our sins, and then ask God to help us again to have his words and attitudes with them? We are, after all, responsible to keep our own hearts tender before the Lord whether they or anyone else does or not. Then when we pray, God will make our prayers more effective than he otherwise would, since James 5:16 tells us the prayer of the righteous is powerful and effective.

After I had been following the Lord seriously for a year or two, I informed my father that I was thinking of joining another denomination. Until that time I had no positive interaction with any of their ministers, and I assumed my father had no good associations either, so I had no idea what his reaction would be. He answered, "Pray about it and do what God wants you to do." That is what I did. And I deeply appreciate him encouraging me to go to God for myself and to place myself consciously under his guidance, instead of giving me some harangue about why he did not like that denomination (if that was the case), and why I should not join them.

I relayed that story to a minister, and he said his father was a pastor, and that he definitely did not give his blessing when he was led to another branch of the Christian church. We naturally prefer that our children continue to have deep ties with us through their love for Jesus Christ if we are Christian, by geography, by ideas and politics and profession if possible. But by far the most important ties are those through the bonds of the Holy Spirit because they last forever.

I believe we will recognize each other in heaven, not necessarily by family, but by the extent to which we have encouraged each other in the Christian faith. Certainly, those who live with each other as spouses and parents and children have the most opportunity to do that, so it is a great sin if we just talk about trivial pursuits.

All other pursuits are relatively trivial, for if we succeed at everything else and fail to be a man or woman after God's own heart, we will have failed our loving creator. Let us pray that we and our children be people after his heart!

Sincere prayer

Many of the Russian congregations under communism would see a new visitor and wonder if the person was a plant who was sent there to spy on them. Several began to ask visitors to pray aloud in their meetings. Now a trained seminarian as Stalin was, could whip off a very convincing prayer for the naive and the backsliders among the congregations, even as trained seminarians can do (and sometimes really do) the same today. But for those who walked with God and who prayed sincerely, they recognized and appreciated prayers of the same ilk.

Whether seminary trained or not, there have always been Christians who valued humility before the Lord and who recognized those who sought to encourage them further in that direction. Real prayer is based on helplessness, wrote the Norwegian professor Ole Hallesby, in his great book simply and profoundly called *Prayer*. None of us really pray sincerely until we see our inability to solve our problems, and our helplessness to change another person who needs to change harmful behavior, etc. But God can solve our problems, and God can change every person.

Some of us have been changed radically by God, and still see our need to be transformed in deeper ways to glorify Jesus Christ. I admit it is still easier to see how others need to improve more than how I should improve, but I know from the Bible not to trust my feelings in this area! Reading the Bible and praying to understand and apply it does help us to get closer to God. Having fellowship with other sincere believers and hearing the gospel preached in the power of the Holy Spirit certainly encourages us to move toward repentance (for the first time or more deeply) and holiness.

And yet we can do all that and if we do not pray ourselves, all those good things will be like water running off a duck's back, for they will not stick. "Pray until you pray," someone has wisely advised. We can pray in ways that may impress our listeners and perhaps ourselves. But do we pray in ways that impress God?

Do we pray, in other words, until we know the mind of God, that he has said yes or no to our request? Do we pray until we know the words we are to preach orally or by written words, or what to say to someone in distress? 1 Peter 4:11 says we are to speak the very words of God, not just in the pulpit but in every conversation, avoiding idle words. How do we know idle words from those that come from God? We will neither know nor care unless we pray as Katy did, not with a canned prayer but a sincere one.

ACTS in our prayers

While I was a student pastor in Windsor, Ontario Canada, the regular pastor noticed that my prayers focused on my own needs (thanks, Rev. Brian Headley). He suggested that I broaden them, using the acrostic ACTS as a framework. ACTS stands for Adoration, Confession, Thanksgiving, and Supplication. These categories include basically the whole range of prayer possible and may help keep us from getting into a rut!

When we spend time adoring God in prayer, this recognizes his wonderful attributes. To praise God because he has all knowledge, all power, and because he is the perfect standard of goodness and justice, allows us to see our situations from his perspective, or to think Christianly. To express adoration to God the Father, God the Son Jesus Christ, and God the Holy Spirit, is to give comfort and peace anew to his followers.

Confession in prayer means that we take seriously the call of Jesus for repentance, or a change of heart and behavior when we conflict with the will of God. We are to pray that God forgive us of open and hidden sins, for the good we have left undone and for the evil that we have done (sins of omission and commission). 1 John 1:9 says, "If we confess our sins, he is faithful and just to forgive us our sins and to cleanse us from all unrighteousness." When we fail to do that, our worship becomes "a form of Godliness, denying the power thereof." But when we truly repent of all sin, the Holy Spirit makes himself known unmistakably in the church services. Unfortunately, this is rare today, although it was the norm in the New Testament (see1 Thessalonians chapters 1 and 2).

Thanksgiving is the third theme of prayer; we should include 1 Thessalonians 5:18, which says, "Give thanks in all circumstances; for this is the will of God in Christ Jesus for you." In the midst of every situation, Christians can deliberately give thanks to God for the assurance of salvation and his other great benefits. All can consciously and regularly be thankful for friends, family, food, clothes, shelter, and so many other things. It is human nature to stress our needs and wants, and to have a sense of entitlement. But when we discipline ourselves to be grateful, this cheers us and also those around us. "Count your blessings, name them one by one, and it will surprise you what the Lord has done." This simple but profound advice makes a huge difference in our spiritual, mental, and emotional health, and affects physical well-being also.

Supplication is certainly legitimate for the needs of others as well as for our own concerns. Since Jesus calls all to love and obey him, we are to pray for those who have not yet done that. We are also to pray for other needs we see, and then God will show us if and how we can be the means of answering our prayers.

Within the supplication section, we also have the right to ask that our own needs be met by God. We should not want to be among those of whom God says, "You do not have because you do not ask." When we deliberately and sincerely put ourselves into his hands and plead for help, he does make a way. Matthew 7:11: "If you then, who are evil (relative to God), know how to give good gifts to your children, how much more will your Father who is in heaven give good things to those who ask him!"

The Titanic

After seeing the movie, I finally saw the Titanic exhibit in Pigeon Forge, Tennessee. I am very glad I did because the movie left out some true and wonderful stories. Over 2,000 were on board when the ship considered by many to be "unsinkable," hit an iceberg and disappeared under the icy waters of the North Atlantic in just over two hours. Around 700 survived, but many more could have been saved had it not been for the arrogance (and criminal negligence) that prompted someone to pack only twenty lifeboats on board.

I was deeply moved by true accounts of so many Godly and brave and unselfish people who died because they helped others. A Baptist minister named Harper did that. He kept yelling, "Women, children, and unsaved men into the boats." He saw one chap floating past him on a plank and asked him if he was saved. The man answered, "No." A few moments he swirling water swept the same guy past the minister and again Rev. Harper asked him if he was saved. "Not yet," he replied. But he was only one of sixteen to live after being pulled from the icy waters (twenty-eight degrees F), and he became a Christian. He recounted that story several times in his country of Canada.

Other ministers were also unselfish and brave. I noticed no Presbyterian ministers were mentioned, and that bothered me some. Hopefully, none were among the men who donned women's clothes to sneak into the lifeboats!

Eight band members were together when their leader told them to leave the ship quickly or it would be too late. They grabbed their instruments and ran. But he stayed, and when he began to play that great hymn, "Nearer my God to Thee," they all returned with their instruments and joined him for that powerful last song, to comfort and encourage their fellow passengers. All of them died, going down with the ship, as the captain Smith did (and unlike another captain who escaped recently when his ship sunk off the coast of Italy, and he left the other passengers there to die).

Another moving event was about a very rich lady (Astor, I think) who was urged by her husband to leave him on the ship and climb aboard a lifeboat. She refused, saying that she had stayed with him in life, and she wanted to be with him in death. She handed her warm fur coat to a woman already in a nearby boat, and said, “Here, I will not be needing it anymore.” Both she and her husband perished soon afterwards. Whether rich or poor or in between, we need to ask ourselves if we would be as loving as Mrs. Astor was, and so many others who sacrificed their lives.

The Rogersville courthouse

I was walking past the courthouse in Rogersville, Tennessee, when I noticed the preacher. He was giving a sermon at the top of his lungs to a group of old men who were always there on Saturdays swapping knives. I thought to myself, "I am glad I do not have to do that; I am Presbyterian."

About two weeks later I was visiting my parents again in that area, and the Holy Spirit was still convicting me of my deep pride and arrogance. I drove out of Rogersville, and I was miserable. I knew it was the Lord's doing, because I was certain the dread was not anything I had concocted. So, I said to God, "All right. I will go back to that courthouse, and I will preach, or read the Bible, or cry, or do anything you want me to do."

As soon as I said that to God, the burden lifted. He did not want me to do any of that. But he certainly wanted me to be willing to set aside my pride to serve him anyway he chose. If you want to be certain if you are Christian or not, get real proud or look up some sin that is mentioned in the Bible and do it. If you do not have the unmistakable dread of the Holy Spirit fall on you, the triune God is not with you. If you sense his displeasure at what he calls sin, congratulations, you are Christian.

If we are from a mainline (now sideline) church we are prone to look down our noses at anything that smacks of emotionalism. This is because we value reason and doing things decently and in order. On the other hand, if we are from a more exuberant tradition, we tend to be arrogant towards those who are less demonstrative. Let's face it, folks. There is some craziness in every denomination. As long as Jesus Christ is worshipped as God and Lord, I hope we wish them well instead of snickering at their more extreme actions. Just choose the zaniness you tolerate best and join them.

The disciples were upset at one point because they saw another group that cast out demons in the name of Jesus, and he said to leave them alone. There are few enough Christians, and when we see another bunch more emotional or more analytical, let us pray for them and wish them well, instead of feeling superior. Professor C.S. Lewis had great admiration for Billy Graham, who reached folks for Jesus Christ that he could not reach. And of course, Graham had the utmost appreciation for Lewis, and his outreach toward intellectuals.

There is a place in this world for all kinds of Christians, as long as we have integrity and put Jesus first in our lives. As far as I know, every Christian group has some who fit that description. Some may prefer wilder congregations for the excitement and adventure. When a passenger was dragged off the United airline for some reason, one guy said he planned to continue flying United, since he was raised Pentecostal and was used to being dragged down the aisles. Others may prefer a more calm environment to ponder and meditate and pray quietly.

When people worship Jesus Christ as God, loving and obeying him, he rewards them. When they do not, Jesus will deal with them. So we do not have to worry about it either way. We just need to be willing to get more starchy or less starchy as the Holy Spirit leads.

Are we failing to be open to all God wants because we are afraid we will embarrass ourselves or others? I hope we get more concerned about whether we are an embarrassment to God or not. I hope we get more concerned about his reputation than our own. I have seen my mom and others shout in church services before, and I am certain at least one was sincerely trying to glorify Jesus Christ (my mom). Are you thinking, "I am glad I do not have to do that; I am Presbyterian, or Baptist, or Methodist, or whatever?"

Pray to our feelings?

At the annual Chicago prayer breakfast, a speaker was applauded when he announced that after September 11, we are all united, and it is wrong to pray to a specific deity. For the first time, the name of Jesus was not mentioned there. We went from a strong Christian nation to a secular one and have been a pagan one for several decades.

According to Barna research, only eight percent of Americans even claim to be Christian in the historic biblical sense (Jesus is God, never sinned, all are to repent and follow him as a God and Lord, etc.). If you talk to high school students in the Bible Belt, they will see the eight percent figure as ridiculously high because it includes parents and grandparents who abandoned evangelism and holy lifestyles for money and pleasure. Thank God for exceptions.

So the progression (regression actually) from a Christian culture, for the most part, to a neutral secular one where any spirituality is mocked, to paganism where any truth claim is opposed, has taken place with most people either not noticing or in agreement. But the good news is that followers of Jesus Christ made converts in such a culture, for the Roman Empire allowed the worship of many gods (sometimes) as long as none of them were taken seriously. Yet Christians proclaimed that Jesus is Lord of all and deserves our worship, from the first generation through Polycarp and the second generation, until now. The big difference between then and now is that all the churches then, whether Jewish or Greek or Roman, held to the deity of Jesus Christ and to the necessity of supernatural conversion.

Now several churches would deny that Jesus is God over all and would be Hindus in drag. Eastern religious leaders have noted the same thing with surprise and gratitude. They have commented publicly how several in the churches share their beliefs while using Christian terms such as salvation. Instead of the historic Biblical meaning of deliverance from sin into fellowship with God through faith in Jesus, some now think of salvation as realizing the potential within each person. When a person mentions the Holy Spirit, some see him as just feelings instead of eternal God who teaches, convicts of sin, confirms in righteousness, and always honors Jesus Christ as God, as in John Chapters 15 and 16:

In other words, praying to our feelings has become popular among those who love to go to church but have not encountered the God who is beyond ourselves. And if we have met someone or some spirit greater than ourselves- how do we know if that entity is loving or not? After all, several who touch the supernatural spend the rest of their lives drawing scary pictures on the walls of mental institutions! In my opinion it is better to remain secular than to unite with an evil power greater than ourselves.

But there are no bad side effects of looking more closely at Jesus Christ of history, who is the same as Jesus of the Bible, full of grace and truth. He is scary only when we make excuses for our sins, instead of repenting before him who died as a substitute for our sins. Jesus is and always was God, entering our world as a human being while he continued to be God. If the Nordics want to paint him as blond and blue eyed, and the Asians and Africans want to paint Jesus to resemble them, fine, although he was Jewish and probably brown. His first followers were ethnic Jews, and then Greeks and Romans and Africans. The apostle Thomas made converts among the Indians in India, so Christianity soon became and has remained, a universal religion.

Once during an airplane trip, I sat by an African woman, and our discussion about Jesus continued after we entered the airport. Hearing the differences we had, an Asian man joined us and handed her a gospel tract. I was very encouraged. Europeans were so effective in missions that over half of Christians have been non-European for several decades, and basically only among white folks is the gospel not growing. Many of the new immigrants to the USA are dedicated Christians. I hope and pray they will not grow ashamed of Jesus and his claims, as so many Europeans and European descendants have done!

Do we live for Christ?

I was deeply moved by two paintings I saw in the Hermitage Museum, Saint Petersburg, Russia. One was by my favorite painter, Rembrandt, and is called "The Return of the Prodigal." It shows the biblical scene of the father embracing the wayward son who has returned home. I identify with that son, as does anyone who has ever known God the Father in the first place. That is because every Christian has turned aside and grieved the Holy Spirit from time to time. But when we repent as the son in the story did, God is always waiting with open arms to welcome us back, whether the rebellion is for five minutes or fifty years.

Meanwhile, the elder brother is shown on the right side of the painting, looking glum and jealous. Technically he was not present when the prodigal returned, but Rembrandt wanted to condense a few verses into one scene. Although he had stayed in the house as a conservative, he still had not embraced the father.

Another painting was of Mary Magdalene, featuring her with red and swollen eyes, for she had repented of her sins with many tears, to become a faithful follower of Jesus Christ. Many of the Czars and their families, as well as more common people, saw these and other paintings of biblical scenes, and yet for the most part, completely rejected the message of the Bible. Godly folks were not plentiful in Russia, either before or after the communist revolution. The last Czarina, or queen, took her sick son to the monk Rasputin. He was a very controversial individual.

We are all tempted to go outside the Bible for comfort, and indeed that may be appropriate with medical care, as long as it does not contradict what the Bible teaches. I received a tough diagnosis recently, and I am considering some options. But there is no option for me to abandon Jesus Christ, and I pray to have his attitudes and prayers about circumstances as well as about people.

I have peace now, and I hope and pray to have peace no matter what happens, however pleasant or unpleasant my life gets. Of course, we are to do all we can within reason, but even then, God has set our times, and they are in his hands.

David Brainard was a great missionary to the Indians who died when he was twenty-nine, while the Chinese church leader Watchman Née was seventy. What is important is not how or when we die, but do we live for Jesus Christ and know for certain that we have peace with him? God reached out through the Dutch masters, the Russians, Americans and others. He calls us individually to repent of our sins and to follow him as God and Lord. No matter how many days we have left, may the Triune God help us to have words and attitudes and actions from him.

Profession of faith inspired by the Holy Spirit?

Christianity is of the belief that God is one; eternally in three persons. The Trinity is God the Father, God the Son Jesus Christ, and God the Holy Spirit. Many churches celebrate Pentecost every year, when the Holy Spirit appeared to the disciples in the book of Acts. Unfortunately, the Holy Spirit is often considered to be the "red headed stepchild" of the Trinity. So many people are turned off by the institutional church because it is "a form of Godliness, denying the power thereof," as Paul phrased it. Many grew up in churches and (depending on the type of church) either walked the aisles and made a commitment, or more quietly made a profession of faith in a church class or at home.

But either way, the profession of Christian faith was in vain unless the person was drawn supernaturally to worship Jesus Christ as God. In 1 Corinthians 12:3, we learn, "No man can say that Jesus is the Lord, but by the Holy Ghost." In other words, a person may make many professions and join several churches, but until the Holy Spirit prompts and supernaturally encourages a person to make a commitment to follow Jesus Christ, one is left with only a form of Godliness- a vain pretense, or perhaps an honest emotional response to try to fit in socially.

The Holy Spirit is God, as Acts 5:3-4 clearly teaches. In these verses Peter said that an individual lied to the Holy Ghost (the word ghost is from the German geist, while the word spirit is from the Latin, meaning exactly the same). The lie was furthermore said not to be to a human being, but to God. So, the early church recognized the Triune God clearly.

The Holy Spirit is also a person. He comforts (John 14:16, 26), and has intelligence. He has will (Romans 8:16, Acts 16:7, 1 Corinthians 12:1:1) and has affections (Isaiah 63:10, Ephesians 4:30). We are not to grieve the Holy Spirit, and 1 Thessalonians 5:19 tells us not to quench the Spirit.

The Holy Spirit is the sanctifier who communicates to Christians. He teaches (John 14:26), and testifies of Jesus Christ (John 15:26). He guides, shows us things to come (my wife in a vision twenty-five years before we met), and always glorifies Jesus Christ (John 16::13-14). So, if one claims to have a spirit, they may have one. But if that spirit does not glorify Jesus Christ, it is definitely not the Holy Spirit! The Holy Spirit is definitely the only spirit I want around me.

Who has the Holy Spirit? Some teach that everyone does, but that is not accurate, and the claim trivializes the third person of the Trinity. No, the Holy Spirit is given only to those who obey Jesus Christ. Acts 5:32 And we are his witnesses of these things; and so is also the Holy Ghost, whom God hath given to them that obey him. Furthermore, Jude 1:19 mentions that some are devoid of the Spirit. The Spirit spoke to Peter (Acts 10:19), and he is witness to us (Hebrews 10:15). The anointing of the Spirit abides in you and teaches, according to 1 John 2:27: The conscience of the Christian bears witness in the Holy Spirit (Romans 9:1).

Every person has a conscience, which is a compilation of societal rules and family traditions. But the true Christian has the Holy Spirit to inform and guide the conscience, often in ways that are against our cultural and family values. Paul would be a good benchmark for us. He made the point that his preaching and speaking was in demonstration of the Spirit and of power (1 Corinthians 4::4, 13). That kind of preaching is so foreign to many churches. Under the influence of the Holy Spirit, Paul taught in 1 Corinthians 4:20, "The kingdom of God does not consist in talk but in power."

To put it bluntly, we can say all the right words and have correct theology, but if the power of the Holy Spirit is not an unmistakable part of our lives, we have not known anything about the kingdom of God, nor have we ever entered it. So, when people speak of having union with the risen Jesus Christ, such words will seem like an illusion until we personally have been supernaturally drawn into such a union also.

Since the Holy Spirit knows all things, of course he does not always lead us in ways we want to go. If we always sense that God is directing us in ways we prefer, rest assured that is an illusion. That is because God's ways are higher than our ways, and often very different. Paul, for example, crossed many mountains and faced dangerous obstacles in order to preach the gospel in a section of what is now modern Turkey. But Acts 16:7 records that he was forbidden by the Holy Spirit to preach in Asia, and when he tried to go into Bythinia, the Spirit also denied him that plan. So, to be a Christian, the Holy Spirit must be a reality within us. Even when the Holy Spirit warns us not to proceed in a particular direction, that is a great comfort. I can say that because as 1 John 3:24 states, we know he (God the eternal Son Jesus Christ) abides in us by his Spirit which he has given us.

Passing on our faith or just culture?

Do you ever wonder why millions of immigrants continue to come to the USA when we are the third most populated country in the world (after China and India)? Even the so-called native Americans came here from other lands. Unless our ancestors were missionaries or criminals, they almost certainly arrived for economic reasons. If the Scots or Germans had a great life in their own countries, they had little or no incentive to leave, unless the Lord or the government prodded them out.

Every American should travel to a poor country and then compare why our nation has several of the billions of human beings wanting to come here. Why is that true? Why are some countries rich and others are poor? There are exceptions, but normally, when an individual stays faithful to a spouse with respect, works hard, doesn't waste money on expensive booze or drugs and doesn't steal or lie, a peaceful and fairly prosperous life results.

The same is true on a national scale. Yes, we have some very evil people in the USA, and waste and incompetence in all layers of government, etc. But we need to appreciate that it takes four times longer to start a business in Europe than in the USA (one good reason not to rush to convert dollars to euros) and 16 to 40 times longer in the Philippines and in other underdeveloped countries. When a crooked government invents layers of bureaucracy to give jobs to their lackeys, the standard of life lowers dramatically for all but the worst criminals.

Virtue brings a good fair government and a society where folks want to come, instead of one they want to leave. Or as the Bible puts it much better, righteousness exalts a nation, but sin is a reproach to any people. Our nation will be as bad or worse than the nations our ancestors left if we cheat on our taxes, have unfair taxes, reward dishonesty, make bribery a way of life, and glorify gambling or prostitution, etc.

What are we doing personally to exalt/lift up/promote the best for our nation? Not much unless we are right with God, and act justly, love mercy, and walk humbly with him. Does our family and others who interact with us, see us encouraging what is good and discouraging what is evil, first of all in our own lives, and then wherever we go? Do they see us not only talking about what is good, but actually doing fair and honest and kind deeds? Can they trust us to treat them as well in private as we do when others are watching?

The USA is on top of the world in many categories. No one questions that economically and militarily and culturally (well, the French would dispute this part) we are far above others. But are we passing on the Christian faith to our children as well as we pass on American culture? Statistically we aren't, with rare exceptions.

After traveling much more than I ever wanted to travel, I am glad to see that most Americans do not care what Europeans or Africans or Asians think about us. At the same time, I am deeply grieved that so few care about what God thinks about us. As individuals and as a nation, we have been given much. God says in his word that where much is given, much is required. Do we have a clear idea of what God requires of us personally in order to be righteous in his sight? As one song so pragmatically proposes, "Come let us pray until the power of the Lord comes down." When we do that the Holy Spirit will cut through our rationalizations and will guide us to be righteous specifically in ways that glorify Jesus Christ.

Four percent of Christian couples pray together.

Those in the hotel/motel/chalet and cabin rental business say that church groups are the worst. They often trash the place, stealing and being very destructive. Some of this may be the fault of wild pagans the Christians take with them. But if this is so, then why do the few wild pagans have more influence on the supposedly spiritual and well-grounded Christian teens than the Christians have on them?

I heard a Christian radio speaker say that only four percent of Christian couples pray together. In other words, only those humbled themselves before God regularly to consciously praise God, to confess their sins to one another, to be thankful, to pray how to best encourage each other, and to pray for the salvation and growth in grace of their children and other loved ones.

When children see this modeled by Godly parents, this normally has a powerful and positive impact, assuming those who pray are Godly, or sincerely repent when they are not. This is not to say that teens will be locked into perfection ever. But I cannot believe that Godly praying parents result in the sort of church group that makes pagans look Godly by comparison. By the way, I do understand that all church groups are not in this category. I applaud the rare exceptions, and I hope you cherish them.

"Why don't you go back to that church group?" The son replied to his father that it was because they were the meanest kids in the school. I would like to think this is an isolated case, but so would the owners of rentals who see them ransacked regularly by church youth groups.

I talked recently with a Christian couple who are missionaries, and I mentioned the four percent finding, adding that I hope they are in that group. Instead of being offended, they said that indeed they do pray together an hour each morning before the work begins. Their three daughters credit their prayer life together with giving them the support they needed, to help them walk with Jesus Christ until they married Godly men.

Yes, I know an individual is responsible himself or herself to love God, and some overcome horrible home situations to do so. But we are responsible to not only point others to the Light of the world, but to walk in that Light ourselves. We are definitely not called by God to raise children in the church to be more evil than those who do not attend church. It is probably better not to go at all than to give others the impression that a form of Godliness that denies the power of God, is all there is.

Why are so many teens who go to church becoming immune to the gospel instead of catching the real thing? Did the parents ever have more than an empty form of Godliness themselves? If so, we are to pray and to live Godly lives before them, then hopefully they will want what we have instead of being repulsed by what we have.

Monica

A friend of mine tells of how his in-laws decided to go to church with them one Sunday. They were not churchgoers at all and were relatively educated and well off. So, he prayed that God would give them a calm and dignified service, because he thought that was important in order to touch them deeply.

When the service began, he noticed that the band played longer than it usually did and was much wilder than normal. A woman in a bright yellow dress jumped up beside them and danced, saying over and over in a very unsophisticated way, "I looove you Jesus." My friend said he felt so embarrassed he wished the floor would swallow him up.

When my friend finally began to preach, a Marine from one of the nearby military bases in North Carolina ran to the front, grabbed the microphone out of his hand, and named several of his sins in detail. Among them he related how he beat his wife up, and sobbingly said how sorry he was. At that time, a woman ran up from the congregation and commenced to hug him and cry. My friend said he really hoped it was his wife. After that event, my friend preached, and the service ended.

On the way home, all was silent until the mother-in-law commented, "That was an interesting service." She added that in all her years teaching school she had seen many children who had been beaten black and blue but had never heard of a parent expressing any regret. When we pray for God to move in the life of someone, he may do so in unexpected ways. When Monica prayed that her son would not leave North Africa and go to Italy, it was because she feared he would be lost to the gospel. But he went anyway and began to listen to the sermons of Bishop Ambrose of Milan.

He was supernaturally converted to Jesus Christ and left his wild lifestyle behind. Today he is known to the world as Saint Augustine, arguably the most influential Christian since Saint Paul.

When we look around us, it is often difficult to trust that God is really answering our prayers, or that we are having an effect at all. We are all tempted to shift our trust from the promises of the Bible to our understanding of how circumstances are unfolding. If we can see how God is working, we tend to relax and to trust that all is well. But when things seem to fall apart, that often is the most effective way for God to move in a particular situation. We do not get to dictate the methods God uses in accomplishing his will (nor do we get to dictate anything else to God, actually).

But we do get to cooperate in the love and power of God when we love and obey Jesus Christ, and then pray as he guides us to pray. James 5:16 assures us that when we are right with God our prayers are powerful and effective. Are we righteous, as Monica and my friend were? Then God promises to guide us to pray in ways that will move others toward friendship with him. But even then, the prayers often will not proceed in ways that we expect. When they do not, do we worry, or do we keep trusting that God reigns and continues to work in ways that honor him best? Sometimes I trust that and sometimes I don't. God help us to love and to trust him for the first time, or more deeply!

God is the ground of our being?

When folks teach that God is really "the ground of our being," or "God is really the God behind God," or some other fuzzy concept, they are saying that Jesus Christ is a crude and out of date way of referring to God. In other words, to claim that God can be known personally as a friend, seems to be empty arrogance to the detractors of historic Christianity.

I understand that when your parents attended church for social or business reasons instead of going to meet with God, such cynicism would naturally result. When ministers preach American cultural norms (freedom from authority, rugged individualism...) with a thin veneer of biblical terms, one would have to look elsewhere for spirituality, as most of the baby boomers have done. One cannot fault them or their parents for failing to pass on supernatural union with Christ to their offspring when they did not have that type of friendship themselves.

But several no doubt have been truly converted, and yet have no interest in passing Christianity on to their descendants or friends. Very few Christians seem to really care about what pleases Jesus Christ, preferring to live as if they were pagans. Is it possible to really be Christian and do this? Yes, I did that for several years. I had no doubt that I was Christian, for the Holy Spirit was with me to convict me of sins of omission and commission (refusing to do what the Bible commanded me to do and doing what the Bible said not to do). If I had children at that time, I would have known what was most important in life—to follow Jesus Christ as Savior and Lord—but I would not have cared deeply enough to have lived out the gospel before them. A vague spirituality that doesn't require any inhibition of our natural impulses to be selfish has gained prominence inside and outside of our churches.

If God is "the ground of our being," then whatever our being wants to do, is blessed by him. If, as the psychotherapist Carl Jung taught, our unconscious has both good and bad and the unconscious is really God, then to follow Jesus Christ as God is not logical. Also, to ask forgiveness of sins of greed or unkindness and all else the Bible condemns, is pointless. Such theories encourage us to live as Israel did during the time of the judges, when "Everyone did what was right in his own eyes." If we want to do that, I hope we have the honesty to say that we are backslidden Christians or not Christian at all!

Jesus says that if anyone wants to be his disciple, he must deny himself (all selfish desires that conflict with the teaching of the Bible) and take up his cross and follow him. Only Jesus and the other writers of the New Testament under the guidance of the Holy Spirit, teach that we are all born with a bent to sinning—in addition to committing individual sins such as lying, adultery, theft... it is that inherent streak of rebellion against God that is counteracted by the Holy Spirit, who begins to live within each person after supernatural conversion. Conversion to what-conversion to follow Jesus Christ as Savior from sin to be Lord (ruler) of our life.

Instead of being, the ground of our being, God is separate and distinct from us. We humans are the creatures that God created. God calls us to choose him. It is offensive to educated and self-made individuals to put ourselves under the power of anyone at all. Yet God has all power and is perfect love, so to volunteer to be under his Lordship does make sense. God became man as he added human flesh to be born as a baby in Bethlehem. At the same time, he continued to be God. While on earth Jesus lived a sinless life and was full of grace and truth. He has all power and is perfect love and will judge each person throughout history. He deserves our love and devotion- so let us not worship our ideas instead!

God determines when and where we live.

With demonstrations and counter demonstrations, the issue of illegal immigration continues to be hot. How should we think Christianly about this matter? If you want clear words about how important the USA is to God, in its present or future form, here they are. "Behold, the nations are like a drop from a bucket, and are accounted as the dust on scales ... all the nations are as nothing before him, they are accounted by him as less than nothing and emptiness," says Isaiah 40:15, 17: This viewpoint extends to Israel, France, as well as the USA and all other countries.

Will we be concerned to "protect our American way of life?" Or is there anyone who values God's point of view? Only the individual has eternal significance to God, not this nation or any other nation or language spoken. Acts 17:26 says, "And he made from one man every nation of mankind to live on all the face of the earth, having determined allotted periods and the boundaries of their dwelling place." In other words, from a human point of view, we and others chose (or our ancestors) to live in this country, but from God's perspective, he inspired everyone who is here, to be here in the USA (or wherever you are).

Why? Acts 17:27 says, "That they should seek God, and perhaps feel their way towards him, and find him (Jesus Christ). Yet he is actually not far from each one of us." Will those who come here legally (my wife and children, for example), or illegally, find the living God through us? Or will they find crabby and inhospitable people who sneer and complain loudly when we hear another language, or see other customs introduced?

Will we who claim to value the Bible as the Word of God let the Holy Spirit who inspired the Bible be our guide? Or will we be guided by our fears and prejudices and discomfort over hearing other languages? Will we be bitter to find that our language or ethnic group has been outnumbered, or will we pray to welcome others with love and respect?

I am sure it does not bother God at all when my color or language is surpassed by other colors or languages, and I pray that we consider important what God considers important, and trivial what God considers trivial. I am also sure that I do not always do that, but I am more and more convicted of sin by the Holy Spirit when I do not. I am not called by God to advance the glory of blue eyed or brown eyed people, or those who call God, Gott or Bog or Deus. As a Christian I am called to glorify Jesus

Christ as God. To do that I must first of all repent- and repeatedly repent, of any and all allegiances that compete with him, whether national or racial or linguistic or whatever. Then I am to ask God the Holy Spirit how to best glorify and honor Jesus Christ by my words, attitudes, and actions.

Fenelon

Fenelon, who was a French Roman Catholic archbishop, said that a baby sees an apple and a diamond and regards them equally, and we should be the same. He wrote this in a letter to a small group of Christians in the royal court of King Louis XIV, arguably the most immoral royal court in the history of the world. When we pass through the Christmas season, probably that is the most greedy time of the year. And on Thanksgiving Day, many employees must work that day or night, so that selfish employers can goad on silly materialists. Thank God for the few businesses who buck the trend to trash Thanksgiving Day. God bless them.

In the interest of full disclosure, I admit that (to paraphrase C.S. Lewis), consumerism/materialism, is one of the few sins not attractive to me. Therefore, I can rail against those who "shop til you drop" without fear of being lumped together with them. But we who are not swayed by the sins of greed for material opulence ought not to look down our noses at those who are. We can be certain that we have other sins, besetting and appealing sins, that those hordes of shopping addicts do not have.

They may be open sins, and by the way, men usually have these more often, and therefore feel less welcome in church than women whose sins are more acceptable to the general public. But all of us veer consciously and radically out of the will of God, since the Bible assures us "the heart is deceitful above all things, and desperately sick." So, if we are not tempted to show off materially, we are prone to be greedy for sexual pleasure, or for status, or comfort, or safety, or for something else we crave more than to worship Jesus Christ as the name above all names. It is not wrong to have money or pleasure or status, etc., unless we get those valued gifts by disobeying the clear teaching of the Bible.

Fenelon says, "Sometimes we find the most surprising faults in otherwise good people ... I ask you more than ever not to spare me if I need correction. Even if you mention a fault which is not really there, there will be no harm done. If I find that your correction wounds me, then my irritability simply shows that you have touched a sore spot in my life." I hope we have his attitude throughout the year, because if we do not need to repent of materialism, we need to repent of hedonism or laziness or some other trait that hinders us from humbly walking with the risen Jesus Christ.

Embrace all cultures?

Anthropologist Carolyn Fluehr-Lobban agonized over the fact that her discipline's prime directive- cultural relativism- left her with no rationale for opposing rape or racial genocide in other cultures. In other words, anthropology asserts that there is no such thing as God, who has communicated absolutes of truth and right and wrong.

Therefore, according to this theory, in Europe and the United States, where Christianity has had strong influence, it may be wrong to rape and commit racial genocide. So, we were right to condemn the slaughter of other ethnic groups in the Balkan, for example. But when Africans or Asians wipe out other tribes or neighboring groups, we as white people have cultural imperialism when we condemn this. Also, in non-European culture when rape occurs, we are being self-righteous and bigoted to oppose it, according to cultural relativism.

This sort of warped demonic thinking has permeated European and American culture more and more, as people have sought to eliminate Christian teaching because it condemns lifestyles we choose. How convenient to steal, commit adultery, etc., and to be able to rationalize that there is no God, therefore whatever we choose to do is okay.

"They thought it was an honor to be sacrificed ... They had a different idea of life and death." These are the words of Mexican First Lady Patricia Valasco Zedillo, as she and her husband escorted President Clinton and Mrs. Clinton around Mayan ruins in the Yucatán Peninsula. She described child sacrifices performed there, explaining that the Mayans believed "the universe was nourished" by the child murders.

There is no basis to condemn such practices unless there is a God who has revealed himself to be opposed to such action. By the way, however one interprets the bloody Old Testament passages, they were not to be followed after Christ came, who says to treat others as you want to be treated. But to be personally disgusted at the Mayan rituals is no more significant than to dislike liver or onions unless our choices reflect a higher power than ourselves.

This is not to say anyone can know truth exhaustively. But as Francis Shaffer said, it is possible to know true truth. "I did it my way," sang Frank Sinatra, without any concern about what pleased God. When a person rapes or murders and says, "I did it my way," we have no legitimate basis to praise or condemn, unless we can appeal to a higher power who has communicated his mind to us.

Christians affirm that God the Father, God the Son Jesus Christ, and God the Holy Spirit exist eternally, and gave a clear and accurate account of what God wants, in the Bible. Those who reject this need to closely examine their own presuppositions. Where do they get their ideas and beliefs? How valid are the sources, and why should you trust the founders of their systems of belief? Are they people of integrity, or did they have one standard for themselves and a higher standard for others?

Even those who do not follow Jesus Christ as God, admit that he was a good man. But he was not a good man. He was a liar or a deluded lunatic unless he was truly God. This is because he made such outlandish claims for himself if he were a mere good man or prophet. John 14:6 says, "I am the way, and the truth, and the life." The Holy Spirit led his follower in Colossians 1:16 to write, "all things were created through him and for him." And in Colossians 2:10 the Holy Spirit teaches that Jesus "is the head of all rule and authority." That is the only legitimate reason ultimately for choosing good, and for even knowing good from evil.

My dog doesn't do that.

I walked my dog past the house of a neighbor with a beautiful flower garden, and she appeared and began to rant about how the dogs in the area were ruining her flowers. By the time she stopped to catch her breath I was a little mad myself. So, I said, "Well, my dog doesn't do that." Immediately my dog hiked his leg and drenched some of her artwork.

We all tend to make excuses when we or our loved ones (or dogs) are accused of wrongdoing, or to confess halfheartedly, if at all. It is exceedingly rare for the Holy Spirit to convict us of sin- otherwise we would have massive revivals with deep conviction for trying to honor ourselves in various circumstances.

C.S. Lewis related hearing a minister preach of how a good family life was the cure for the ills of society and waxed lyrical about the joys of family. One of his daughters told him that if he were ever invited to lunch with them, for God's sake please go, for it would make the meal less dreadful. Sure enough, once he went, and saw the parents treat their children with far less civility and grace than they would have shown ordinary criminals.

How could that pastor—and the rest of us—see so clearly the sins of others and so little of our own sins? It is pride that makes us see the sins of spouses/children/conservatives/liberals to be so much worse than our own. We are all affected by great pride- the poor as well as the rich, and people of every color and language. We do have common grace—folks can be and often are hospitable and kind and helpful, apart from Christianity, and sometimes more than some Christians. We who follow Jesus have no monopoly on virtue at all- we just have the Holy Spirit within us. In addition to normal human nature, each Christian has the Holy Spirit or God within. This makes us miserable when we sin (have words or attitudes or actions God calls sin). And the same Holy Spirit gives us peace and joy when we really want to glorify Jesus Christ in our circumstances.

But what if we do not have peace in our family? Then we should do all that we know to do in order to gain peace, and there is no use to pretend, or sooner or later we will be exposed, as Lewis discovered what was really going on with the family he visited. I hope we are more concerned with honor going to Jesus than to us for being a model person or having a model family. To have the goal of honoring Jesus above all, is always a struggle. We may gloss it over when situations are pleasant, and we have most of what we want in life. Self-doubts as to meaning and purpose may not appear so important when material needs are met.

But when material needs are difficult to accomplish, then stresses will be terrible, and will tend to tear apart even the best of families. Especially during these times, I hope and pray that we explore all possibilities to make the situation better, repent of our sins, and ask God for guidance and help. Perhaps it may be necessary to go to friends who may know of work or other opportunities for using our gifts and abilities in ways that best honor Jesus Christ.

In this year, please pray that God let us be encouragement to others in deep and meaningful ways. I know many individuals and families are hurting in several kinds of situations. Perhaps they are self-destructive or maybe circumstances have knocked them over through no fault of their own. Either way, I pray that God helps us to search our hearts to make sure that any problems we have are not of our own making, to repent when they are, and to remain faithful to follow Jesus and to trust his great and precious promises. I know that is not always easy, but it is the best life possible.

The water strider

As I ate my lunch quietly by a creek in the Great Smoky Mountains National Park, I saw an otter and fish swimming by with the greatest of ease. But what most impressed me was a water strider. I identified with him, because for about fifteen minutes he tried to go upstream and gained around an inch at most! If he had a human mind, I am convinced he would have wondered why his progress was so slow, and why the water was so swift, and why he did not have stronger and longer legs.

I recalled a seminary professor who was talking informally with a small group of us students, when he began to recount how he had prayed for someone (a beauty queen—it seems to always be a beauty queen and not a waitress or lawyer) who had one leg shorter than the other. After the prayer, the shorter leg grew to be as long as the other one.

As we pondered silently on that, I mentioned that I had always wanted to be taller, and I requested that he pray that both of my legs grow longer. My petition was not granted. Years later I realized that my hope may have sounded sarcastic, but it was not. I was sincere, and I could have proven my height before and after the prayer. I would have given the glory to God, and I would even have mentioned him favorably.

Why have you made me this way? This has been a question for devout (and less devout) people throughout history when we lapse into distrust of God. Perhaps my maternal grandfather wondered why he was short, until a certain battle during World War 1: He was loading a cannon when another soldier rudely demanded "Get out of the way, shorty." The very next instant a German cannonball took his head off.

God has blessed each of us with a gift mix of abilities and limitations, in order to bring his purposes to pass. We may prefer to be taller or richer or different in several ways. And sometimes by repentance and study and hard work, we can improve our circumstances (And I read that now legs can be lengthened for around $70,000). At other times we may do all that, and still seem to be like the water strider. We may not be able to impress others very much with our abilities. So what?

The Bible requires that we act justly, love mercy, and walk humbly with God. No person or circumstance or limitation can keep us from doing that. Then our life will be a powerful witness for folks or against them. Saint Paul tells us to stand firm, to let nothing move us, but to always give ourselves fully to Jesus, knowing that our labor in the Lord is not in vain. Life may seem like the water strider, but then we are to trust the Word of God more than our feelings and observations. The many and great promises in the Bible that our life matters and has great impact when we love and obey Jesus Christ, ensures that our work/labor/efforts to please him are not in vain.

Following Christ kills boredom

"When you work for the Lord, you don't get bored," is a joyful expression. When I began to take Jesus Christ sincerely, I attached myself to some folks in Knoxville, Tennessee, who were both very Godly and very colorful. One of the couples came up from the state of Georgia and called themselves Junior and Sissy. While riding with them in their car one day, they taught a song to their little daughter that included the words, "When you work for the Lord, you don't get bored." I do not know if the little girl benefited from that song or not, but I did.

I had been bored often while growing up in rural east Tennessee, and later in Amsterdam, Paris, etc. After a few days, the thrill of museums, canals, towers, and all other sights (and relationships) become mundane, unless we are working for the God of the universe. Since all things were created through Jesus Christ and for him, and he has all power in heaven and in earth and assures us that those who love and obey him are guided by him into the best life possible, boredom for such an individual is never an option. We may be puzzled or bewildered, or even mad or sad at times when our hopes and plans are blocked. But life is always fascinating, for the follower of Jesus knows that every circumstance is conforming us into his image more and more.

There are no accidents since Jesus has all power, and therefore blocked or open doors are there for a purpose. Maybe we are to keep knocking until the door opens, or perhaps we are to give up, or to refuse to enter when it does open. But do not be like the witty Irish, who claim, "When God shuts a door, he shuts a window too." The Christian can be confident that everything happens for a reason, or for several reasons, whether we can understand in a few moments, or maybe never. How can I bring honor to Jesus Christ in the midst of my present situation? That is a question when asked sincerely, may make us glad to see the answer or sad, but never bored.

What can I learn from this circumstance? That is another question that prevents monotony. That will help us to grow in favor with God as we develop our minds. We all like to be entertained, some with crude humor and others with witty humor or attention or praise. But consciously and daily asking God to help us to learn all he wants us to learn, and then praying to honor Jesus Christ, delivers us from boredom and into fruitful fellowship with the Triune God.

I know very well that it is sometimes difficult to keep on following him and not our own feelings and logic that are naturally predisposed against God. I am thinking now of an Indian missionary to Nepal, whose pregnant wife was just raped repeatedly by soldiers. I have confidence that both are sincere Christians, who rarely if ever have the problem of being bored.

As the British writer and professor C.S. Lewis said, Christianity is either the most important thing in life (as Jesus and his disciples claim clearly in different ways) or it is not important at all. It cannot be just a little bit important but not enough to live by and to pass on to our children and grandchildren and friends.

Perhaps we have no opportunity to pass Christianity on as directly as we prefer. That is okay. It is just as wrong to speak when we should be silent, as it is to be quiet when we should say a good word about Jesus Christ.

As we are willing on a daily basis to be faithful friends of his, we must pray in order to maintain that openness. Otherwise, our consciousness can be seared as with a hot iron if we pile up rebellions, and it will be easier and easier to miss that "still small voice." But when we pray to be open to hear and to obey whatever he says to be and to do, boredom will never be a problem in our lives!

Hymns born through pain

Some of my favorite hymns have flowed from deep personal tragedies the authors experienced. Thomas Dorsey received word that his wife and child had died during childbirth. But instead of getting bitter, he then penned the lines that have comforted so many in his song, "Precious Lord, Take My Hand."

Joseph Scrivener, a native of Ontario, Canada, received the news that his family had perished at sea. Instead of getting resentful and turning his back on God, we can be truly thankful that he chose to draw closer to Jesus Christ, whom the Bible calls the author of life. The result was the powerful song, "What a friend we have in Jesus."

Another saint was suicidal, and in such a mood he requested that a taxi driver take him to the London Bridge. The fog was so thick that the driver apologized because he could not find the bridge. But he assured William Cowper that he could find his way back to his home. Once home, Cowper wrote a song with words from the first line that have become common usage in the English language.

"God moves in a mysterious way, his wonders to perform. He plants his footsteps on the sea and rides upon the storm." And the last verse affirms his belief in divine guidance. "Blind unbelief is sure to err, and scan his work in vain. God is his own interpreter and he will make it plain."

When severe trials come, I hope and pray we go to God for strength and comfort, as these authors did. Do not depend on fog or another intervention to preserve us if we worry or otherwise harm ourselves or others. Instead, I encourage each of us to turn to the Bible, and to the God of the Bible in prayer, and to precious hymns to lift us up in times of need.

One of the most moving examples of a hymn giving peace under extreme duress was when an African saint was tied up and about to be shot for being a Christian. Before the bullets ripped into him, he was given a last request, and he sang this song.

"Out of my bondage, sorrow and night, Jesus I come, Jesus I come; into thy freedom, gladness and light, Jesus I come to thee." His last few words and the last verse are as follows. "Out of the fear and dread of the tomb, Jesus I come, Jesus I come; into the joy and light of thy home, Jesus

I come to thee. Out of the depths of ruin untold, into thy peaceful sheltering fold, ever thy glorious face to behold, Jesus I come to thee."

Fear not.

Isaiah 43:5 tells those who are friends with God, "Fear not." As we enter each new year I hope this good advice is heeded by each of us. As a high school student, I remember hearing a group sing about being three, four, and finally 500 miles away from home, and how scary that sounded to me. I was awed to even think about that distance, because trips to Nashville and Louisville were my farthest journeys from east Tennessee. I was impressed to imagine myself that far from my home. But later I worked in different countries and married someone 12,000 miles away. Believe me, she is much less scary than any other woman in the world, because I am dead certain that she is the one God wanted me to marry.

When Corrie Ten Boom was worried how she could stand it if she were captured by the Nazis and told her father her fears, he related this powerful story. He asked her if she remembered riding the train when she was a small girl, and she answered that she did. When he asked her if he gave her the ticket way in advance or just before she boarded, she told him it was just before she got on the train.

Then he said that God is like that. He gives us courage and strength when we need it. After Corrie and her sister Betsy were prisoners of the Nazis, she saw what her father said about God was true. I have not counted them, but someone noted that 365 times we are commanded in the Bible not to fear.

May Jesus help us to walk as humbly with him this year as the father of Corrie did, so we can give our children and others such profound and Godly counsel. And if we do not have such parents or friends to advise us against silly or evil ways, we can go to God directly in prayer and take courage from his many promises for those who worship him.

A favorite scripture of mine (which I often forget in the midst of a difficult circumstance) is Romans 8:28: "And we know that for those who love God all things work together for good, for those who are called according to his purpose." We cannot love God and trust his promises, and fear at the same time. So may we trust our Lord for peace. Here is one of my favorite hymns, based on 2 Timothy 2:19, Hebrews 13:5, and Isaiah 44::1-2, called "How Firm a Foundation."

How firm a foundation, ye saints of the Lord, is laid for your faith in his excellent Word. What more can he say than to you he hath said, to you who for refuge to Jesus have fled?

Fear not, I am with thee, O be not dismayed, for I am thy God, and will still give thee aid; I'll strengthen thee, help thee, and cause thee to stand, upheld by my righteous, omnipotent hand.

When through the deep waters I call thee to go, the rivers of sorrow will not overflow. For I will be with thee thy troubles to bless, and sanctify to thee thy deepest distress.

When through fiery trials thy pathway shall lie, my grace, all sufficient, shall be thy supply: The flame shall not hurt thee; I only design thy dross to consume and thy gold to refine.

The soul that on Jesus hath leaned for repose I will not, I will not desert to its foes. That soul though all hell should endeavor to shake, I'll never, no never, no never forsake.

Seeds sprout and grow.

My Toronto pastorate was by far the most productive, in terms of results that I could see. My other congregations may or may not have been more deeply moved, but only God knows. When Corrie Ten Boom was mocked by her Nazi guard because she worked with handicapped children, she replied that in the eyes of God perhaps that kind of work was much more valuable than any other.

But it was very encouraging to see God bringing very Godly volunteers (thanks, Frank Scavuzzo and others) to set up programs for children lasting several years. I became especially close to two little Italian girls who participated in Bible studies I led. But one day the older sister was crying, and I asked her what was wrong. She answered that her grandmother had told her she was not Christian. I am sure she had testified about Jesus to her, and although she meant well, she had hurt her granddaughter by claiming that since she had not been baptized, she was not Christian. I asked my little devastated friend if she had prayed that Jesus take over her life. She answered, "Yes." I then asked if she had meant it, and again she responded, "Yes." I assured her that she was Christian because I had seen her draw closer to God over time, so I was convinced that she was sincere and knew what she was doing.

Female volunteers finally dried up for several reasons, so after a while, we males who continued grew increasingly concerned that someone could unfairly accuse us of improper behavior. So, we decided we should shut down the programs. I was very sad about that, but thought it was the right thing to do. I think it was not long after one of the boys stole all the microphones for his brother's rock band. We did get them back, but support for the children's programs was waning.

At a church event about two years later, however, the same little girls from down the street on Ramsden Road showed up. They asked if they could have some Bibles. Of course, I was very happy to give some to them and inquired why they wanted them. The reply was that they had started Bible studies for children in the neighborhood and needed more Bibles for that reason!

Mark 4:26-27: "And he (Jesus) said, The kingdom of God is as if a man should scatter seed on the ground. He sleeps and rises night and day, and the seed sprouts and grows; he knows not how." What toughness and courage and love for God those two girls had! I still pray for them. Decades later I took my family to the church I pastored and looked for them on the same street, but they had all moved.

There is no use wishing I could see them, and several other children I adored. God brings people into our lives for an hour for some, and decades for others, by his appointments and with his timing. Love the ones you are with, appreciate them, and pray for them and for those we will never see again. Sow the seed of the gospel when we can, live it, repent when we do not, so that our prayers for others will be powerful and effective.

A written prayer

Prayers to God can either be written or unwritten, and sincere or insincere in both categories. One of the most meaningful prayers to me has been an ancient Roman Catholic litany, penned by a person known only to God. There is a clear wish that the petitioner be kept by Jesus from the desire to be glorified, and also be kept from the fear of not being glorified.

"O Jesus, meek and humble of heart. Deliver me Jesus, from the desire of being loved (Being desperate for love often prevents a person from seeking first the kingdom of God, and then trusting that all things that we need will be given to us. When we live for love we become the easy victims of predators who will take advantage of us).

Deliver me from the desire to be extolled (This means that we admit that all we have we received from God, as the Bible teaches, and that all credit belongs to him and not to us).

Deliver me from the desire to be honored (This normal tendency is the cause of whining and manipulation to gain applause, and is not appreciated by God or mortals either).

Deliver me from the desire to be praised (There is nothing wrong with being loved, praised, etc., but we are not to desire it or we do things for our gain instead of to glorify Jesus Christ. We surround ourselves with flatterers who try to use us when we do not want to honor Jesus Christ above ourselves and all others).

Deliver me from the desire of being preferred to others (We all want to be chosen first for the sports team, academic team, or for a date. It takes supernatural help to avoid these tendencies in order to have peace whether we are preferred or not, and we have that aid from above when we do everything as unto the Lord).

Deliver me from the desire to be consulted (The older and more educated I get, the more I naturally expect to be asked my views on theology or travel, ad nauseam, unless I humble myself enough to ask God for help in this area).

Deliver me from the desire to be approved (Who does not want to be considered one of a group of close friends, a good old boy, one who is always cheerfully greeted? I hope that happens to all of us, but how much more important it is to know that we are approved by God, a workman who does not need to be ashamed)?

And Jesus, deliver me from the fear of being humiliated. This fear may keep us from trying great things for God. So what if we fail when we intend to honor God by our efforts? How much better to fail trying to do something for God than to succeed in doing some work for the devil or for our selfish selves!

Deliver me from the fear of being despised. This fear has prevented many from saying a good word for Jesus Christ when he calls us to speak for him. It is selfish to be more concerned about our reputation than for the reputation of Jesus Christ when he really is our Lord.

Deliver me from the fear of suffering rebuke. If we do nothing or something or anything in between, someone is going to criticize us, so we might as well determine to live for the one who created the heavens and earth anyway.

Deliver me from the fear of being forgotten. As a child I would dread a grown up asking "Do you remember me," and I would answer "No," as often as not. What an arrogant question! But God has numbered every hair on our heads, and he remembers us always—our name is written on the palm of his hand, the Bible assures the follower of Jesus Christ.

Deliver me from the fear of being wronged. This dread has kept many of us from reaching out to do good. Be in prayer about who to help and how to do that, and God will give us balance and peace.

Deliver me from the fear of being suspected. Others may think we have bad motives when we try to do good. But we are to check our own motives, repent of all selfish ones, and pray to be open before God, and then worry free of what others assume.

And Jesus, grant me the grace to desire that others might be loved more than I, that others may be esteemed more than I, in the opinion of the world, others may increase and I may decrease. John the Baptist prayed this regarding Jesus, and so should we.

And Jesus, grant me the grace to desire that others may be chosen, and I set aside, that others be praised and I unnoticed (even when I consider myself smarter or more experienced or more holy…), that others may be preferred to me in everything, that others become holier than I, provided that I become as holy as I should."

The hope that we will be glorified and the fear that we will not be glorified is common to all of us. The writer of this prayer admitted this and pleaded with Jesus to help him/her to overcome this sin. May God help us to go and to do likewise.

Pray for the salvation of loved ones.

Especially for those who have higher education, the onslaught of rationalism and post modernism has tried to gut faith in the Bible as the Word of God. Those who survive such immersion in skepticism often become very timid of biblical claims that do not fit into what the "cool" or "woke" leaders of society think. Historic mainline denominations have become sideline denominations, suffering wholesale desertions, as many ministers water down the gospel to basically teach Americanism—the pursuit of life, liberty, and happiness.

But the Bible instead promotes holiness—to be set aside to follow God. "The fear of God is the beginning of wisdom." This awe of God and call for all to worship God the eternal Son Jesus Christ is sometimes downplayed when only the love of God is stressed. Several who gave their lives to Jesus Christ seem to accept the attacks against evangelism, and to ignore the many clear verses promising eternal punishment for those who reject Jesus Christ as Savior and Lord.

It is impossible to read through the New Testament and not to notice both the great love of Jesus and also his great grief over those who reject him. It is not intellectually honest to accept the one side and to gloss over the other. When we have his love for those who do not follow him, we also have his burden for those who have not yet begun to worship him, as well as for those who began and then let the cares of this life choke out the Word of God and make it unproductive in their lives.

When the parent or spouse puts confidence in the Bible as the teaching of God, there is the same thinking that Abigail Adams had. She was the wife of John Adams, the second president, and the mother of John Quincy Adams, the sixth president. Once when John Quincy was in Europe as a young man, she wrote that she would rather read that his ship had sunk and that he had drowned, than to read that he had abandoned Jesus Christ. Few of us will have children as gifted as this son was, and yet it is rare to hear of a parent who values a Godly life for our children more than the relatively small successes possible for them.

Brilliant scholars have debunked attempts to lower the Bible down to the level of other literature, and no archeological discovery has ever contradicted a biblical claim—it either supported the Bible or had no relevance. So, it is not intellectual problems but concerns for money or pleasure other selfish pursuits that have made us complacent about the salvation of our loved ones.

Can we really call them loved ones if we claim to believe the Bible, and then do not have the deep anguish Jesus had for those who did not become his faithful followers? Is it possible to truly love others and not be concerned about their salvation? If we do not believe the Bible- I understand and I respect that kind of honesty. But how is it possible for a Christian to be satisfied with the great achievements of our spouse or children and to think their lives are fulfilling, if they have not yet consciously and deliberately come under the Lordship of Jesus Christ, who spoke three times more about hell than he did about heaven?

Ted Turner

The high school boy led Bible studies at McCallie in Chattanooga among his teenage peers and seemed to be very devout. Then his sister died of a disease, and his father committed suicide. "Christianity is for losers," said Ted Turner, the founder of CNN news, in his later years.

Have you lost anything valuable as you tried to serve God? Then you know something about the severe pain involved. All Christians have huge disappointments. And of course, those who are not Christian also lose loved ones to disease or suicide or murder or have other severe disappointments to overcome.

When we lead Bible studies or do other Christian ministry, we may get the idea that God owes us more than he does those who do not stand out. Job noted with resentment that the wicked saw their little ones dance about (while his children had died). When we feel we are treated unfairly by God, do we cast off restraint and join those who do whatever the Bible teaches not to do? Yes, unless we have supernatural union with God, and value that friendship more than all else.

Who knows whether those who turn their backs on God were ever really converted or not? The individual knows, and God knows. I am completely convinced that once the Holy Spirit enters a person through faith in Jesus Christ, God remains within the individual to confirm them in righteousness, and to convict them of all sin (certainly that happened with me when I turned away from God for far lesser reasons than Mr. Turner had).

When a fellow believer does experience great disappointment, I hope that we are there to encourage and to comfort that hurting individual. We are to bring God's perspective on the situation as we pray for words in due season (or just be present but be quiet: that would have kept Job from calling his friends "worthless physicians").

Since the USA is a rich country, many Christians (and others) often assume that we should go to higher and higher levels of comfort and status. And we are tempted to be quite bitter if we do not fare much better than those we consider to be more wicked than ourselves! So, it is a hard sale to convince Christians that we are called to holiness, and not necessarily to have an easier life than others. But only pride and arrogance makes us think that we deserve more comfort and ease than

Christians in Africa or Pakistan or China, when often they are at least as Godly as we are.

It is strange to me that the more we have, the more difficult it is to be truly thankful to God (I am sure I am not the first to notice this). Probably we just tend to take for granted our families are healthy, our job is steady, and our tables are full. "He must increase, I must decrease," said John the Baptist about Jesus Christ. Can we as Americans say that sincerely? When we can, we will have unbroken fellowship with the risen Christ, even in the most difficult trials.

Jan Hus

The church needs revival, both in the USA and in Europe. In Prague there is a statue of Jan Hus, the brave reformer who was promised protection if he appeared at a church court. Instead, he was grabbed and told they did not have to keep their promise because he was a heretic. Then he was burned at the stake, about one hundred years before Martin Luther. He was the president of the university of Prague and was translating the Bible into the Czech language so they could read it in his and their native tongue. Also very importantly, he preached repentance and the necessity of supernatural conversion to Jesus Christ. Today his stature is about the only Christian influence left in that land.

I was surprised how stunningly beautiful Prague was, and to know that many cities were about as gorgeous before Hitler demolished them (with much assistance from our bombers in the process or rooting the Nazis out of Dresden, Hamburg, etc.). In Berlin we saw about five churches in a city-wide tour of 3:5 million inhabitants (down from 4:5 million in 1940). But the good news for those who do not accept Jesus Christ is God, is that there are many thousands of Muslims there.

After pouring many billions of dollars into Berlin for rebuilding, we saw empty spaces in almost every block, so the city is still suffering from the effects of bombing during World War 2, when 70 percent of the city was destroyed. The few Godly Germans who were there during the time of Hitler, did not find fertile ground for the gospel after his defeat either.

London has many more churches, and we attended a service at Westminster Abby, where the kings of England have been crowned for the last 600 years. I was pleasantly surprised to hear a great sermon encouraging a deep encounter with Jesus Christ to keep us going in the midst of the dry spells of life. About half of the priests in the Church of England now claim to be evangelical/historic Christian, and as a result they try to rotate the Archbishop of Canterbury, or leader, among the liberal and evangelical factions in that body.

Amsterdam, with its wide open tolerance of everything, is full of very pleasant people, great cheese, and the Dutch have almost totally rooted Christianity out of their society. Anne Frank is well known, but the Christian witness of Corrie Ten Boom and her family, who died in the midst of saving many Jews from death, is not so appreciated. I admire and respect the Dutch very much, since I worked there in the past and got to know several. Even though I was on the other side when I was there the first time, I was amazed how far from God they were then, and they have regressed much farther in that direction over the years. There is a great hymn that will spread revival in both continents when it is prayed sincerely. The title is "Renew Thy Church."

Real Christian faith?

I read of a teenage boy who does not drink or smoke or take drugs. Neither is he sexually active, nor rude nor lazy. He sounds like a good Christian, right? Actually, he is an atheist. In a tourist area such as the Great Smoky Mountains of east Tennessee, many who work in hotels call teenage church groups "thieves for Jesus." That is because most church groups cause much more damage and are rowdier than other teen groups that visit and steal more also.

What is going on? Of course, we should teach our children to be sober, to be sexually active only after marriage, and to be polite and hardworking and respectful. But are we encouraging them to be supernaturally converted to follow Jesus Christ as God and Lord? Alter calls or church membership classes can be opportunities to do that. Or they can just be ways to fit into our social expectations. Then we can expect neither inward change, nor outward change to be holy. Often only God knows whether such a declaration of faith is real or not.

In my own case it was real, at age nine: Yet for several years I was leading a life basically the opposite of that of the atheist teen. No one (including my parents) would have thought that I was Christian by either words or attitudes or actions. But I was Christian, and with no doubt whatsoever. The Holy Spirit stayed with me to remind me of sins of commission (things I did which the Bible calls sin) and sins of omission (omitting what the Bible says to do).

If our child or grandchild (or parent for that matter) has ever been truly saved/converted, we can be sure that if that person is not walking humbly with God, he or she is miserable. The person may be doing well on the outside, but inside there is dread and darkness. That is because such a person knows that God is real and the individual going in the opposite direction is just waiting for the hammer to drop, so to speak. In such a case, the unconverted who goes his or her own way has more joy in life, with only cultural or personal goals to achieve, instead of being faced with the demands of a holy God.

"For me, to live is Christ," said Saint Paul. We have a rift with God when that is not our highest goal. In that case we are either unconverted or backslidden, having slid back from what we know is right and from close communion with the Holy Spirit.

What a privilege it is to have his presence, even when we do wrong, for that is how we know to retrace our steps, repent and ask forgiveness when appropriate, in order to again have unbroken fellowship with the risen Jesus Christ. So, the atheist teen is a good role model, up to a point.

But Jesus says that unless our righteousness exceeds that of the Pharisees, we will not enter heaven. For that we must be born again, or to be saved, or converted, in other words. Then we have the power to keep his commandments inwardly as well as outwardly, and the ability to repent and get back in fellowship with God when we do not.

Excuse making

In the book *The Scarlet Letter* by Nathaniel Hawthorne, Hester's husband went to another country, and she committed adultery while he was there. Many church-going high school students in the Bible Belt south argued that the adultery was the fault of her husband. So, churches are effectively teaching that when we sin, it is not our responsibility, but it is because someone else made it difficult for us to stay righteous.

Perhaps her husband was wrong to leave her and to go to a far country, although in some cases temporary separation may be necessary because of jobs or other commitments. But even if the one going away is being inappropriate, we are taught in the Bible that we are responsible to keep walking with God anyway.

Many Mennonites in Russia were left behind as the others fled to South America and other countries. Spouses were often divided during World War II by prison or other persecutions and could not find each other. When a spouse who emigrated wanted to marry again after hearing nothing from the first spouse for several years, the Mennonites prayed about this difficult problem. They decided that after seven years of not hearing anything from the first spouse, the survivor was free to remarry if they wished. Of course, a few remarried, and only after a search of more than seven years could the missing spouse reach them.

If spouses were involuntarily separated for a long time and one seriously considered remarriage, I am convinced that the Christian who truly wants to do the will of God would have no peace to remarry if the other spouse were still alive and trying his/her best to reunite. The Holy Spirit within each follower of Jesus would not be pleased when we consider going against his teaching that a man (singular) shall cling to his wife (singular) until separated by death. What a terrible reunion it would be when a missing partner finally found his or her spouse, only to learn that the person did not wait, but remarried!

Follow your conscience (follow your bliss, as Joseph Campbell taught) is the kind of advice given by those who do not have the Holy Spirit within as a guide. But when God lives within a person, then God the Holy Spirit supersedes our conscience and informs our conscience about what is right or wrong. We may still be too cowardly to do what we know is right before God, but we will not make excuses for what the Bible labels as sin.

Conservative or liberal convictions may shape our views for or against political or sexual or financial choices. But whatever our personal inclinations are, God has his point of view. Are we willing to say to God that we will change our views on any or all of these matters if they are not his will? It is not important that you agree with me or that I agree with you about what is right. But it is very important that we sincerely want to have the mind of Christ. He promises that his yoke (leading and direction) is easy (relatively) and his burden (work for us) is light.

Those of us who have disregarded the words of Jesus in the past have discovered that "the way of the transgressor is hard." To transgress or to sin may seem impossible for a teen who is convinced of his or her invincibility. But even a bit of Bible study and reflection will show us how we do not naturally follow God at all.

Our conservative or liberal traditions are not enough to support us in life as we face temptations to sin. The Germans proved what a thin veneer indeed there was between them being the most refined and civil of Europeans during the 1930s, to being the worst European monsters of the 1940s. Only the most deluded and naive fail to look in the mirror and to see the potential for evil that could come out in trying circumstances. We are different only when the Holy Spirit is within us, convicting us of sin beyond what our conscience tells us is right or wrong.

Otherwise, we weasel out of blaming ourselves for our sins and shortcomings. According to an Associated Press poll, six in ten Americans who are overweight by government standards say they have a healthy weight, for example. Dr. William Dietz, of the Center for Disease Control and Prevention in Atlanta, says that people are unlikely to admit how bad their weight problems are for fear of being seen in a bad light.

Well, I am not naturally inclined to blame myself for anything, or to admit my sins either. But when the Holy Spirit is within an individual, he or she cannot rationalize sins for long without experiencing his convicting power. Then repentance brings us back into fellowship with God, and the resulting loss of pomposity helps us to have better relations with people also.

Making excuses for the sins of others is not just the habit of church going high school kids in the Bible Belt. It is the mode for all of us when we want to convince someone that when we do the same sin, we should not be held accountable to a holy and righteous God. Have our lifestyle and attitudes contributed to such excuse making among our children—or do we have Godly lives, confessing our sins and turning from them, to walk humbly before the God of the universe?

John Lennon

"Imagine there's no heaven …." John Lennon of the music group The Beatles wrote and sang that song and lived it. Millions have since joined him to sing about love and to have children who hate them, as John's son said about him. Millions have dumped their spouses as John did, to live for today.

The Bible can be interpreted different ways about the details of where heaven and hell are, but even a casual reader cannot deny that the Bible clearly teaches that both exist. Worship of Jesus Christ as God is emphasized, while heaven and hell are lesser motivations to act justly and to love mercy and to walk humbly with God. When the Beatles announced that they were more popular than Jesus Christ, several were offended but I believe they were right. Later polls confirmed that in terms of how folks lived their lives, even often when they professed to believe in Jesus Christ.

"Imagine all the people living life in peace…" He had no peace in his own family, and ignored the Nazi and communist movements that took power when Christianity was suppressed. Puppet clergy blessed both dictatorships, but Jesus Christ was always on the side of justice and mercy throughout history. Religion will never die out- it always takes the form of Christianity or another world religion, or of one concocted by an individual. So we either worship Jesus or Shiva or another world recognized religious person, or we worship ourselves. We may take a bit out of the Bible, the Koran, a favorite novel and our feelings, and set ourselves up as God. Few do this deliberately for such arrogance is mind boggling, but many do this unconsciously. Such folks filter out those teachings of Jesus or Mohammed, etc., that we do not like and follow our own feelings for meaning and purpose in life (as Thomas Jefferson did).

To say we will have peace on earth if we all live for today, setting each person up as a God to determine our own standards of good and evil, is a recipe for disaster. When a Hitler says his notions of right and wrong should be accepted, we have no logical reason to oppose him if it is merely his opinion/feelings that contradict our logic/feelings. If God does not exist and has not revealed his will to us, then no one has a right to praise or blame anyone for anything. After all, in such a world we are only following individual logic and feelings. Or as Dostoyevsky said, "If there is no God, anything is permissible."

But Jesus Christ is God who left heaven to add human flesh in history, and who revealed his will to us- to worship and to love and to obey him and to treat others as we want to be treated. To love God and human beings is the summary of the Old and New Testament, and the whole Bible is basically a commentary on how to do that.

We all naturally want to substitute our own selfish desires for those of God and to "follow your bliss," as one Beatle co-thinker taught. But it is bliss for some to lie, steal, torture, and to do other sins that make earth a foretaste of hell. There is, however, no right or wrong, meaning or purpose in life except selfish animal pursuits, unless God is real and can be known, at least partially. But God is just a cultural concept catering to our whims, except for the historic facts of the life and death and resurrection of Jesus Christ.

Whether single or married, no Christian has ever lived a consistent Christian life perfectly. But each Christian has the Holy Spirit inside to convict him or her of sin. I would like to be able to say that every true Christian repents and then ceases sinning, but my family would not agree. I admire greatly Dr. Stephen Olford, a Welshman who pastored Calvary Baptist Church in New York City. When he died his wife said he was the holiest person she had ever known. May God help all of us to be that sort of Christian. I heard him preach in the power of the Holy Spirit on the radio and in person, so I do not doubt the truth of her statement about him.

When we live for Jesus instead of living for today, we have his attitudes and a standard of goodness above every culture or personal opinion/feeling. After writing a few books or songs adored by millions, it is nearly impossible to humble ourselves and to pray, "God have mercy on me, a sinner." But when we do that under the prompting of the Holy Spirit, God forgives our sins, and we have his peace and friendship.

Prayer of a Civil War soldier

One of the best prayers I have read was prayed by an unknown soldier from the American Civil War. No one knows which side he was on, for there were Godly troops on both sides. Very little is known about the prayer. This is appropriate since he seems to be like John the Baptist, who said about Jesus: "He must increase, I must decrease." Here is his prayer.

"I prayed for strength that I might achieve; I was made weak that I might obey. I prayed for health that I might do greater things. I was given infirmity that I might do better things. I prayed for riches that I might be happy. I was given poverty, that I might be wise. I prayed for power that I might have the praise of men. I was given weakness that I might feel the need for God. I prayed for all things that I might enjoy life. I was given life that I might enjoy all things. I received nothing that I had asked for but all that I had hoped for."

The highest prayer is to do the will of God. Then within that will of God, sometimes he gives us the freedom to pray specifically. Obviously, the Holy Spirit did not give the unknown soldier freedom to pray when he asked for wealth, power, and other things he might allow another dedicated Christian to have. These gifts valued by him and others are not necessarily wrong, but they may be a hindrance to a particular individual at a certain time.

Health is certainly not bad in and of itself, but at one point Paul left Trophimus sick at a certain city. Does that mean the faith of Paul or Trophimus was deficient? No, it means that God was honored by the sickness of that individual more than he would have been honored by his health then.

Ruth Bell Graham said, "God has not always answered my prayers. If he had, I would have married the wrong man- several times." I am sure Billy Graham and their children appreciated that God does not always answer prayer as we prefer. The Bible promises that God does what is best for those who love and obey him (Romans 8:28). Sometimes we can look back as Ruth Graham did and see clearly how God has provided what is best for us. I like the story of the country singer who was rejected by a girl in high school, went to a high school reunion, and was inspired to write the song, "Thank God for Unanswered Prayer." So sometimes we really do get to see how a refusal from God is for our own good. And if we really do need to see and to understand God in a particular situation, I hope we trust that he will provide that insight. Otherwise, we are to trust and obey blindly on faith.

I am aware that the more educated we are, the more we tend to emphasize reason. Therefore, the more we search for meaning, and for understanding of the ways of God. This can be beneficial when it leads us to a deeper faith. But when such questioning leads away from trust in God, it is a curse to us. Saint Teresa of Avila noted that if God treated his friends better, he would have more of them. Yes, I know that is bad theology, but all of us have probably thought the same on occasion! God does not owe us explanations for his every move. He does not have to give regular reports for us to grade with an "A" or "B" or "F." When I recognize that I am in the role of a teacher grading God on how he performs in my life, I am responsible to repent and to pray to love and trust him more.

Ole Hallesby

I have not doubted the existence of God once in my entire life. That is because when I was a boy, the power of God was so real in the churches I attended. God met with us in such a way that lives were changed, so that we were in awe of Jesus Christ.

Although church history is filled with such stories, now even many evangelicals who claim to have a high view of the Bible look at me blankly when I talk about unmistakable encounters with God. The times are past when, according to Dr. William Fitch, Scottish elders would ask this of a prospective pastor, "Does he have the anointing?"

Today, most in the West would interpret that as a question regarding the eloquence or winsome personality of a prospective pastor. It bothers me to think that children growing up now may not even meet others who are touched deeply by God to live in his presence.

What were the ingredients of those churches in my childhood? I do not believe that denomination or race or age or education had anything to do with God filling us with himself. Instead, it was a brokenness before the Lord that brought forth the awareness of his presence to us. This has happened to people of different denominations, races, languages and economic groups. It may be more difficult for rich, healthy, or respected folks to get humble before the Lord, but it has been done throughout history.

In his magnificent book simply entitled *Prayer*, Dr. Ole Hallesby, who taught at the university of Oslo, Norway, states this: "Prayer and helplessness are inseparable. Only he who is helpless can truly pray." As long as we have money and health and safety, few care what it means to know and to do the will of God.

But the persecuted Christians in Barnaul, Russia, understood the importance of helplessness. When anyone joined their group, they would ask them to lead a prayer aloud. The informers would then become very clear to them!

How much more clear does it become to God when we pray and are not really casting all our cares on him, to do with us as he wishes? When we say in our hearts that we can depend on the government or spouse or parent or our own resources if God doesn't help us, then we are really going to idols instead of to God wholeheartedly. God knows the difference, and he rewards such prayers with the absence of himself.

How do we achieve this helplessness that is necessary for God to meet with us? When we read the Bible and pray that God will show us ourselves as he sees us (not others) and then show us himself, he will. The contrast will drive us to our knees. When we compare the love of God with our love, his power with our power, his knowledge with our knowledge, and then really begin to believe that he is sovereign as the Bible repeatedly teaches, a sense of helplessness without God will be seen as appropriate. Then he fills us with himself when we have that attitude.

Some will always go to church for social or business or other reasons. But some will also always go to meet with God. To those the Bible says in Matthew 5:6, "Blessed are those who hunger and thirst after righteousness, for they shall be satisfied." Let us pray that we and those we love will know that this is different than an emotional or psychological uplift.

The Cross

As a small boy I remember an older cousin sitting beside me in church while the congregation sang "The Old Rugged Cross." He ridiculed the song and the message by substituting silly words and singing them. Although I liked him and wanted his friendship, I did not join him, for I had already been drawn by the Holy Spirit to give my life to Jesus Christ.

I forgot his mocking words, but still remember that great hymn. "On a hill far away stood an old rugged cross, the emblem of suffering and shame ... and I love that old cross, for the dearest and best, for a world of lost sinners was slain." The cross was used by the Romans to crucify criminals with a slow and painful torture until they died. It was a mark of horror and disgrace. Yet today it adorns the flags of Finland, Sweden, Norway, Denmark, Iceland, Great Britain, and Switzerland. Why the turnaround?

God the eternal Son, through whom all things were made and for whom all things were made (Colossians 1:16), conquered death to make the cross a mark of triumph. It has been misused sometimes, as Europeans carried it to Jerusalem to kill Muslims for whom Jesus died. Today some criminals use it to advertise so that those who honor the cross can be taken advantage of in business.

But the cross is loved by those who have been crucified with Christ, who have given themselves to him consciously to love and obey. God the Father allowed himself in the person of the second person of the Trinity, to be handed over and murdered, although Jesus could have called legions of angels to prevent his suffering and death. But God is holy and hates sin. As a lamb without blemish was necessary to be sacrificed in the Old Testament times to turn the wrath of God from the sinner, so in New Testament times to the present, Jesus Christ, the eternal God the Son, offered himself as the perfect and sinless substitute for us. He took the punishment that we deserve- Jesus made an atonement for us, in other words.

Does that mean we are all one in Christ then? The gift of salvation is offered to us, but until we accept it, we are not converted to follow Jesus. The theologian Karl Barth confused many when he spoke of all being positionally in Christ as a result of the crucifixion. No doubt his mistress was included in his theory. But we have no benefit whatsoever from the death and resurrection of Jesus except for vague sentimental feelings, until we pass consciously from the kingdom of darkness into his kingdom of light. This is done by the supernatural drawing of the Holy Spirit until the individual asks for forgiveness of sins and invites Jesus Christ to come into his or her life, and to reign there. Mere membership classes or alter calls are not enough, although they may encourage that step of faith. No amount of emotion or logic or tradition can take a heart that is void of the Spirit (Jude 1:19) to a heart where the Holy Spirit lives.

When conversion happens, then we see the cross with love and respect. Once I asked a woman in an elevator in Toronto if she were Christian, since she was wearing a cross. "It is not a cross, it is a *t*," she replied. That is fine—the symbol does not give life, as in the movies someone may hold up a cross to scare werewolves away. But when we are joined by faith to be a follower of Jesus Christ, we do love the cross. I hope we can all say sincerely with Saint Paul, "In the cross of Christ I glory." He gloried/bragged/boasted not in his achievements or ethnic heritage, but because the God of the universe died on the cross as a substitute for his sins. He consciously became a follower of Jesus Christ and lived for him. Nothing else we can do has one whit of significance compared to that.

Unconverted ministers

Gilbert Tennent, a Presbyterian minister who along with Jonathan Edwards and George Whitfield, was a catalyst for the great American revival in 1735, wrote a pamphlet called "The Danger of an Unconverted Ministry." He basically countered the spiritually dead ministers who had opposed the recent work of God. Mark 6:34 Jesus himself pointed out that people "were like sheep without a shepherd." The Pharisees and Sadducees were plentiful, but where were those Jesus considered Godly shepherds/pastors? Tennent was sharp to point this out.

No one will have a heart for the conversion of sinners unless he himself has been supernaturally converted. As Paul noted in 1 Corinthians 4:20, the kingdom of God is not in word, but in power. Many can speak well naturally, but one must be converted to have words from the Holy Spirit that move the listeners to repent and follow Jesus Christ. No unconverted minister is endured with power from on high but must substitute emotion or funny or interesting stories to entertain the congregation.

So, are these unconverted ministers spawns of Satan, hell bent on destroying congregations? Perhaps. But I was friends with two who were converted only after they became pastors. They became pastors to help people, with the best of intentions. They really did not understand the need for supernatural conversion until they had pastored a while. One remained in the ministry, and the other left it.

Tennent said, "To trust the care of our souls to those who have little or no care for their own ... would signify that we set light by our souls, and did not care what would become of them. For if the blind lead the blind, will they not both fall into the ditch? And O! That vacant congregations would take due care in the choice of their ministers."

These words are at least as important now as they were in 1740. Do we not consider the fact that an unconverted minister can be well intended, eloquent, intelligent, and with a charming personality? Most can copy a sermon of someone else and add a few interesting or wise stories, deceitfully passing them on as theirs when the details gave them away as from another! I have heard that done.

1 Corinthians 2:4 says, "And my speech and my message were not in plausible words of wisdom, but in demonstration of the Spirit and of power ... that your faith might not rest in the wisdom of men, but in the power of God." Without supernatural conversion and a distinct call from God to preach, at best all the unconverted minister has is what he can muscle from his own meager resources. This is because such a person knows nothing of the power of God.

Unconverted ministers know nothing about the supernatural conversion power of God, who drags folks from the kingdom of darkness into the kingdom of God. We do not need a kingdom of fast-talking quacks, because as someone has noted, if we marry the spirit of the age, we will be a widow in the next. Thank God for converted and holy ministers like Jonathan Edwards and Gilbert Tennent, and other ministers in every age, who were supernaturally drawn to worship Jesus Christ as God and Lord, and who were called consciously and definitely by him, to preach the gospel/ good news of Jesus Christ.

Re-examine all received wisdom?

"In a world where rapid change is constant, all received wisdom, including what is virtuous, must be regularly re-examined." So said Mary Loftis, associate editor of *Emory Magazine* in 2013. That is thinking normally, because each generation tends to think that we are smarter than all the ones before us and after us. All but the coolest of us tend to prefer the styles of clothes we wore in our early twenties, for example. But if the "received wisdom" is revealed to us from God, then it should be re-examined in order to know how to best apply it to new situations.

In other words, biblical teachings for honesty, faithfulness in marriage, abstinence before marriage, etc., should be continued in every generation in every culture. Barna research shows that the vast majority of single adults who consider themselves Christian, do feel that sex before marriage is okay. So, this discussion is not just academic.

If "received wisdom" is merely human in origin, then it should be re-examined and dumped whenever we want to ditch a spouse for a younger or richer or more understanding one. "Situation ethics" is another way of describing that idea. Under this system of thinking, humans have invented "what is virtuous," and therefore we have no obligation to be honest, kind, or hardworking as unto the Lord, who is just created by us anyway, such folks feel. By this type of thinking, neither do we need to seek peace and pursue it, or to forgive those who have wronged us, etc.

Then these are merely cultural norms to be discarded when a Hitler or Stalin or Pol Pot or Idi Amin comes along, or when a spouse wants us to lie or steal to improve our situation, or when an acquaintance wants us to have sex.

When the law of God is not written in our hearts through supernatural conversion to follow Jesus Christ, then of course his laws seem disposable when they conflict with our selfish desires. Recently, some parents were troubled because not only did their offspring denounce Christianity, but they were also hostile to it and turned from it. I doubt very seriously if the children were ever Christian in the first place. Even if their parents were hypocrites who pretended to follow Jesus, real Christian children would be called to repentance.

We all want to re-examine "received wisdom" when it conflicts with our perceived well-being. But the Christian reads the Bible and prays to have God's view on people and circumstances. We accept, as the Bible teaches, that our hearts are desperately wicked, and therefore are not the trustworthy corner stones of our decision making.

Therefore, we should re-examine our hearts to see if they line up with the unchanging Word of God, call virtuous what God forever calls virtuous, and call sin what he forever calls sin. And no, that is not easy for me to do either. But it is necessary in order to have peace with God, or people.

Preaching with excitement or anointing?

I grew up in east Tennessee eating corn bread and soup beans (which I still love), but broadened my food tastes to learn the best chocolate is Belgian, the best cheese is Dutch gouda (not the fake Wisconsin stuff), the best bread is French, etc. So, I was disappointed when the only world class pizza place in Gatlinburg, Tennessee, began to substitute cheaper and inferior products for their food. I have sent thousands there, and many thanked me after they ate. But I do not send anyone there now, nor will I.

Much more importantly, do we notice when we hear the gospel watered down with excitement or personal charm substituting for preaching in the power of the Holy Spirit? Or do we recognize the difference? I did a wedding, and the groom was so moved that he cried, and he explained that he had not heard such preaching since he had left Kentucky many years ago. In Florida he had made a fortune, but it was a poor substitute for the historic Christian gospel.

Are we like the restaurant, unashamed to proclaim we have the same pizza, when we have substituted inferior ingredients? Have we replaced holiness with unholiness, humble prayers with arrogance, and being more irritated at the sins of others than our own sins? It is true that we all drift away from God at times and grieve and quench the Holy Spirit. But I hope we repent sincerely and often.

Do we have a spouse or church leaders who will confront us when we lower God's spiritual standards? That is much better than continuing in a backslidden condition. Vance Havner said for a Christian to be in fellowship with most Christians, we must be backslidden ourselves! That sounds about right from the churches I have pastored.

I was not only raised on cornbread and soup beans, but in churches where God was there unmistakably in power. People were afraid to play church in such an environment, and folks were either converted, got closer to God, or were so uncomfortable that they departed. Do you think your minister would muscle a sermon out when God did not give words, or be humble enough to ask someone else to preach?

Do you know the difference between playing church and historic Christian services? I remember one church member testifying and noting that they might as well have gone to a ball game, because God was so far from that church service. He was right.

God is holy. Whatever the Holy Spirit who inspired the Bible calls sin, ensures that we are just playing church unless we repent and turn from it. The official words may be the same with good doctrine, but just as the restaurant dropped the quality ingredients and still calls the product by the same name, we can drop holiness and still play church! But 1 Corinthians 2:4 assures us, "My speech and my message were not in plausible words of wisdom, but in demonstration of the Spirit and in power." We can substitute anything we want and still call it church if we wish. But when the preaching is not anointed with the power of the Holy Spirit, it is fake and not worthy of the name Christian.

Corrie Ten Boom

The Amsterdammer Miep Gies was one of the few Dutch who helped protect Jews from the Nazis. For two years she was one of those who hid Anne Frank, and she saved her diary for posterity. Miep was modest and did not see herself as a hero, but as a normal person. But she risked her life to do her good deeds.

I do not know what inspired Miep to be so brave and caring. But I do know why the Ten Boom family put themselves in similar danger. When Casper Ten Boom, a watchmaker in Harlem, tenderly held a Jewish child, another Dutch person warned him that he could be killed by the Nazis for doing that. He replied that he would consider it an honor to die for that child. Later he and others of his family did perish in the German death camps for hiding Jews in their home.

A film called *The Hiding Place* (based on the book by the same name) shows how the Ten Booms made a fake closet where Jews would hide when anyone knocked on the front door. They were part of the Dutch underground that, among other things, harbored them in city homes until they could find safer places in the countryside. But finally, a Dutch informer told the Germans what they were doing, and the Germans came for the family. The Jews, who were there at the time, managed to reach the closet and were safe, but the Ten Boom family was carted off to the Nazi prisons. Only the daughter Corrie Ten Boom survived the death camps.

After the war Corrie began a speaking ministry all over the world. Following a speech in Germany, a man who did not recognize her approached her to shake her hand, commenting what a good sermon she had given. Corrie immediately knew that he was a particularly brutal guard at her concentration camp and wanted to kill him. But she prayed that Jesus would help her to forgive him, and as she extended her hand also, the peace of God filled her.

Her books also include *Tramp for the Lord*, with stories of her speaking engagements, and *My Father's House*. The latter one is an account of her upbringing with her parents, and how caring and hospitable they were with family and strangers also. My wife and I read it aloud as our children grew up, and I recommend it highly. At one point, the father Casper would not allow them to use pacifiers, because they were dishonest.

Another story Corrie told was when a customer came into the shop and complained that the son of a watchmaker in Harlem could not fix his watch, so he plopped down a big wad of money for a very expensive one. Casper asked to see the old watch, repaired it easily, returned his money, and suggested that the customer return to the son of his competitor who had died, for he was confident he would do a good job. They were always near financial ruin, so as soon as the customer left, Corrie rushed to her father and asked, "Father, how could you?" Casper replied that there is good money and bad money, and God only wants us to have the good money and to trust him. Do we? If we are not faithful in the small things, how can God trust us to do what is right as Miep Gies and Corrie Ten Boom did, in the dangerous times?

When I had sex outside of marriage, I was convicted by the Holy Spirit.

So were you if the Holy Spirit is a part of your life. Then why do so many teen church leaders have sex and pretend that it is okay with God? They do so for the same reason that older adults have sex outside marriage between a man and a woman, and pretend it is okay. When a person is devoid of the spirit of God, as in Jude Verse 19, then it is ridiculous to expect a person to walk with God in holiness. But we can expect a person not to pretend to be walking with God and doing the opposite of what he requires.

Certainly, sin can be pleasurable. But the pleasure does not make it right, any more than to say if something is difficult to do, then that is wrong. I have stolen before and gained some benefit, but it was wrong. It is difficult to be honest or sexually pure, but it is possible, and necessary if we hope to have fellowship with the God of the universe. The gospel or good news of Jesus Christ is offensive to all of us, Christian or not. That is because we must deny ourselves or put behind our natural inclinations many times in order to love and obey him. Even when we are truly Christian and therefore have the Holy Spirit dwelling in us, it is still counter intuitive to obey him. But we have life more abundantly when we do, even though selfish and demonic reasoning is to the contrary.

And do not let others tell us that Jesus did not mention sexual ethics as much as Paul did, and therefore it is okay to follow Jesus and to reject Paul. Christians worship God who is Triune, and the Holy Spirit inspired Paul and the other writers of the Bible. No one can drive a wedge between the Holy Spirit and Jesus, and no one can say (truthfully) that Jesus is Lord except by the Holy Spirit. As the gospel was preached, people were converted and churches were born, and situations arose that needed specific teaching to address, which the Holy Spirit did through Paul and Peter, and other writers in the New Testament.

Some object by saying that we should care only about social justice and not be concerned about personal morality. I am about as socially concerned as anyone else can be, and I am for justice and mercy on grand as well as personal levels. In 1950 the average paycheck ratio of the executive to the average worker was thirty to one, and from 2000 until now the average was between 300-500 to one (Business Insider, July 15,

2010). Christians are to work for justice and holiness on all fronts possible, and to support those who advocate the good in areas where we are not gifted to participate (with Jim Wallis of *Sojourners Magazine*, for example).

But we can all be holy in our private lives. We all occasionally want to take advantage of others sexually or economically or otherwise. But such inclinations are sins to repent of, not to make excuses about or to brag about and promote! Especially in the churches if nowhere else, we are to pray we do not grieve or quench the Holy Spirit, but to be open to whatever honors Jesus Christ best. Whatever else that is, and it will vary with the individual, it is never the opposite of what is clearly taught in the Bible. Godly revival comes when we build our lives on truth—not lies.

"Stop the service. My son wants to be saved!"

I was sitting by my father at age nine in a church in Rogersville, Tennessee, when the preacher began to read the Bible. I started to cry, and my father asked, "What is the matter with you?" I did not understand what was going on, so I answered, "Nothing." I did not know what else to say. A few more verses and a few more tears later, my father asked, "Do you want to be saved?" I nodded yes, and he yelled, "Stop the service—my son wants to be saved!" We gathered at the alter and prayed, and the dread conviction of the Holy Spirit turned into peace when I gave my life to Jesus Christ.

My father had been a paratrooper before he broke his foot, and I never saw him afraid of anyone or anything. He was brave enough to do whatever honored Jesus Christ, no matter what anyone else thought. Fathers are usually interested in getting children to be independent, self-sufficient, to be adventurous, and to stand on their own two feet. So, when I wanted to go to Europe he was in favor while mom only reluctantly agreed. Mothers are normally more nurturing and protective by nature and concerned with feathering the nest. Fathers tend to take more risks with jobs and money, with confidence that somehow things will work out.

A neighbor worked with my father and was speaking very disrespectfully to him at one point. Then Dad took out a knife, held it to his stomach, and promised to kill him if he said another word. I am glad he trusted my father to be honest and kept quiet. Otherwise, I would have been visiting him in prison for several years. Perhaps he scared the hell out of our neighbor, for he later gave his life to Jesus Christ and showed evidence of a changed life. No, I do not recommend that as an evangelistic method, and it certainly was not done with that in mind by my father. God in his mercy protected two families that day (and me in almost identical cases later).

So, I am sure that no one gets higher and higher in the Christian life. We either repent daily and again humbly depend on Jesus Christ for his values, or we get caught up in greed, desire for revenge, etc. If you have not noticed that happening to you, then it is because you have had a sheltered life and have not had to face difficult situations yet. A very Godly preacher from Bean Station, Tennessee, named Johnnie Coffee, had a daughter who was murdered by her husband. At the courthouse trial he took a pistol and planned to shoot her murderer dead. Yes, he was wrong. And he had walked so closely with God that he preached in the power of the Holy Spirit. In that case he did not, but I hope we have humbled ourselves enough to preach or to speak or sing under the influence of the Holy Spirit, otherwise we grieve the Holy Spirit even if we have not threatened to murder our tormentors. I am confident that in addition to King David (Acts 13:22), Rev. Coffee and my father, were fathers who were men after God's own heart. I hope we pray that God can say that about us (or women after God's own heart for the females).

God loves winter.

I always feel much better in winter, and I love the cold. So, I am glad to see such verses as Psalm 147:16, "He gives snow like wool; he scatters frost like ashes." Who can help but admire the crunch of snow beneath our feet, the icicles as long as spears at Alum Cave Bluff in the Great Smoky Mountains, and the frozen ponds around us?

I delight in my cross-country skis, and children of all ages climb aboard sleds and zoom down slopes. Animals also frolic, chomping snow, sliding around and developing "snow boots" that melt only after they come inside. What glorious beauty surrounds us when even the weeds hold ridges of snow. I hope you have had the privilege of hearing the heavenly music that results when the wind blows the branches of trees encrusted in ice!

Yes, I have seen winters colder than those in east Tennessee, and I still appreciate them. The first winter I pastored in Montreal, I went to church on Christmas day when the temperature warmed up to minus thirty-five (Fahrenheit and Celsius are about the same then). I would ski for twenty miles at a time in zero degree weather and felt better than walking a few yards in an eighty degree climate.

What a joy it is to introduce others to snow for the first time. Adults as well as children go berserk, laughing and putting it in their hair, but are always shocked at how cold it really is. While I was at seminary in Boston, I saw the kind of blizzard that probably made some of the Pilgrims doubt the love of God for sending a storm that blew them so far north of their intended destination in Virginia. As I watched the first snowfall of one season there, I noticed an African student from Nigeria standing beside me crying. I asked him what was wrong. He answered that he finally understood what Isaiah was talking about when he said in Isaiah 1:18, "Though your sins are like scarlet, they shall be white as snow."

In the cities, crime decreases in winter because evil people do not like to wait to rob others when it is uncomfortable. The cold weather makes people more reserved to do good or bad to others. Therefore, the northern countries have folks who are less demonstrative and more restrained in their social interactions.

Perhaps even fewer of us would appreciate winter if we were in Siberia, the eastern part of Russia. There the temperature reaches – negative sixty, and many believers were exiled there. Even those there who love animals wear fur coats in order to keep from freezing to death! And the Christians there held fast to their faith in the midst of huge obstacles. Despite fierce persecution and severe winters, the believers wrote, "Helpless are your icy blizzards to quench God's flame within our hearts." Since they can say that, surely in our much milder winters we can find reasons to praise the living God.

Literal or figurative

I read a Baha'i publication and the author was convinced that many in the churches are much closer to eastern religious beliefs than to historic Christian beliefs. I agree, and that is not news to any pastor. His position was based on findings published by George Barna in his book *Second Coming*.

For example, Barna found in 1999 that fifty-nine percent of Americans believe "Satan is not a living being but is a symbol of evil." In this category are seventy percent of Roman Catholics, sixty-two percent of mainline Protestants, and forty-five percent of those born again. By 2020 the percentage is much higher for all these groups. The Baha'i Guardian teaches "the devil or Satan is symbolic of evil and dark forces," which have no independent reality of their own.

Baha'i teaches that the Holy Spirit is only a symbol of God's power and not truly God. In 1997, fifty-five percent of all who considered themselves born again Christians defined the Holy Spirit in a figurative manner—as a symbol of God's power but not a living entity. Again, by 2020 far fewer Americans considered themselves born again Christians.

In 1999, forty-two percent of Americans and thirty-three percent of self-described born again Christians deny that Jesus Christ was raised from the dead. That percentage is much higher in 2020. But according to the Bible, such folks have faith that is useless! Baha'i and Islam and other eastern religions see the resurrection as somehow spiritual but not historical, and even in conservative evangelical churches their world view is increasingly accepted, and historic Christian views are increasingly rejected.

Authentic Christianity, however, accepts the Bible passages on the resurrection, the Holy Spirit, and Satan, as the authors clearly intended them to be understood, and as the first followers of Jesus lived and died for them. One can honestly read the Bible and reject it as false, but it is intellectually dishonest to ignore the way those of that day interpreted the passages.

If I said my father died, and I claimed to see him alive afterwards and touch him and talk with him, one could believe me or not. But if I spent the rest of my life going around the world trying to convince others that he bodily rose from the dead, it would not be because I thought he just somehow spiritually overcame death. The first followers of Jesus Christ based their lives on the conviction that Jesus was alive after his death on the cross, had communicated to them, and had sent the Holy Spirit as eternal God to be with all who gave their lives to him. John 16 and other passages teach that the Holy Spirit is God who communicates with the Christian to remind us of his great and precious promises.

I am convinced that many reject a shell of Christianity instead of the real faith of the Bible and Godly people throughout history. God has revealed himself through the Bible, his characteristics and will are repeatedly proclaimed to us. The Holy Spirit is with every Christian, but when most ministers preach as though everyone who hears them are already Christian, those who are not, get bored and contemptuous at what an empty shell it seems to be. Truly, without the Holy Spirit, Christianity is just another cultural set of beliefs, better or worse than other world views only by personal preference!

Best friends in the first grade

My best friend in the first grade, Alan Broyles, just died (farm mishap). My family moved right after the first grade, and the next time I saw him was about twenty years later at the funeral of my father. I was too broken to converse, so I just thanked him for coming. I did appreciate it. About twenty years later at another funeral, we talked seriously and laughed a lot together. It was as if we had never been apart.

His wife had this to say about him: "He was loving. He was understanding. He was a man who kept his word. He was the best husband in the world. I really mean that." Even in the first grade, he was a good guy.

I found out much later after the first grade that he lived in a mansion and I lived in a shack, relatively speaking. He was landed gentry while I was basically peasant stock. He had good connections in Greene County, Tennessee. Although I loved the people there (both sides of my family are from there) and the mountainous area, God had no future for me there. My calling was to pursue radically different paths, so much of my nostalgia was not realistic at all.

Romans 8:28: "And we know that for those who love God all things work together for good." That includes being torn away from my friend because my father got a much better job. That verse also applies to friends now in different countries, because God says, "Grow in grace," and then arranges circumstances in ways that best helps us to do that. I can choose to trust my feelings and prefer my good friends all be close by, or I can think Christianly.

It is normal to sometimes miss our birthplace and friends and family- my wife gave up that when she left Russia. But God either wants us to return and he will give us peace and open doors to do so, or he will give us the grace to thrive where we are. I know that is easy to say, and at times difficult to do.

We are to pray that God helps us to learn from our past, to be thankful for it, and to bloom wherever he plants us. I am persuaded that if I had stayed in Greene County, Tennessee, grabbing on to my friend's coattails would have been the only way I could survive- not to mention, thrive. So, I accept that God never wanted me to return to beautiful and deeply loved Greene County, except to visit.

The best is yet to come.

Every now and then, I get a little bit nervous that the best of all the years have gone by," Bonnie Tyler sang. More and more of us can identify, since a very small percentage of Americans get richer and a bigger and bigger percentage of Americans get poorer. I certainly made more money in the past with higher status jobs. As I get older, one reason that I would like to get another Great Pyrenees dog is so when I walk around drooling, the Great Pyrenees will drool with me and make it much cooler to drool!

I do not think the singer was worried about drooling, but after age thirty or forty, most of us see missed opportunities for glamor or adventures. On my worst days I do also. But on my best days, I take the view of my father, who would say, "The best is yet to come." I never actually heard him say that, for I rededicated my life to Jesus very shortly before he died, so I had little opportunity to talk about things of God with him. A cousin related that he would say that often, and she was older than I, and if I heard it as a small child, I missed the significance then.

But for the Christian, no matter how terrible or how great our situation is, we can be certain that the best is yet to come. The Bible promises that heaven is much better than any of us can imagine. My best nature thoughts are of the Great Smoky Mountains (where I picked blueberries recently and plan to again soon), the Swiss Alps, and the Norwegian mountains, and Great Pyrenees dogs. My best thoughts of food are Paula Dean type fried chicken, French bread, Belgian chocolate, Dutch Gouda cheese, Rooibos tea from South Africa, and Lunetta Pizza in New York City.

But 300 Bible references promise that Jesus will return as the judge of all, and those who love him will have the best years, much better than anyone can guess, for eternity! Christians can take different views of exactly how Jesus will return, but every eye shall see him, so it will not be a secret or symbolic return. And if a person thinks this is a fairy tale, it is based on the historic resurrection of Jesus Christ, for which there is much evidence. Where is the evidence for views to the contrary? It is only the feelings or wistful thinking and not in historic evidence, so in those cases there is logic to be "terrified that the best years have gone by." But for the one who has been drawn by the Holy Spirit to accept Jesus as Savior and Lord, even if we start to drool as we walk, the best is yet to come. As the Bible promises, the eye has not seen neither has the ear heard, what good things God has in store for those who love him.

To have friendship with God, we must be more irritated at our own sins than the sins of others!

"There are things which a man is afraid to tell even to himself, and every decent man has a number of such things stored away in his mind." Dostoyevsky

Or as the Bible puts it, "The heart is desperately wicked."

Anthropologist Caroline Fluehr-Lobban agonized over the fact that her discipline's prime directive-cultural relativism-left her with no rationale for opposing rape or racial genocide in other cultures. Her pessimism is logical unless there is a supernatural God who transcends culture.

About the Author

Rev. Dr. Alden Marshall pastored Presbyterian churches in Montreal and Toronto, Canada, spearheaded new churches in Portuguese and Spanish, then returned to his native Tennessee to pastor and teach college courses. He has a B.A. and M.S.S.W. from The University of Tennessee (Knoxville), a M.Div. from Gordon-Conwell (Boston), and a D.Min. from Fuller Seminary (Los Angeles). After living in New York City for several years, Rev. Dr. Marshall has returned to Knoxville, Tennessee, near the Great Smoky Mountains.

For inquires, contact aldenmarshall8@gmail.com.

www.ingramcontent.com/pod-product-compliance
Lightning Source LLC
LaVergne TN
LVHW041102080826
845145LV00007B/1669

* 9 7 8 1 9 7 0 0 3 7 9 0 6 *